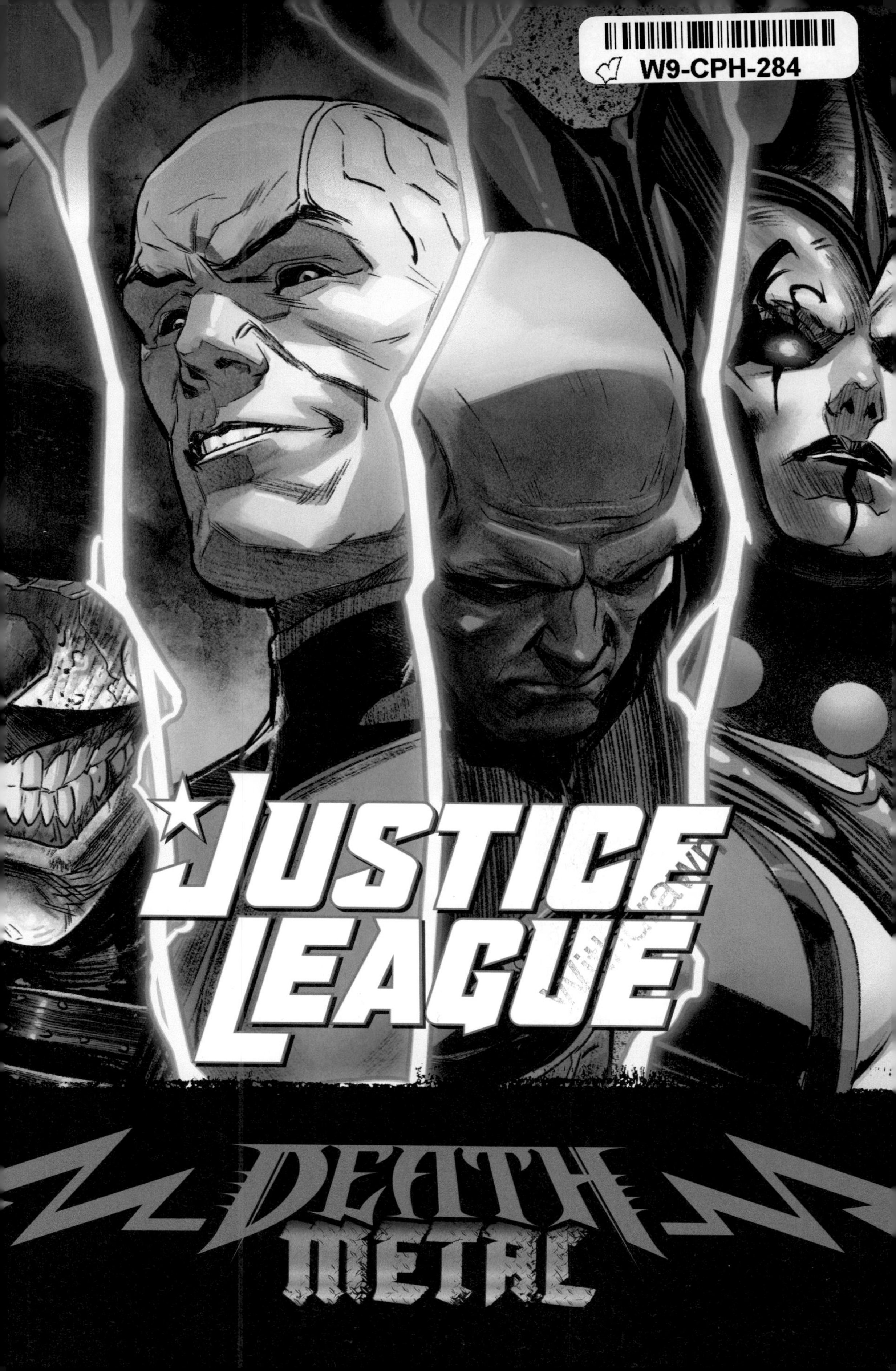
JUSTICE LEAGUE
DEATH METAL

JUSTIC

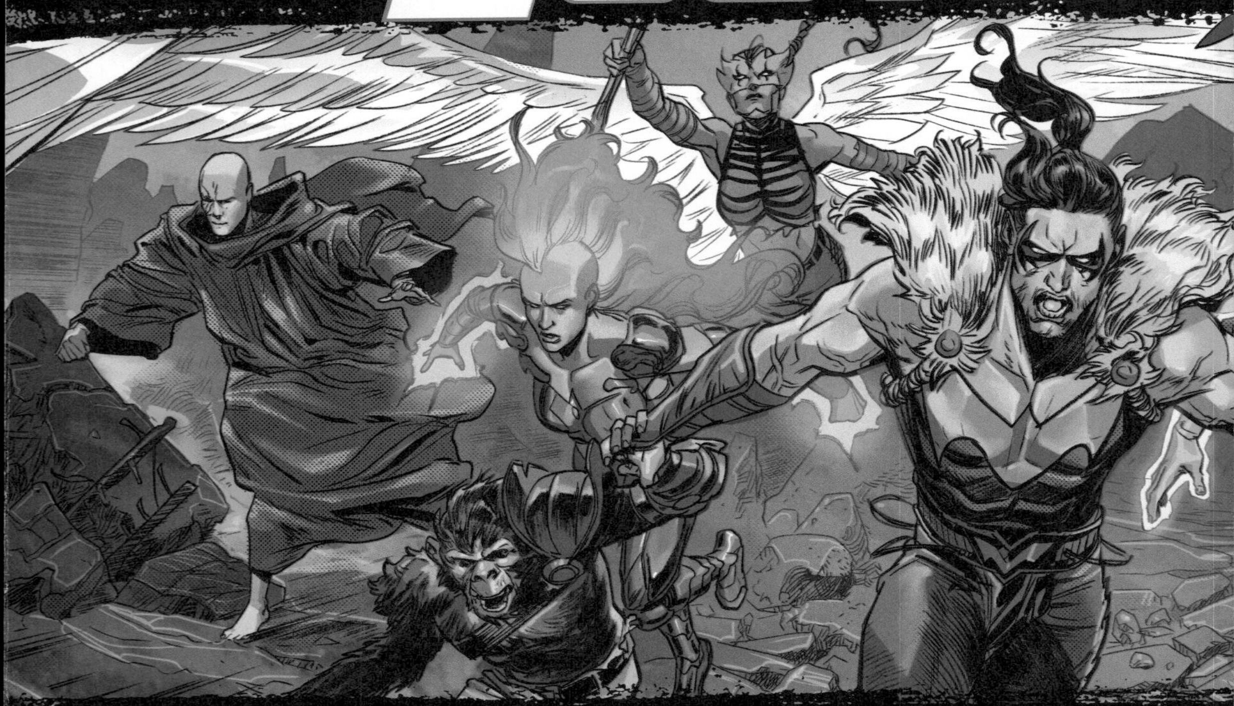

DE
ME

Joshua Williamson
writer

Xermánico | Robson Rocha
pencillers

Xermánico | Daniel Henriques
inkers

Romulo Fajardo Jr.
colorist

Tom Napolitano
letterer

Howard Porter & Hi-Fi
collection cover artists

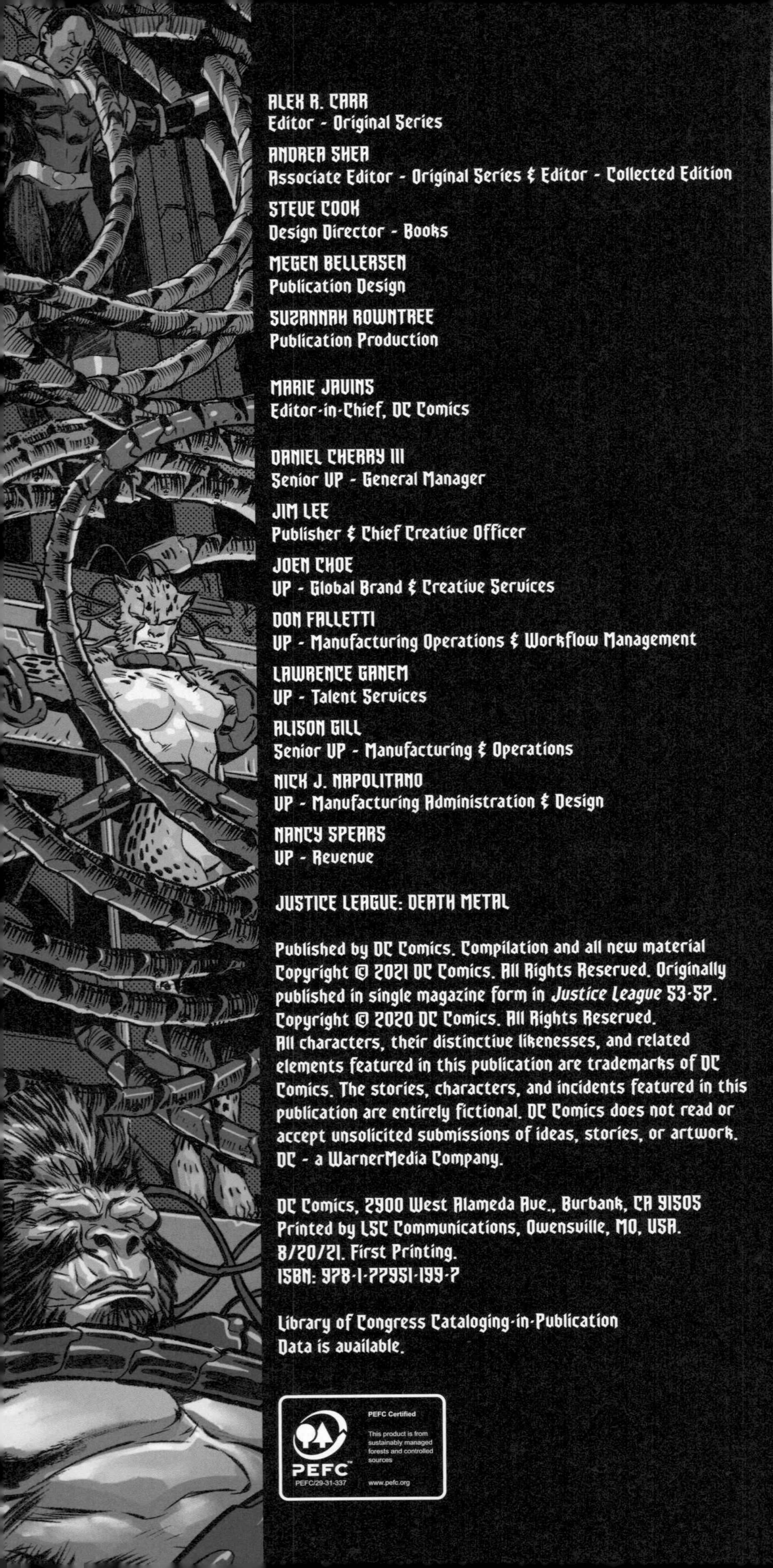

ALEX R. CARR
Editor - Original Series

ANDREA SHEA
Associate Editor - Original Series & Editor - Collected Edition

STEVE COOK
Design Director - Books

MEGEN BELLERSEN
Publication Design

SUZANNAH ROWNTREE
Publication Production

MARIE JAVINS
Editor-in-Chief, DC Comics

DANIEL CHERRY III
Senior VP - General Manager

JIM LEE
Publisher & Chief Creative Officer

JOEN CHOE
VP - Global Brand & Creative Services

DON FALLETTI
VP - Manufacturing Operations & Workflow Management

LAWRENCE GANEM
VP - Talent Services

ALISON GILL
Senior VP - Manufacturing & Operations

NICK J. NAPOLITANO
VP - Manufacturing Administration & Design

NANCY SPEARS
VP - Revenue

JUSTICE LEAGUE: DEATH METAL

DC Comics, 2900 West Alameda Ave., Burbank, CA 91505
Printed by LSC Communications, Owensville, MO, USA.
8/20/21. First Printing.
ISBN: 978-1-77951-199-7

Library of Congress Cataloging-in-Publication
Data is available.

PEFC Certified
This product is from sustainably managed forests and controlled sources
PEFC/29-31-337
www.pefc.org

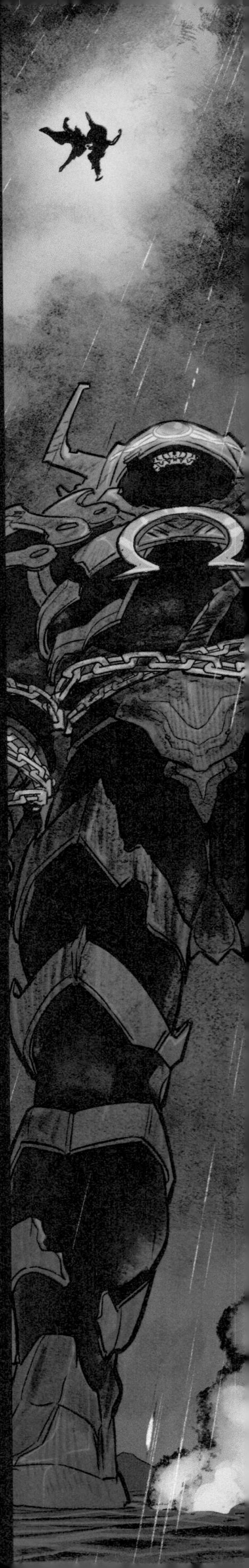

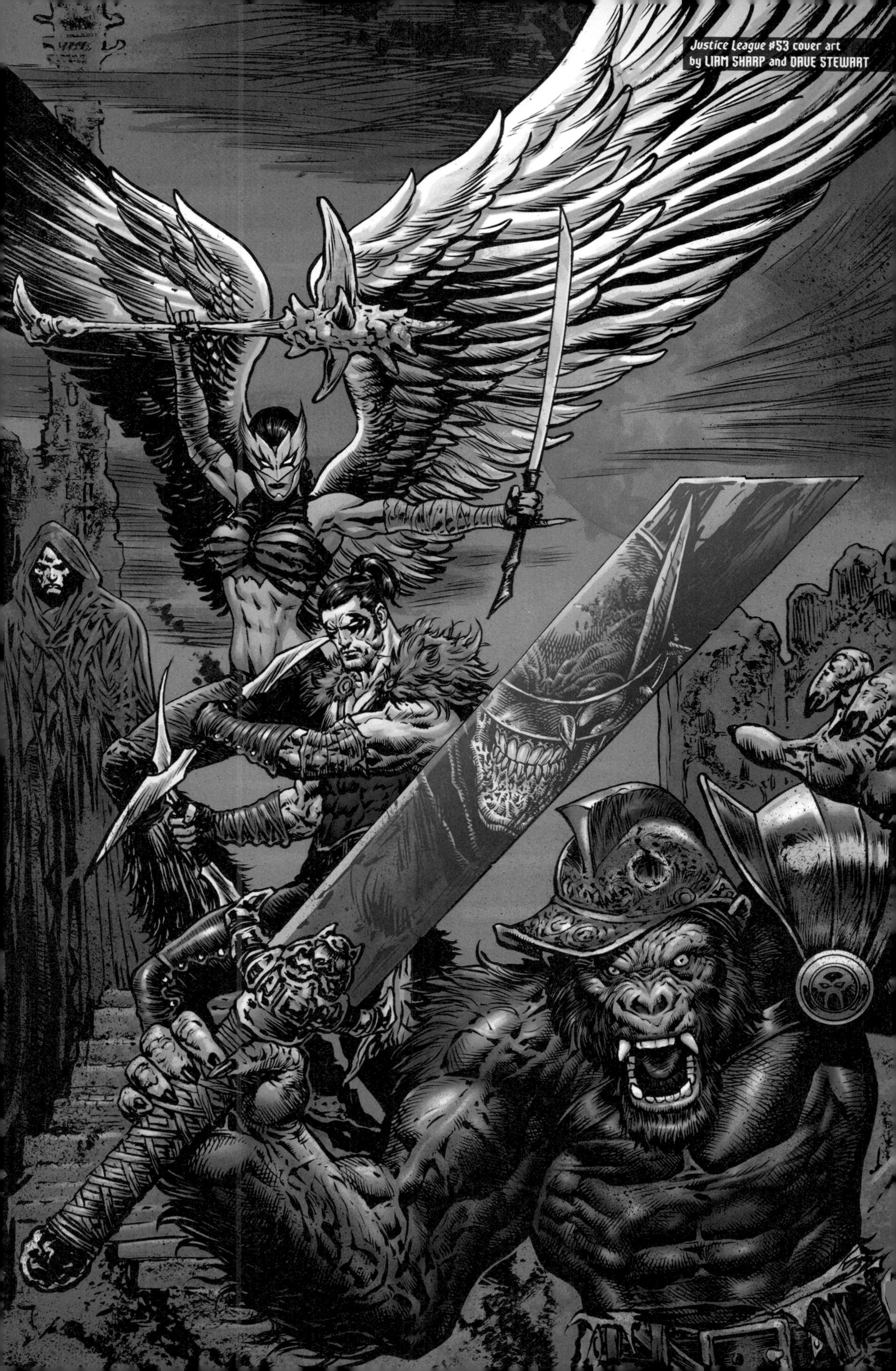

Justice League #53 cover art
by LIAM SHARP and DAVE STEWART

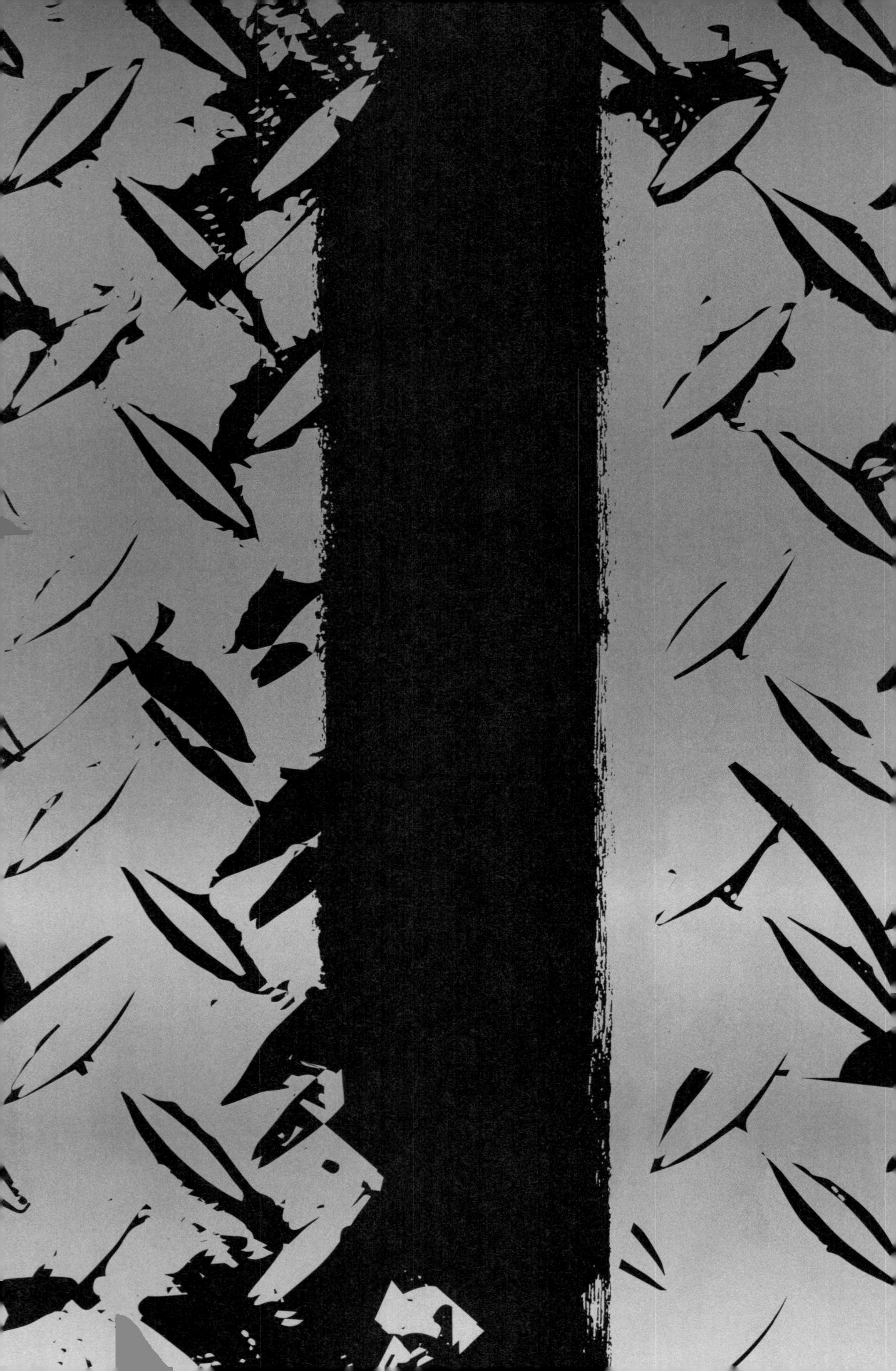

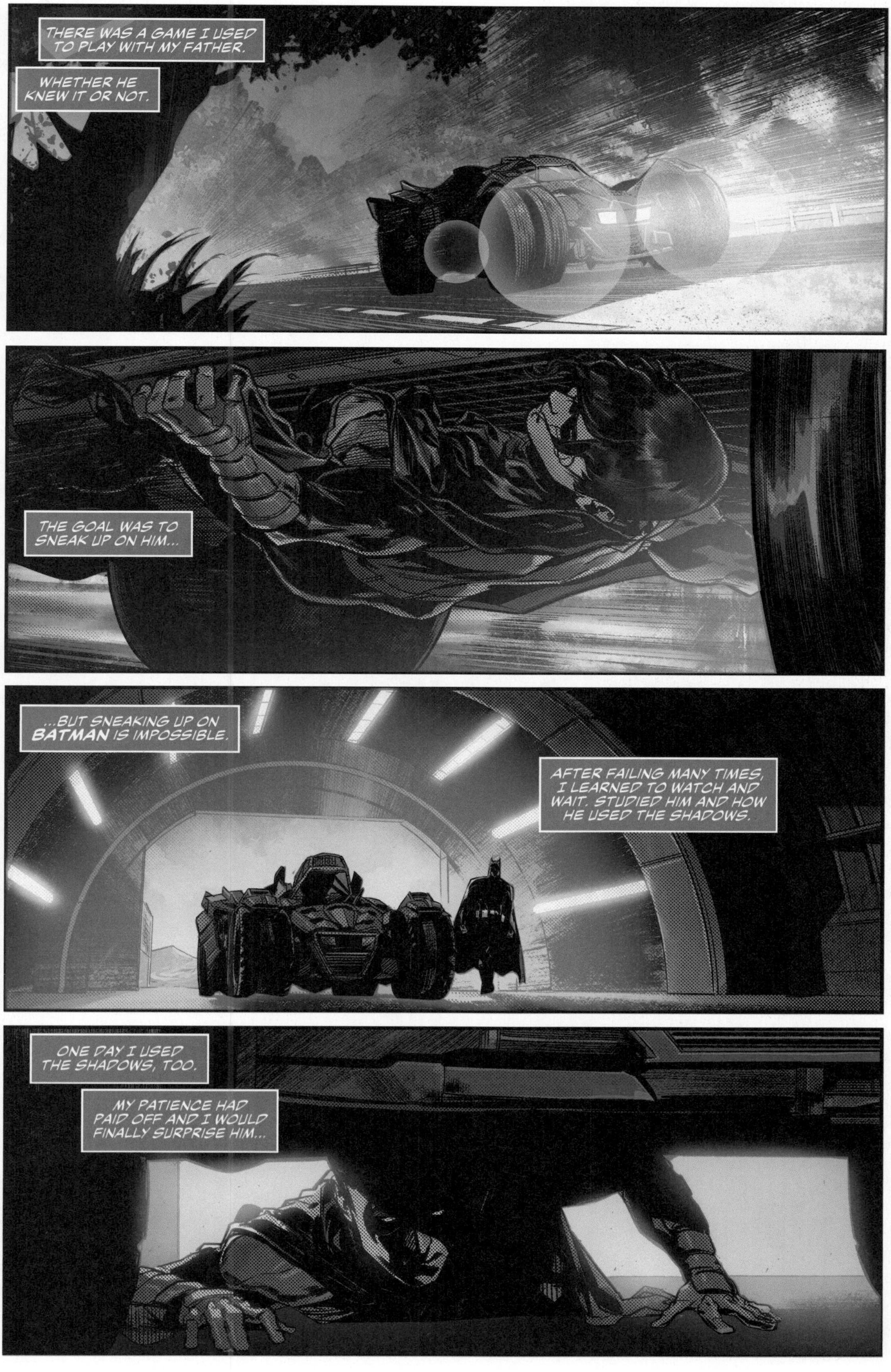

THERE WAS A GAME I USED TO PLAY WITH MY FATHER.
WHETHER HE KNEW IT OR NOT.
THE GOAL WAS TO SNEAK UP ON HIM...
...BUT SNEAKING UP ON BATMAN IS IMPOSSIBLE.
AFTER FAILING MANY TIMES, I LEARNED TO WATCH AND WAIT. STUDIED HIM AND HOW HE USED THE SHADOWS.
ONE DAY I USED THE SHADOWS, TOO.
MY PATIENCE HAD PAID OFF AND I WOULD FINALLY SURPRISE HIM...

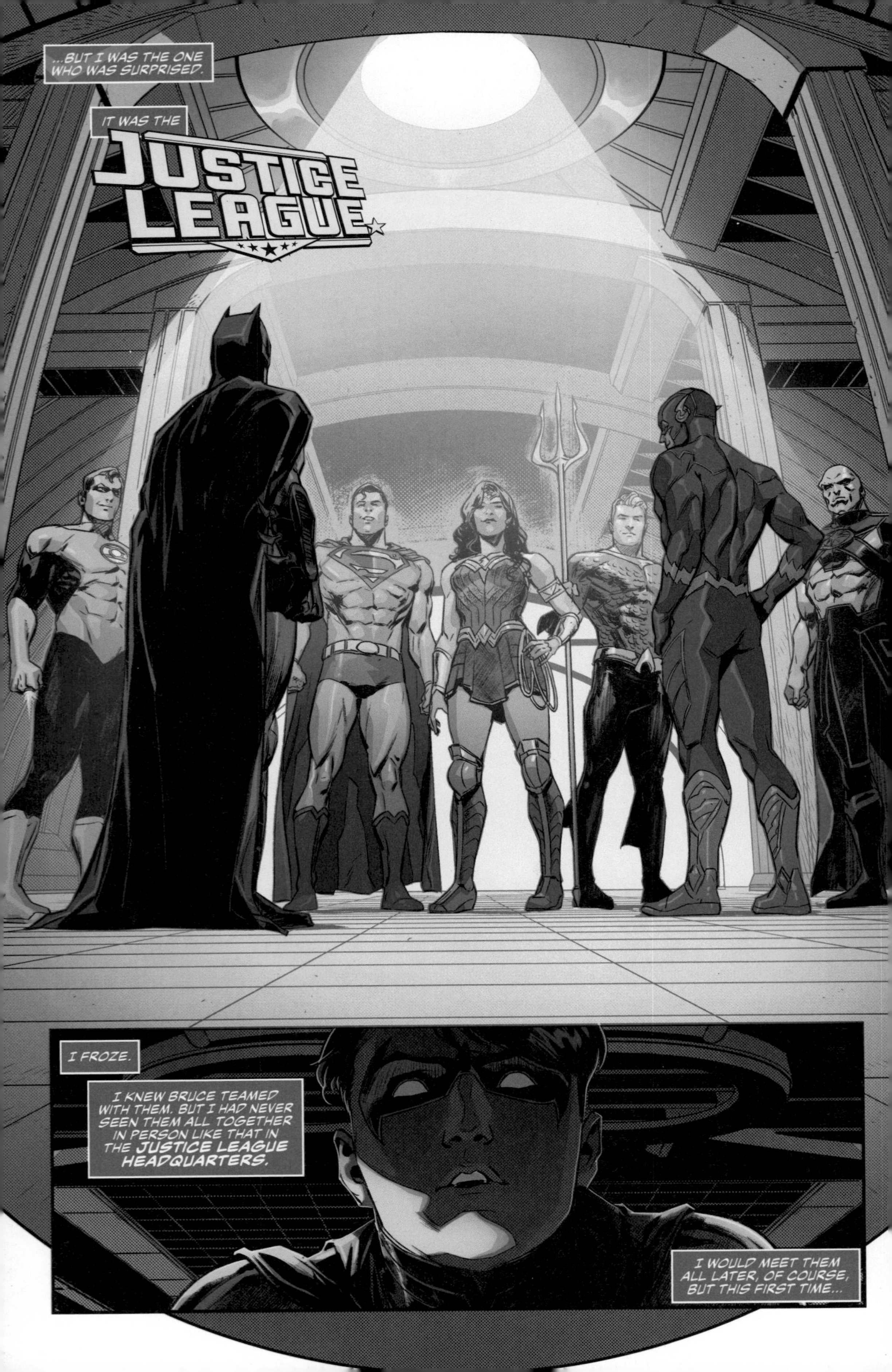
...BUT I WAS THE ONE WHO WAS SURPRISED.
IT WAS THE
JUSTICE LEAGUE
I FROZE.
I KNEW BRUCE TEAMED WITH THEM. BUT I HAD NEVER SEEN THEM ALL TOGETHER IN PERSON LIKE THAT IN THE JUSTICE LEAGUE HEADQUARTERS.
I WOULD MEET THEM ALL LATER, OF COURSE, BUT THIS FIRST TIME...

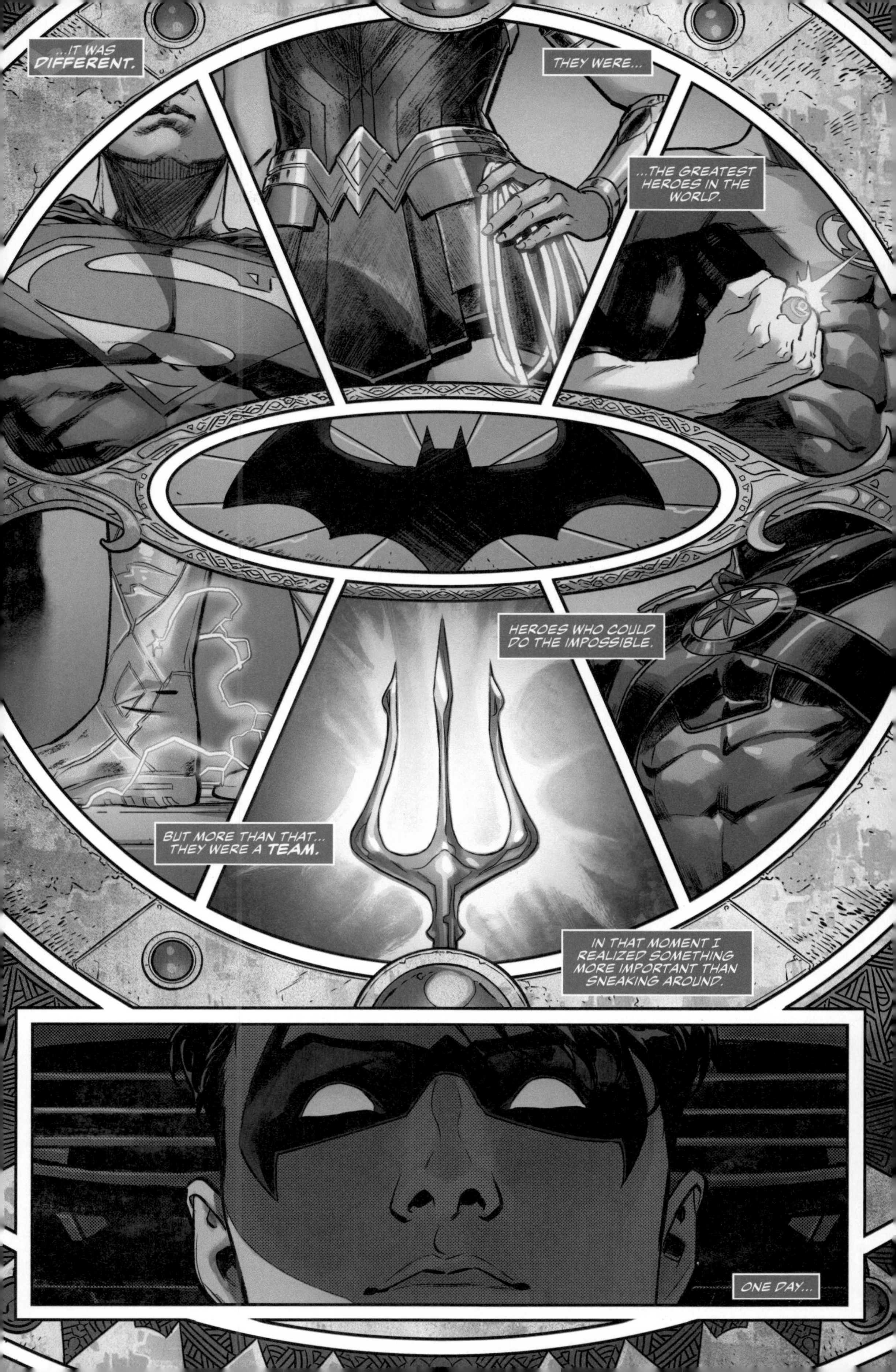
...IT WAS DIFFERENT.
THEY WERE...
...THE GREATEST HEROES IN THE WORLD.
HEROES WHO COULD DO THE IMPOSSIBLE.
BUT MORE THAN THAT... THEY WERE A TEAM.
IN THAT MOMENT I REALIZED SOMETHING MORE IMPORTANT THAN SNEAKING AROUND.
ONE DAY...

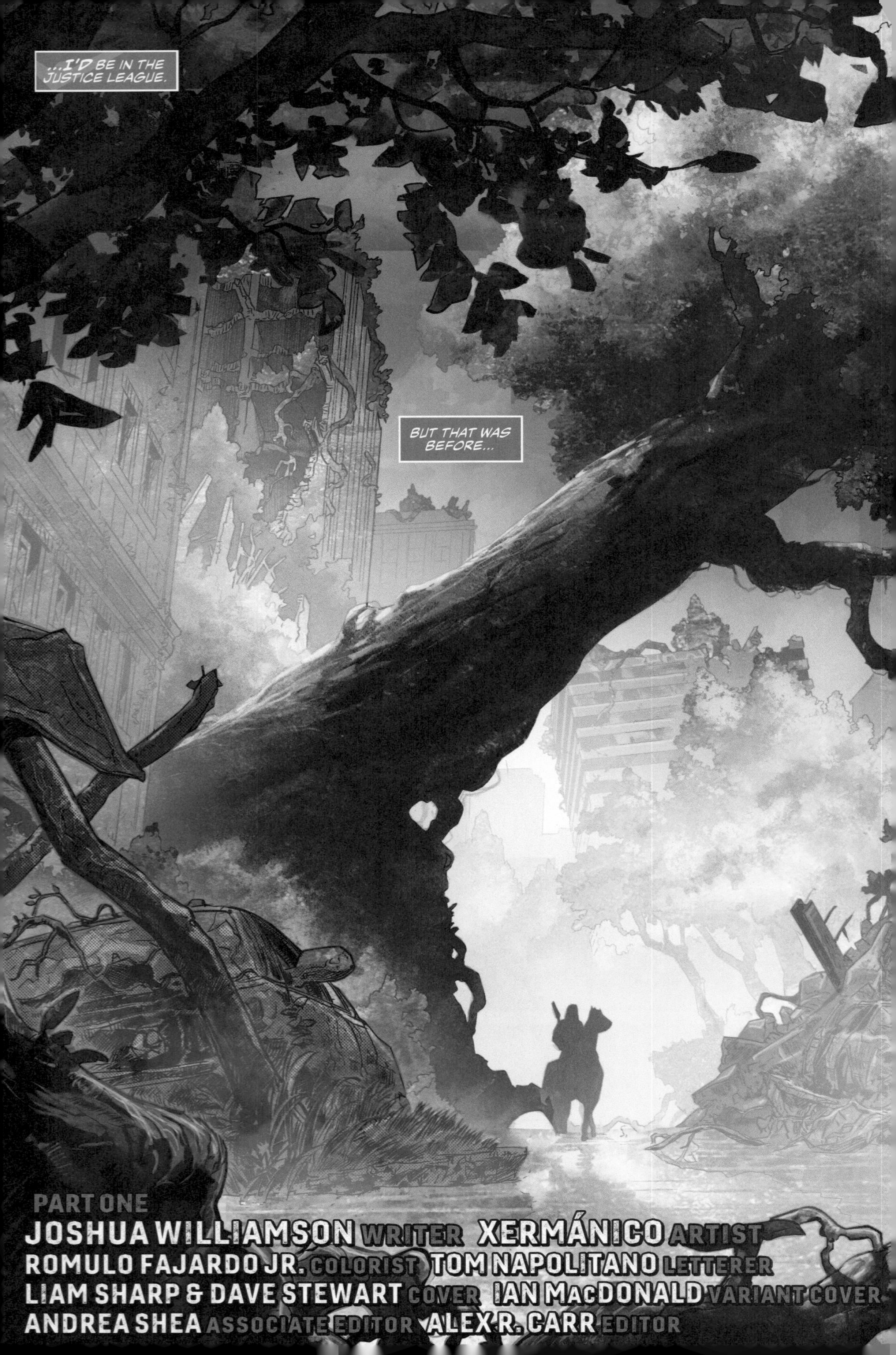
...I'D BE IN THE JUSTICE LEAGUE.
BUT THAT WAS BEFORE...
PART ONE
JOSHUA WILLIAMSON WRITER XERMÁNICO ARTIST
ROMULO FAJARDO JR. COLORIST TOM NAPOLITANO LETTERER
LIAM SHARP & DAVE STEWART COVER IAN MacDONALD VARIANT COVER
ANDREA SHEA ASSOCIATE EDITOR ALEX R. CARR EDITOR

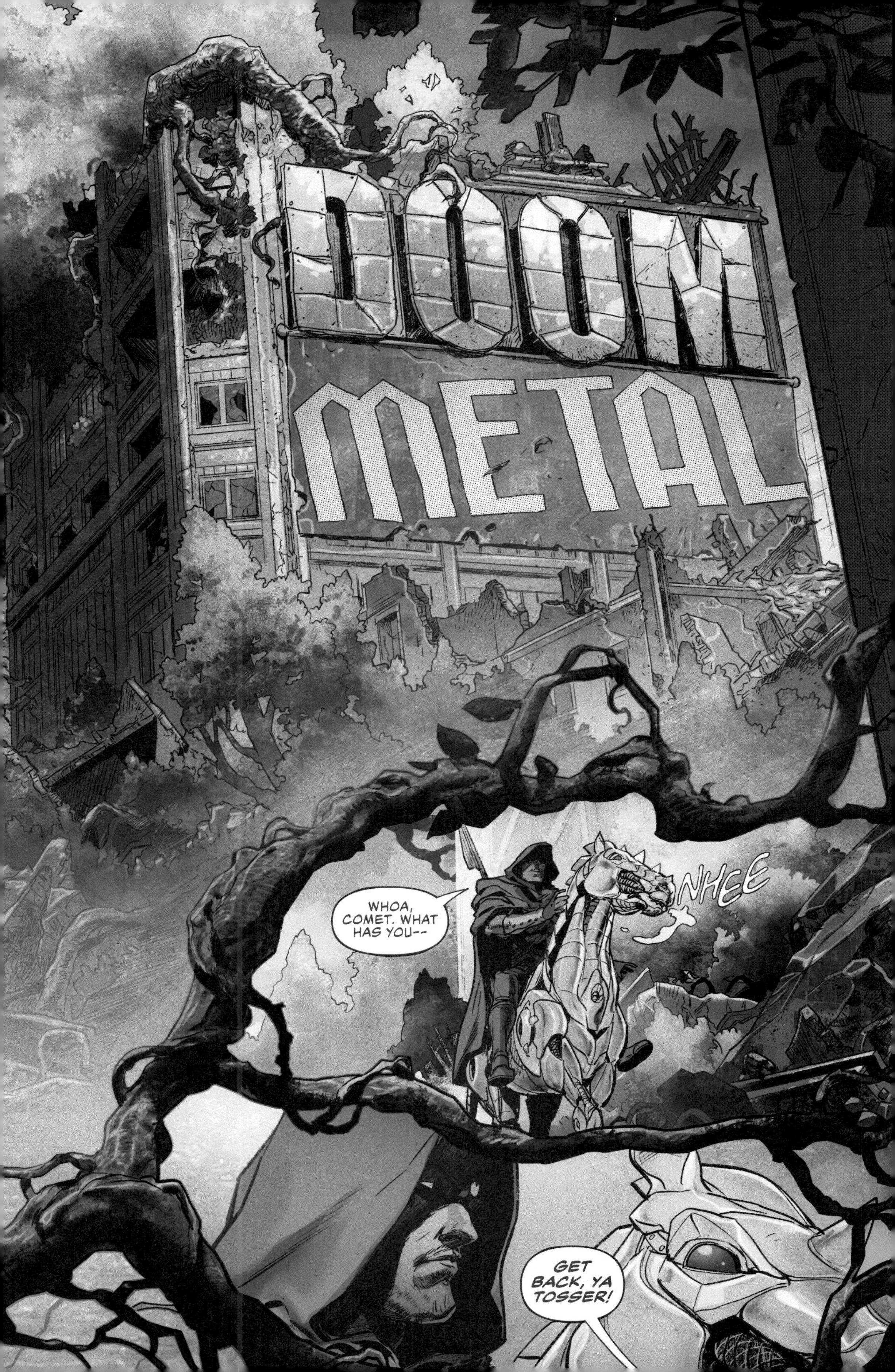
DOOM
METAL
WHOA, COMET. WHAT HAS YOU--
NHEE
GET BACK, YA TOSSER!

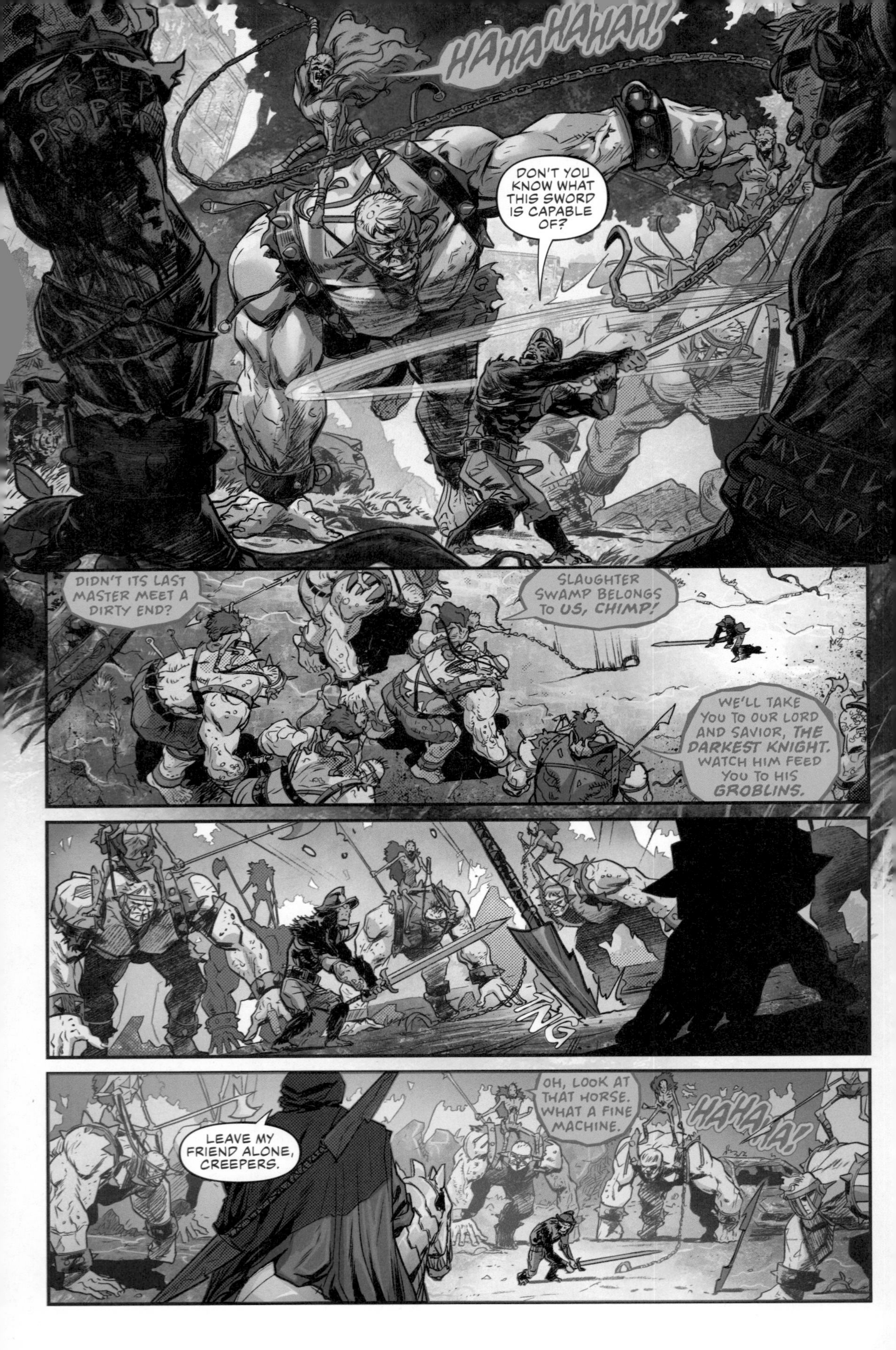
HAHAHAHAH!
DON'T YOU KNOW WHAT THIS SWORD IS CAPABLE OF?
DIDN'T ITS LAST MASTER MEET A DIRTY END?
SLAUGHTER SWAMP BELONGS TO US, CHIMP!
WE'LL TAKE YOU TO OUR LORD AND SAVIOR, THE DARKEST KNIGHT. WATCH HIM FEED YOU TO HIS GROBLINS.
TING
LEAVE MY FRIEND ALONE, CREEPERS.
OH, LOOK AT THAT HORSE. WHAT A FINE MACHINE.
HAHAHA!

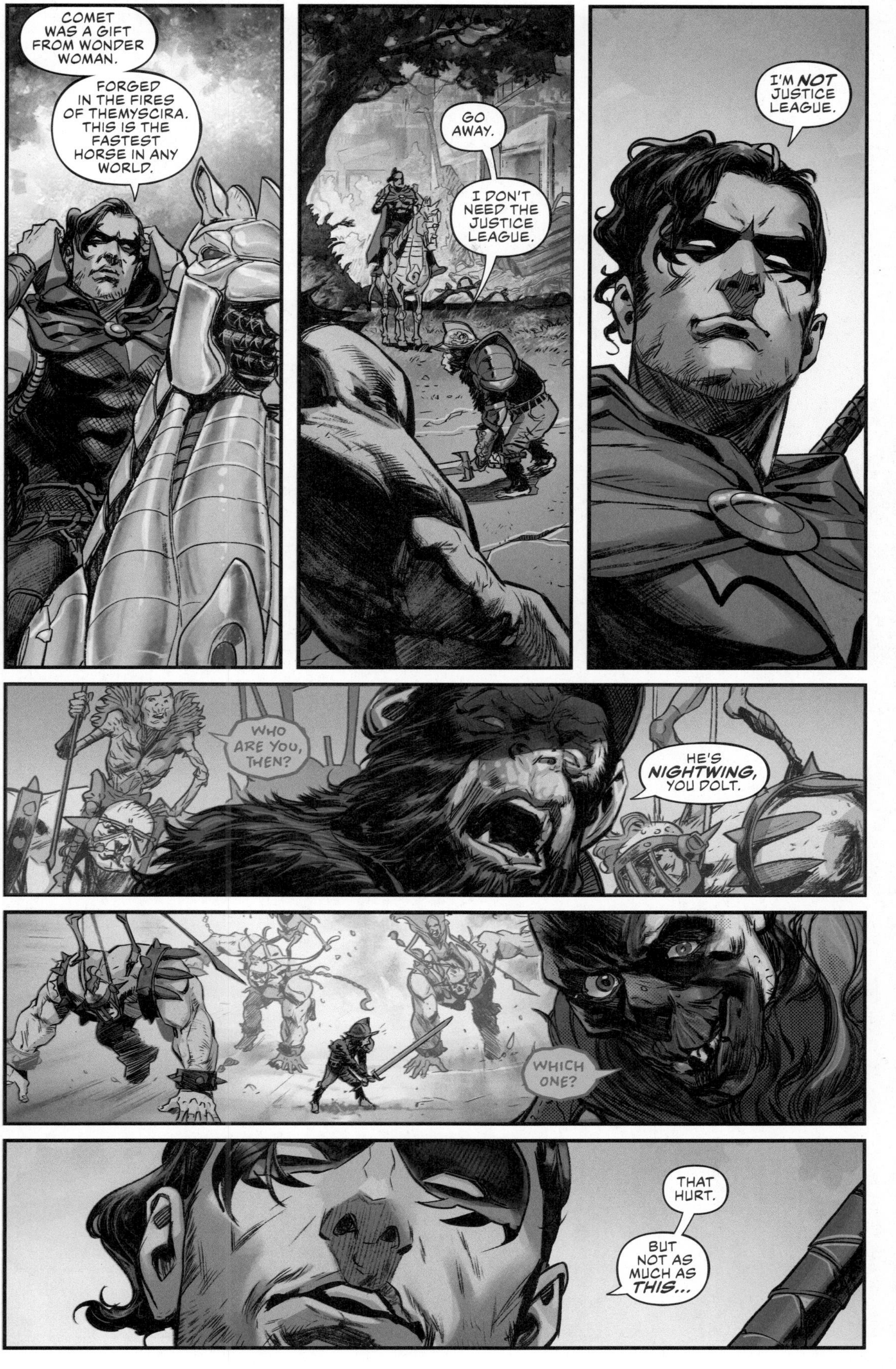
COMET WAS A GIFT FROM WONDER WOMAN.
FORGED IN THE FIRES OF THEMYSCIRA. THIS IS THE FASTEST HORSE IN ANY WORLD.
GO AWAY.
I DON'T NEED THE JUSTICE LEAGUE.
I'M NOT JUSTICE LEAGUE.
WHO ARE YOU, THEN?
HE'S NIGHTWING, YOU DOLT.
WHICH ONE?
THAT HURT.
BUT NOT AS MUCH AS THIS...

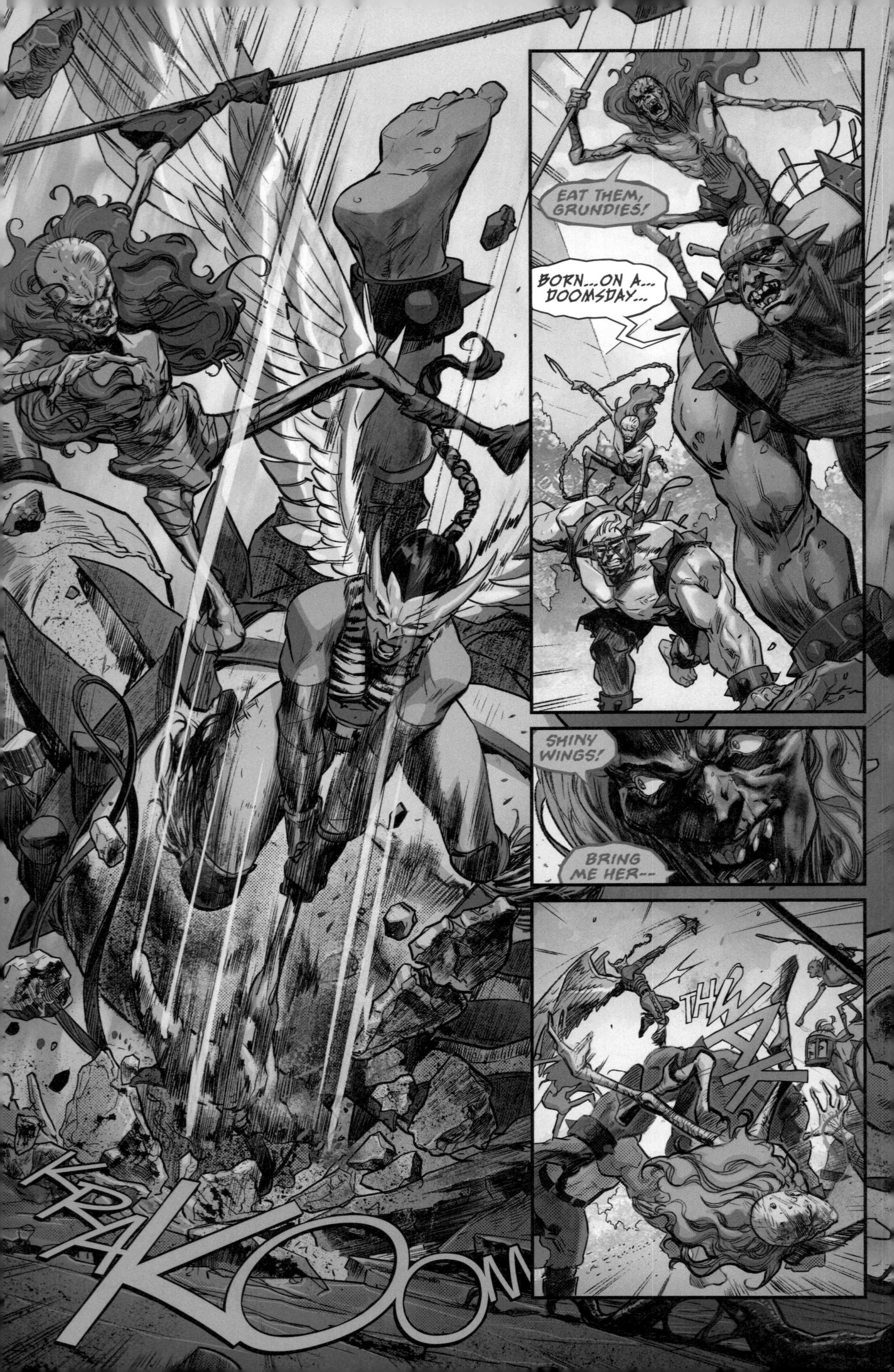
KRAKOOM
EAT THEM, GRUNDIES!
BORN...ON A... DOOMSDAY...
SHINY WINGS!
BRING ME HER--
THWAK

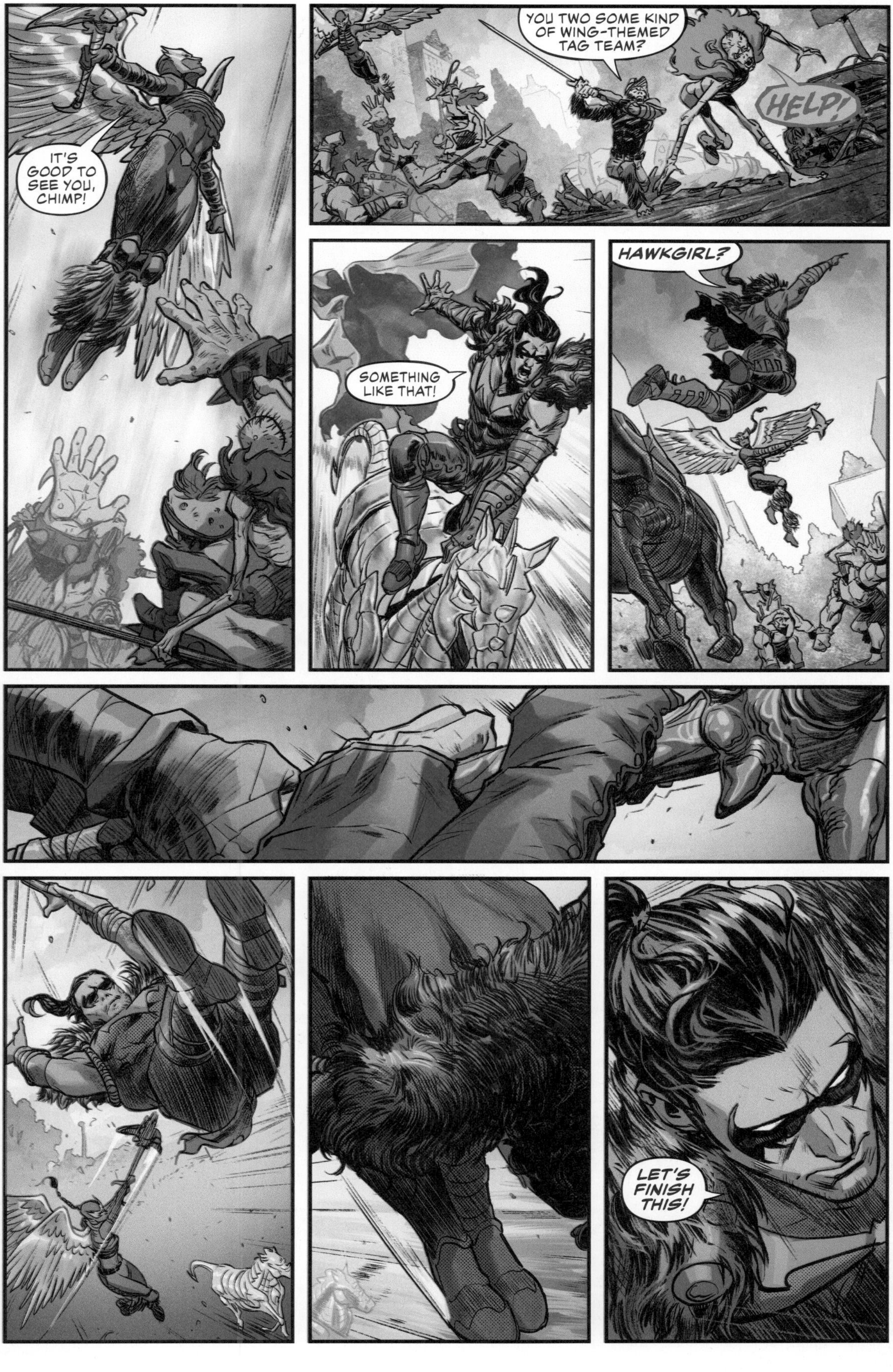
IT'S GOOD TO SEE YOU, CHIMP!
YOU TWO SOME KIND OF WING-THEMED TAG TEAM?
HELP!
SOMETHING LIKE THAT!
HAWKGIRL?
LET'S FINISH THIS!

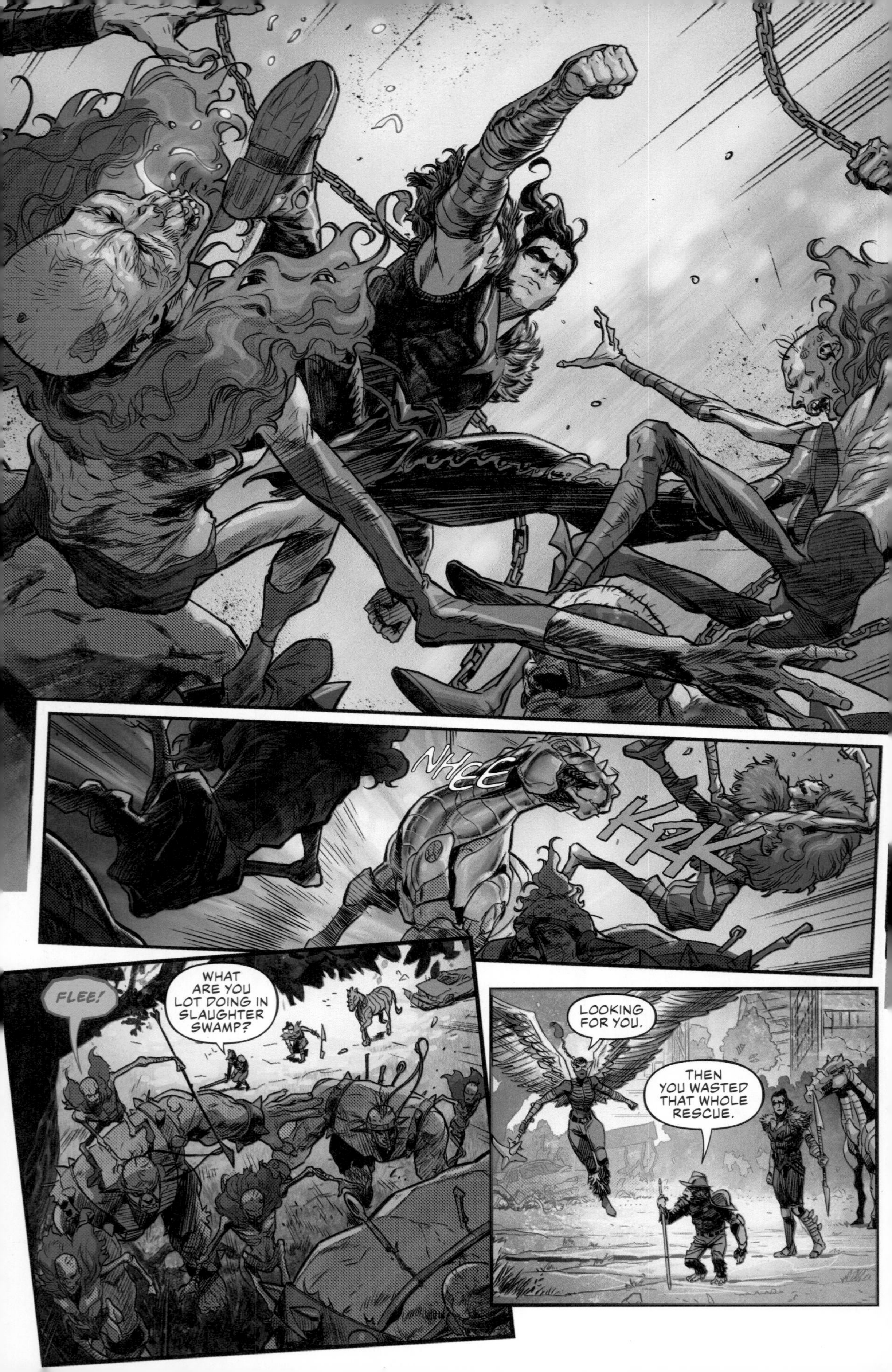
NHEE
KRK
FLEE!
WHAT ARE YOU LOT DOING IN SLAUGHTER SWAMP?
LOOKING FOR YOU.
THEN YOU WASTED THAT WHOLE RESCUE.

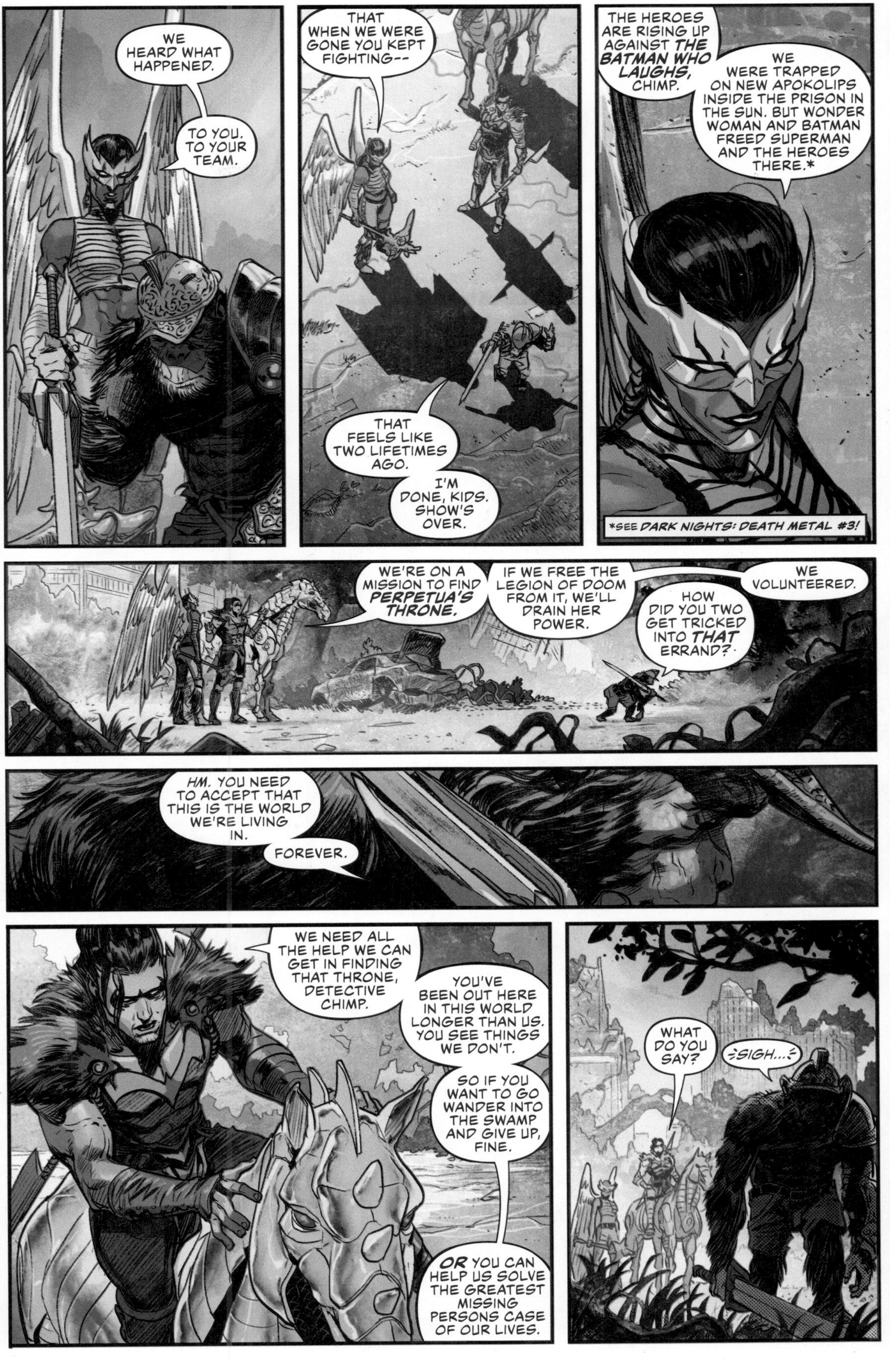
WE HEARD WHAT HAPPENED.
TO YOU. TO YOUR TEAM.
THAT WHEN WE WERE GONE YOU KEPT FIGHTING--
THAT FEELS LIKE TWO LIFETIMES AGO.
I'M DONE, KIDS. SHOW'S OVER.
THE HEROES ARE RISING UP AGAINST THE BATMAN WHO LAUGHS, CHIMP.
WE WERE TRAPPED ON NEW APOKOLIPS INSIDE THE PRISON IN THE SUN. BUT WONDER WOMAN AND BATMAN FREED SUPERMAN AND THE HEROES THERE.*
*SEE DARK NIGHTS: DEATH METAL #3!
WE'RE ON A MISSION TO FIND PERPETUA'S THRONE.
IF WE FREE THE LEGION OF DOOM FROM IT, WE'LL DRAIN HER POWER.
WE VOLUNTEERED.
HOW DID YOU TWO GET TRICKED INTO THAT ERRAND?
HM. YOU NEED TO ACCEPT THAT THIS IS THE WORLD WE'RE LIVING IN.
FOREVER.
WE NEED ALL THE HELP WE CAN GET IN FINDING THAT THRONE, DETECTIVE CHIMP.
YOU'VE BEEN OUT HERE IN THIS WORLD LONGER THAN US. YOU SEE THINGS WE DON'T.
SO IF YOU WANT TO GO WANDER INTO THE SWAMP AND GIVE UP, FINE.
OR YOU CAN HELP US SOLVE THE GREATEST MISSING PERSONS CASE OF OUR LIVES.
WHAT DO YOU SAY?
SIGH...

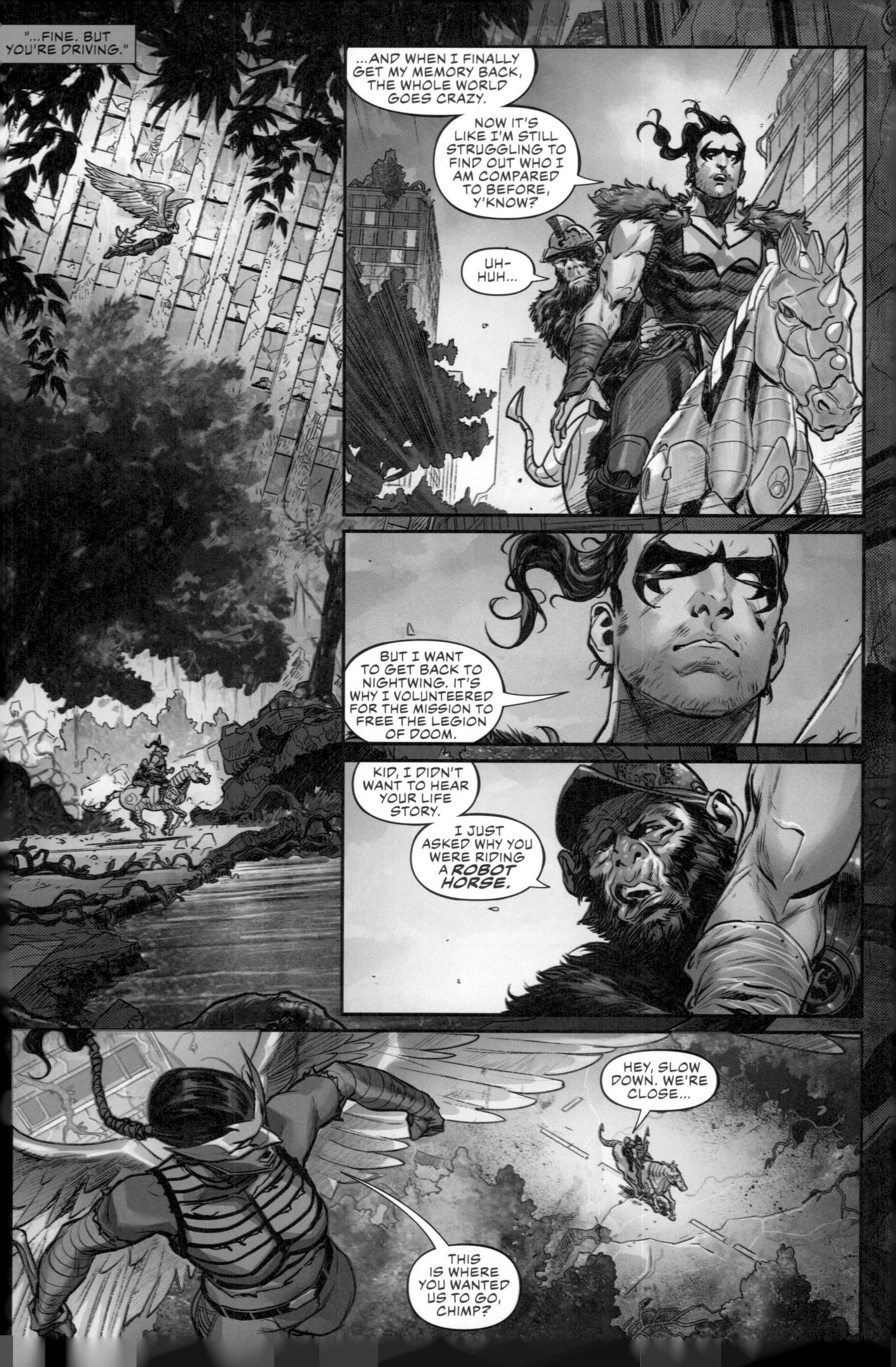
"...FINE. BUT YOU'RE DRIVING."
...AND WHEN I FINALLY GET MY MEMORY BACK, THE WHOLE WORLD GOES CRAZY.
NOW IT'S LIKE I'M STILL STRUGGLING TO FIND OUT WHO I AM COMPARED TO BEFORE, Y'KNOW?
UH-HUH...
BUT I WANT TO GET BACK TO NIGHTWING. IT'S WHY I VOLUNTEERED FOR THE MISSION TO FREE THE LEGION OF DOOM.
KID, I DIDN'T WANT TO HEAR YOUR LIFE STORY.
I JUST ASKED WHY YOU WERE RIDING A *ROBOT HORSE.*
HEY, SLOW DOWN. WE'RE CLOSE...
THIS IS WHERE YOU WANTED US TO GO, CHIMP?

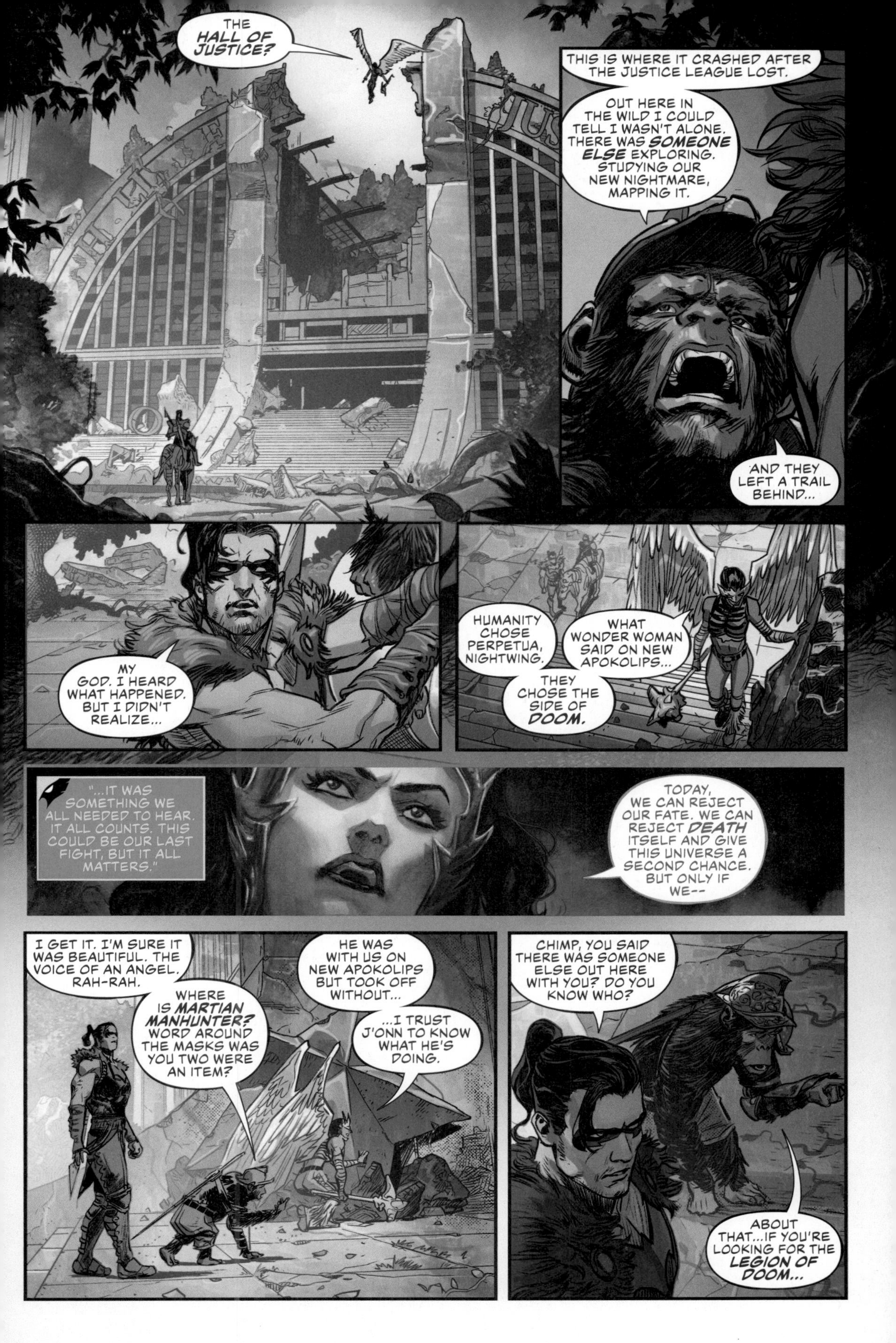
THE HALL OF JUSTICE?
THIS IS WHERE IT CRASHED AFTER THE JUSTICE LEAGUE LOST.
OUT HERE IN THE WILD I COULD TELL I WASN'T ALONE. THERE WAS SOMEONE ELSE EXPLORING. STUDYING OUR NEW NIGHTMARE, MAPPING IT.
AND THEY LEFT A TRAIL BEHIND...
MY GOD. I HEARD WHAT HAPPENED. BUT I DIDN'T REALIZE...
HUMANITY CHOSE PERPETUA, NIGHTWING.
THEY CHOSE THE SIDE OF DOOM.
WHAT WONDER WOMAN SAID ON NEW APOKOLIPS...
"...IT WAS SOMETHING WE ALL NEEDED TO HEAR. IT ALL COUNTS. THIS COULD BE OUR LAST FIGHT, BUT IT ALL MATTERS."
TODAY, WE CAN REJECT OUR FATE. WE CAN REJECT DEATH ITSELF AND GIVE THIS UNIVERSE A SECOND CHANCE. BUT ONLY IF WE--
I GET IT. I'M SURE IT WAS BEAUTIFUL. THE VOICE OF AN ANGEL. RAH-RAH.
WHERE IS MARTIAN MANHUNTER? WORD AROUND THE MASKS WAS YOU TWO WERE AN ITEM?
HE WAS WITH US ON NEW APOKOLIPS BUT TOOK OFF WITHOUT...
...I TRUST J'ONN TO KNOW WHAT HE'S DOING.
CHIMP, YOU SAID THERE WAS SOMEONE ELSE OUT HERE WITH YOU? DO YOU KNOW WHO?
ABOUT THAT...IF YOU'RE LOOKING FOR THE LEGION OF DOOM...

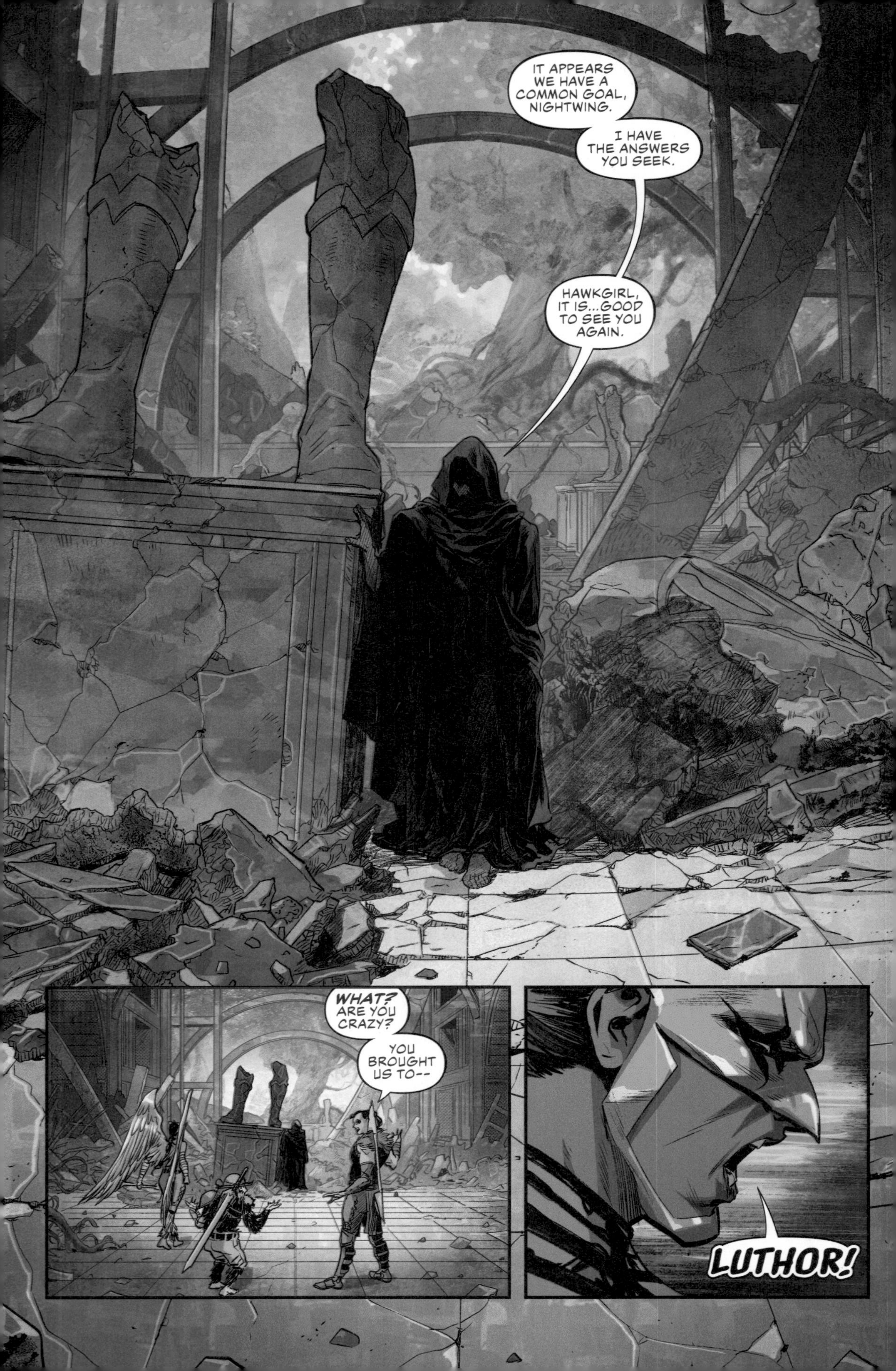

IT APPEARS WE HAVE A COMMON GOAL, NIGHTWING.
I HAVE THE ANSWERS YOU SEEK.
HAWKGIRL, IT IS...GOOD TO SEE YOU AGAIN.
WHAT? ARE YOU CRAZY?
YOU BROUGHT US TO--
LUTHOR!

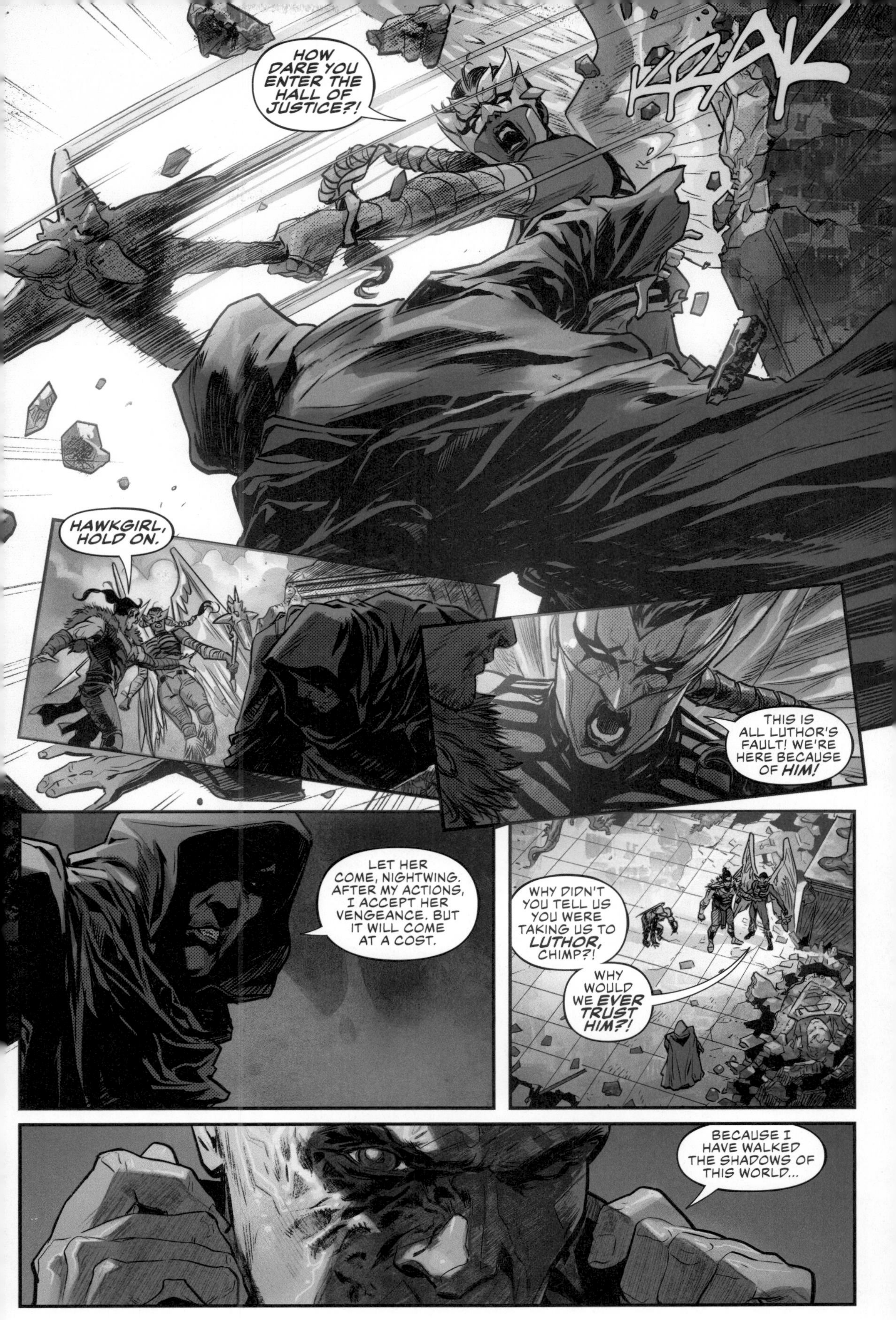
HOW DARE YOU ENTER THE HALL OF JUSTICE?!
KRAK
HAWKGIRL, HOLD ON.
THIS IS ALL LUTHOR'S FAULT! WE'RE HERE BECAUSE OF HIM!
LET HER COME, NIGHTWING. AFTER MY ACTIONS, I ACCEPT HER VENGEANCE. BUT IT WILL COME AT A COST.
WHY DIDN'T YOU TELL US YOU WERE TAKING US TO LUTHOR, CHIMP?!
WHY WOULD WE EVER TRUST HIM?!
BECAUSE I HAVE WALKED THE SHADOWS OF THIS WORLD...

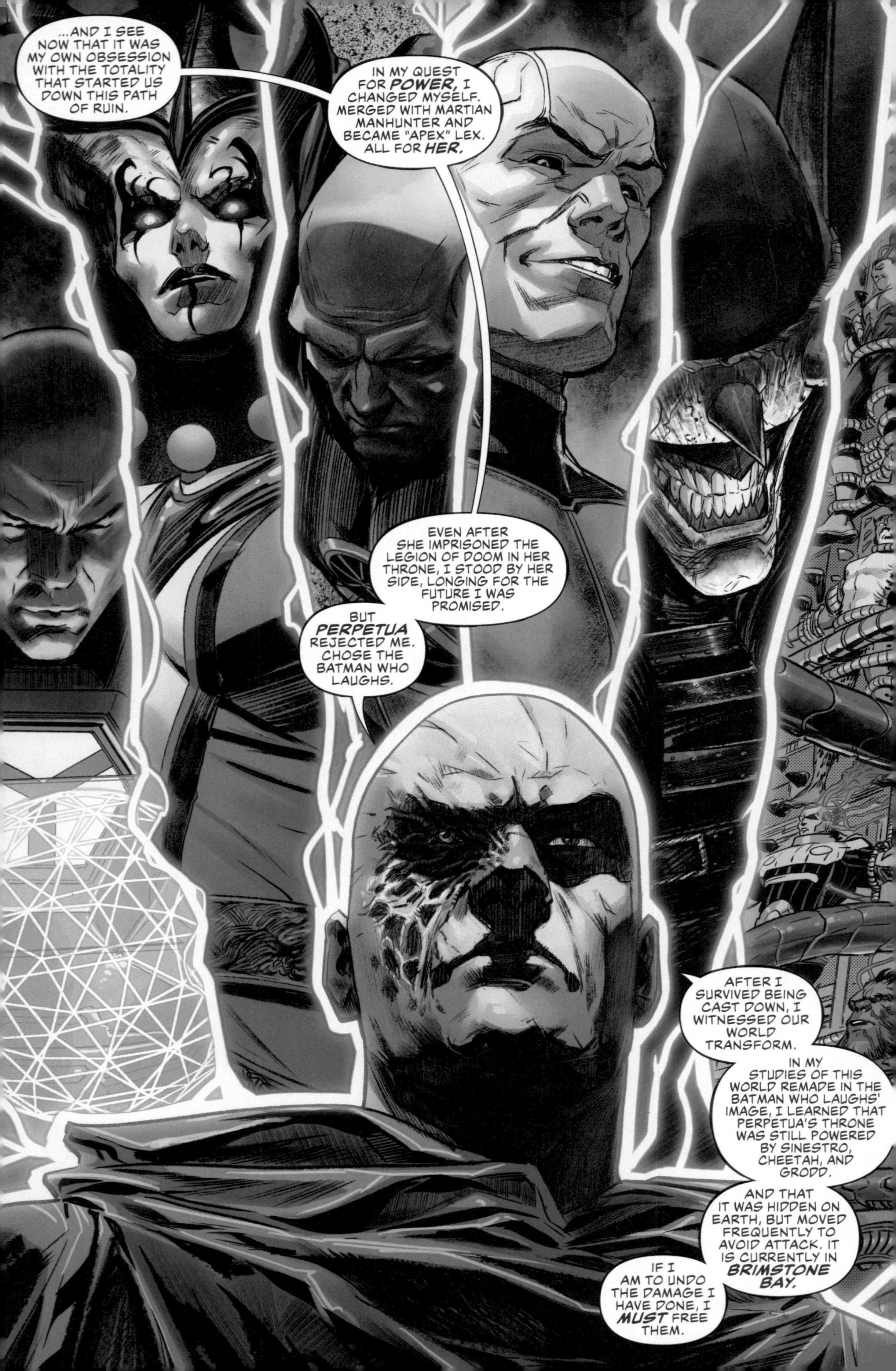
...AND I SEE NOW THAT IT WAS MY OWN OBSESSION WITH THE TOTALITY THAT STARTED US DOWN THIS PATH OF RUIN.
IN MY QUEST FOR POWER, I CHANGED MYSELF. MERGED WITH MARTIAN MANHUNTER AND BECAME "APEX" LEX. ALL FOR HER.
EVEN AFTER SHE IMPRISONED THE LEGION OF DOOM IN HER THRONE, I STOOD BY HER SIDE, LONGING FOR THE FUTURE I WAS PROMISED.
BUT PERPETUA REJECTED ME. CHOSE THE BATMAN WHO LAUGHS.
AFTER I SURVIVED BEING CAST DOWN, I WITNESSED OUR WORLD TRANSFORM.
IN MY STUDIES OF THIS WORLD REMADE IN THE BATMAN WHO LAUGHS' IMAGE, I LEARNED THAT PERPETUA'S THRONE WAS STILL POWERED BY SINESTRO, CHEETAH, AND GRODD.
AND THAT IT WAS HIDDEN ON EARTH, BUT MOVED FREQUENTLY TO AVOID ATTACK. IT IS CURRENTLY IN BRIMSTONE BAY.
IF I AM TO UNDO THE DAMAGE I HAVE DONE, I MUST FREE THEM.

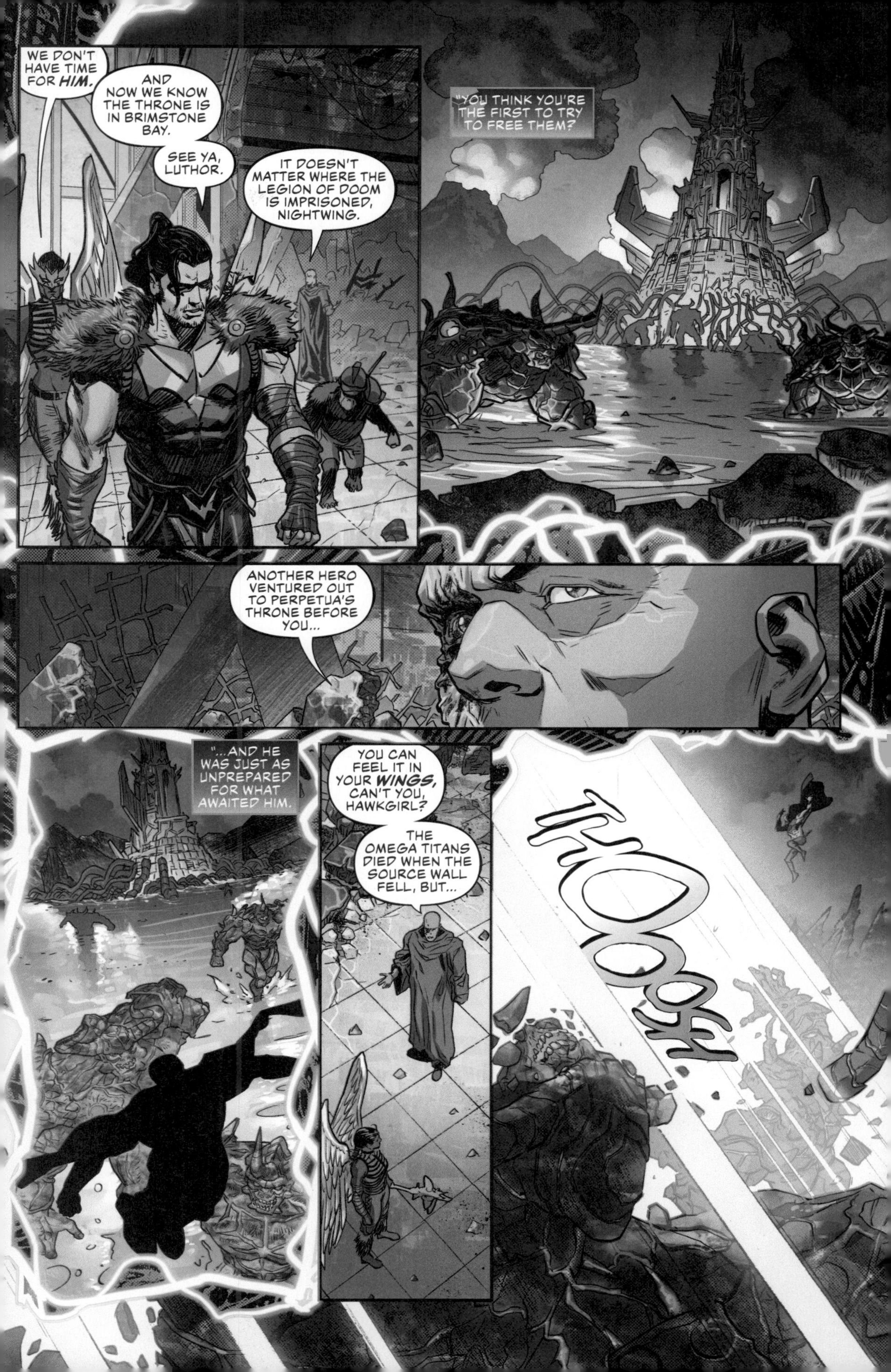
WE DON'T HAVE TIME FOR HIM.
AND NOW WE KNOW THE THRONE IS IN BRIMSTONE BAY.
SEE YA, LUTHOR.
IT DOESN'T MATTER WHERE THE LEGION OF DOOM IS IMPRISONED, NIGHTWING.
"YOU THINK YOU'RE THE FIRST TO TRY TO FREE THEM?
ANOTHER HERO VENTURED OUT TO PERPETUA'S THRONE BEFORE YOU...
"...AND HE WAS JUST AS UNPREPARED FOR WHAT AWAITED HIM.
YOU CAN FEEL IT IN YOUR WINGS, CAN'T YOU, HAWKGIRL?
THE OMEGA TITANS DIED WHEN THE SOURCE WALL FELL, BUT...
THOOOSH

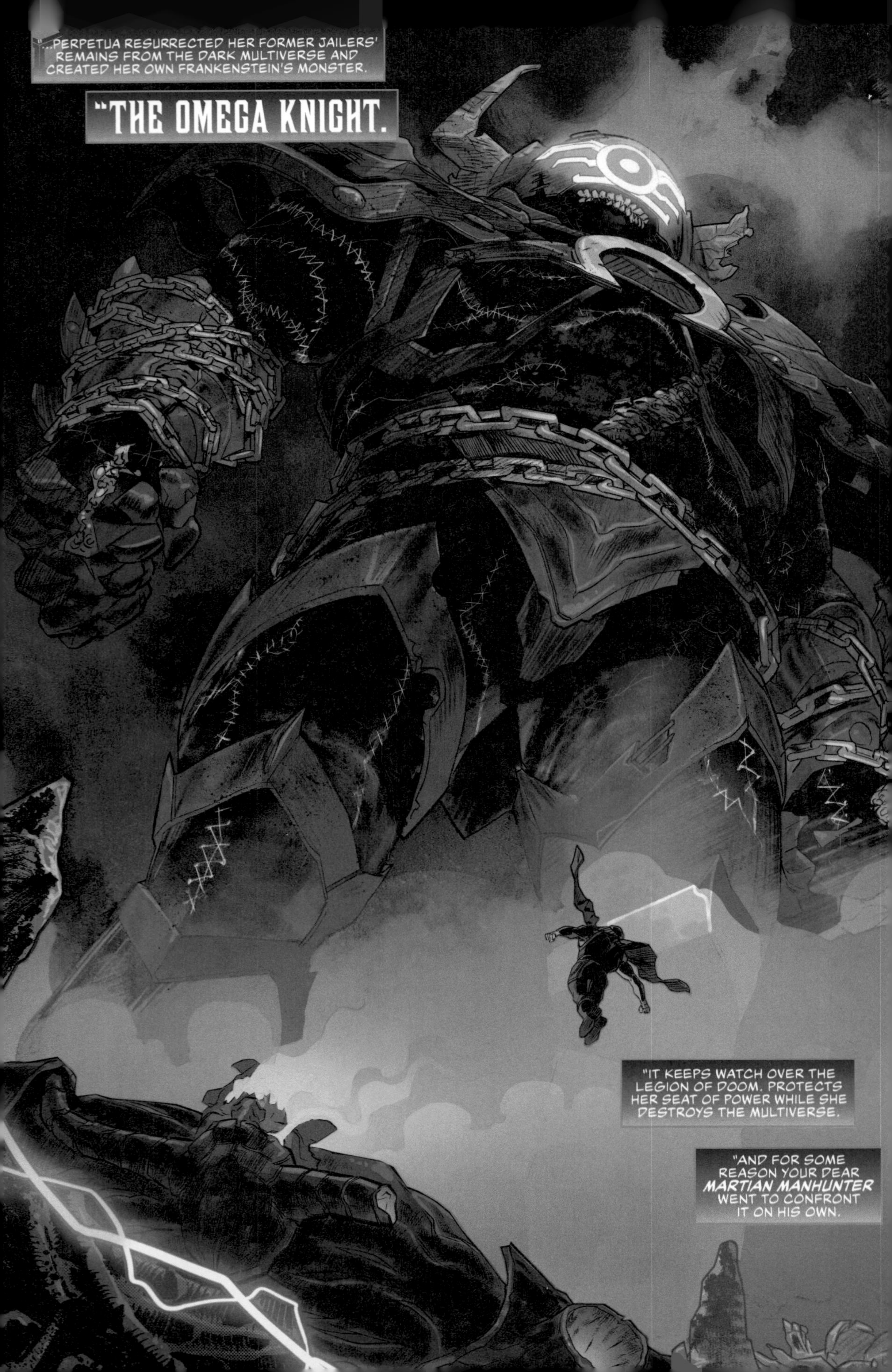
"...PERPETUA RESURRECTED HER FORMER JAILERS' REMAINS FROM THE DARK MULTIVERSE AND CREATED HER OWN FRANKENSTEIN'S MONSTER.
"THE OMEGA KNIGHT.
"IT KEEPS WATCH OVER THE LEGION OF DOOM. PROTECTS HER SEAT OF POWER WHILE SHE DESTROYS THE MULTIVERSE.
"AND FOR SOME REASON YOUR DEAR MARTIAN MANHUNTER WENT TO CONFRONT IT ON HIS OWN.

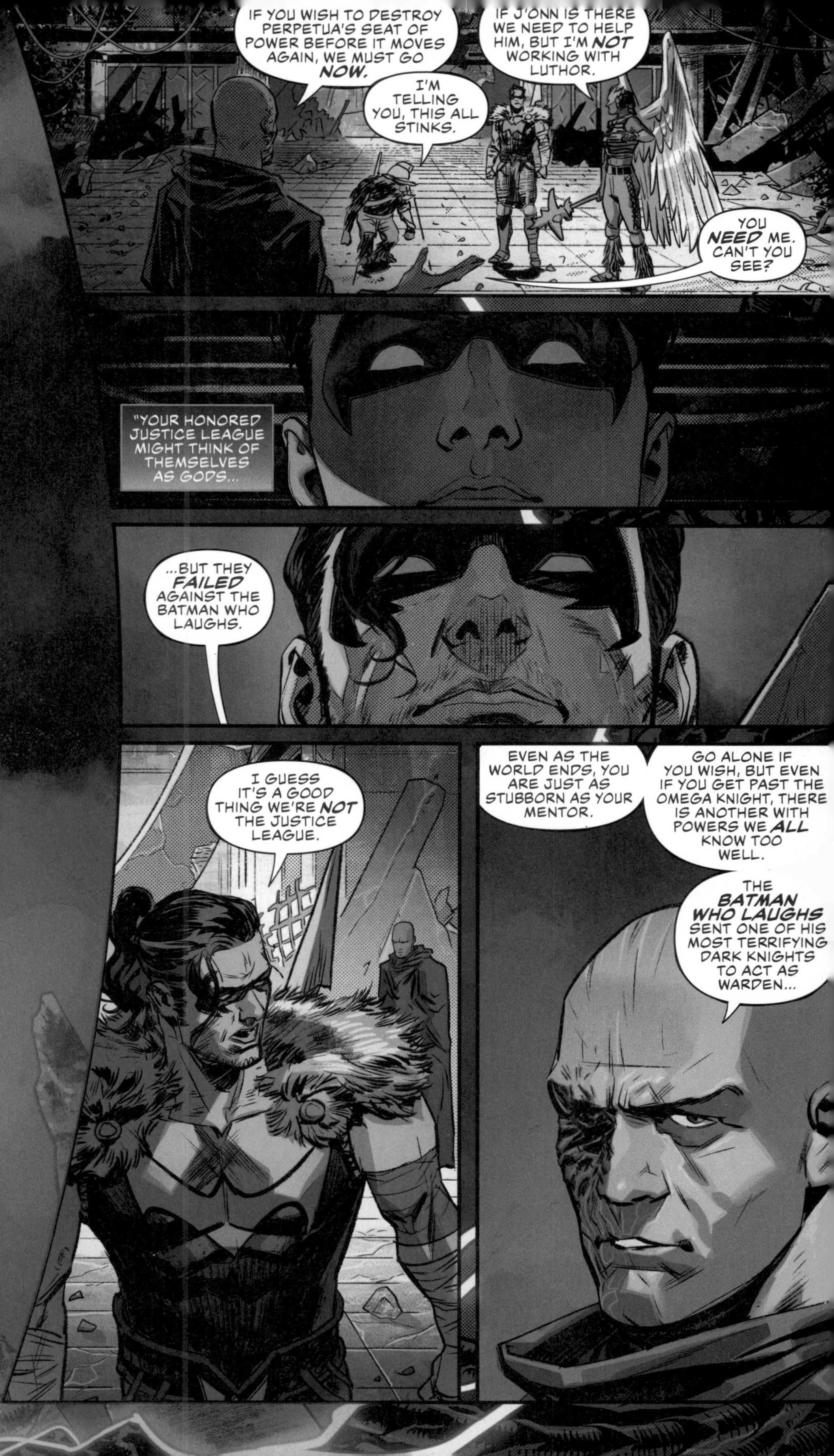
IF YOU WISH TO DESTROY PERPETUA'S SEAT OF POWER BEFORE IT MOVES AGAIN, WE MUST GO NOW.
I'M TELLING YOU, THIS ALL STINKS.
IF J'ONN IS THERE WE NEED TO HELP HIM, BUT I'M NOT WORKING WITH LUTHOR.
YOU NEED ME. CAN'T YOU SEE?
"YOUR HONORED JUSTICE LEAGUE MIGHT THINK OF THEMSELVES AS GODS...
...BUT THEY FAILED AGAINST THE BATMAN WHO LAUGHS.
I GUESS IT'S A GOOD THING WE'RE NOT THE JUSTICE LEAGUE.
EVEN AS THE WORLD ENDS, YOU ARE JUST AS STUBBORN AS YOUR MENTOR.
GO ALONE IF YOU WISH, BUT EVEN IF YOU GET PAST THE OMEGA KNIGHT, THERE IS ANOTHER WITH POWERS WE ALL KNOW TOO WELL.
THE BATMAN WHO LAUGHS SENT ONE OF HIS MOST TERRIFYING DARK KNIGHTS TO ACT AS WARDEN...

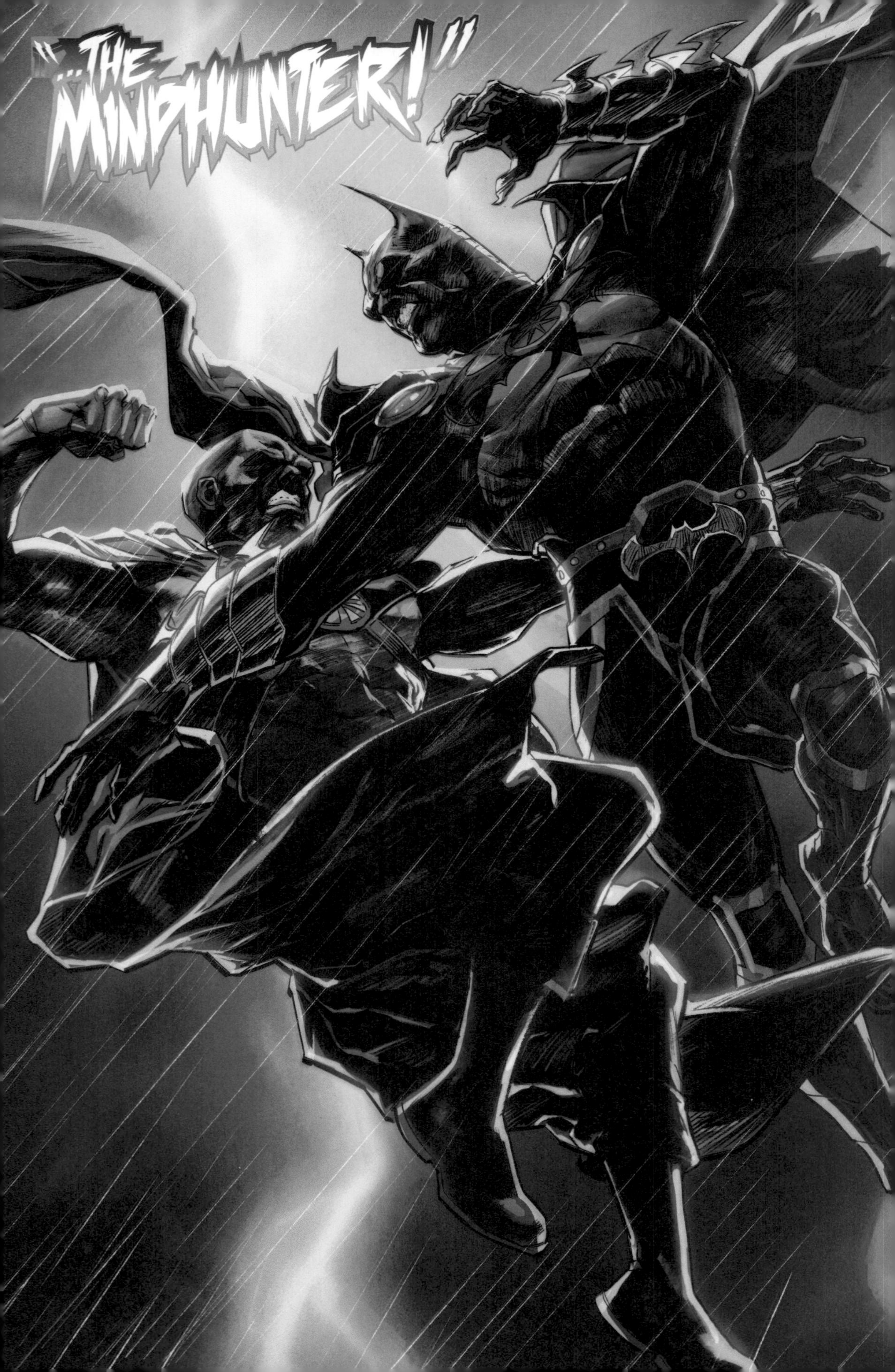
"...THE MINDHUNTER!"

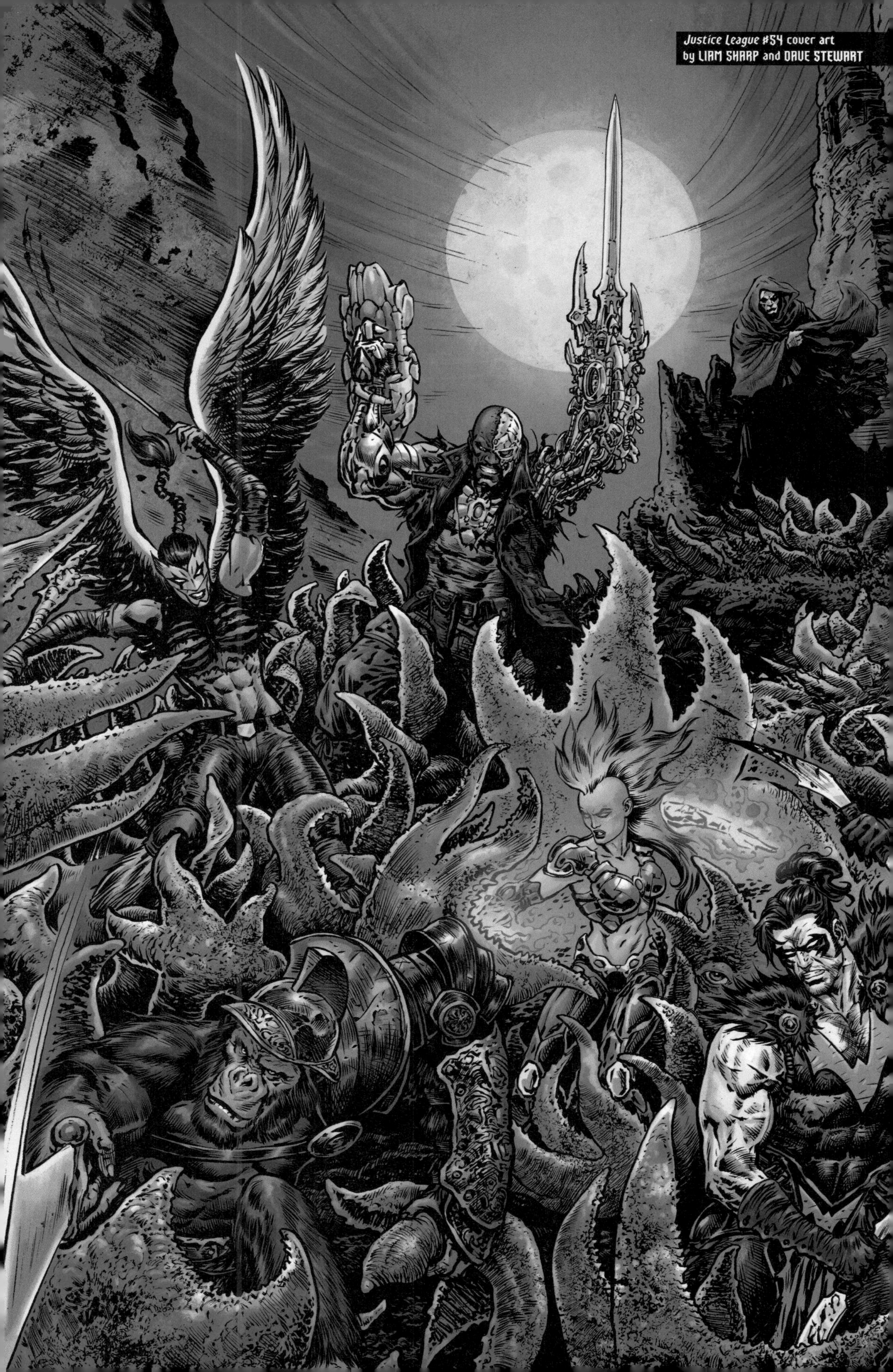

Justice League #54 cover art
by LIAM SHARP and DAVE STEWART

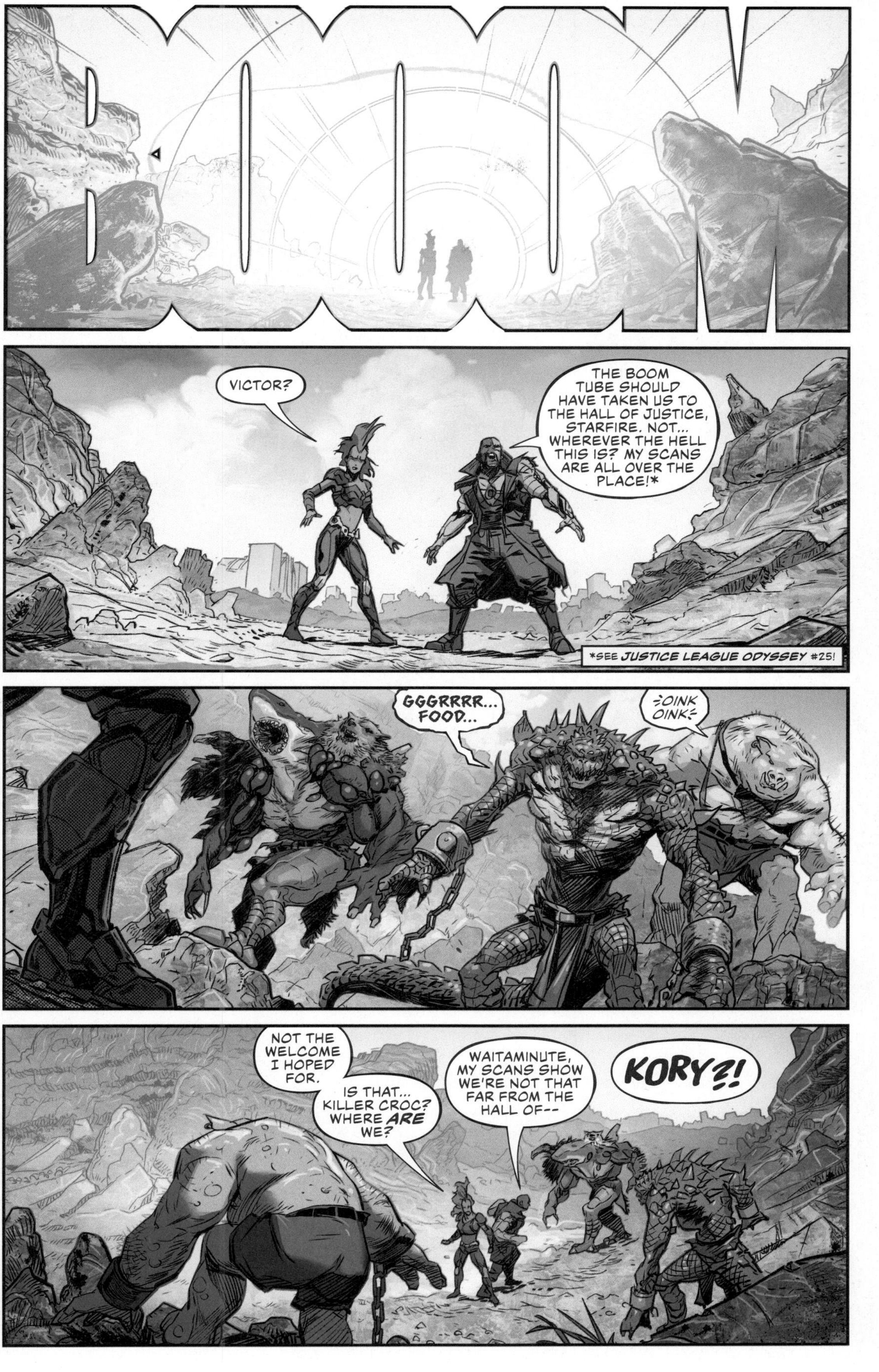
BOOOOM
VICTOR?
THE BOOM TUBE SHOULD HAVE TAKEN US TO THE HALL OF JUSTICE, STARFIRE. NOT... WHEREVER THE HELL THIS IS? MY SCANS ARE ALL OVER THE PLACE!*
*SEE JUSTICE LEAGUE ODYSSEY #25!
GGGRRRR... FOOD...
OINK OINK
NOT THE WELCOME I HOPED FOR.
IS THAT... KILLER CROC? WHERE ARE WE?
WAITAMINUTE, MY SCANS SHOW WE'RE NOT THAT FAR FROM THE HALL OF--
KORY?!

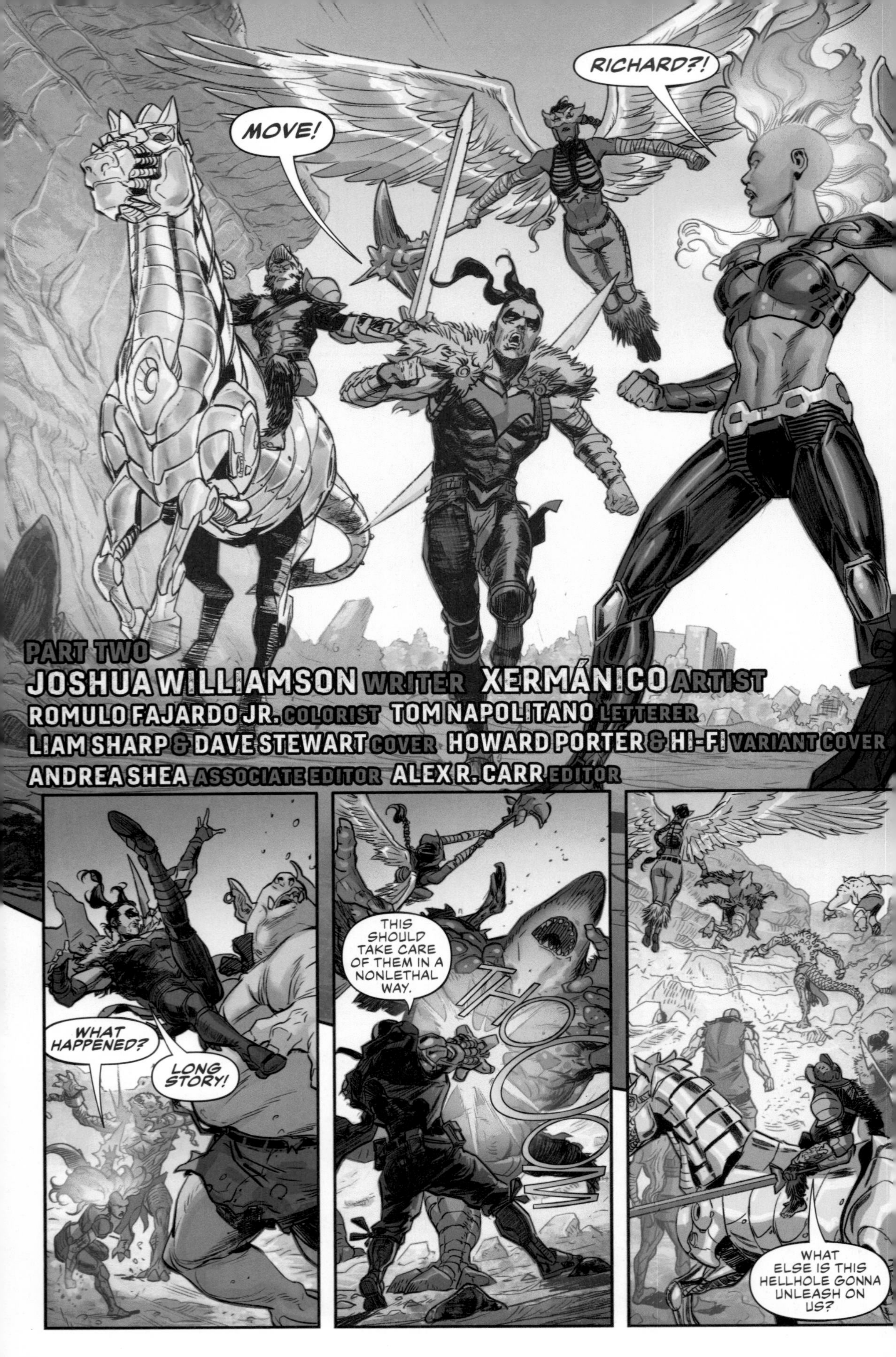
RICHARD?!
MOVE!
PART TWO
JOSHUA WILLIAMSON WRITER XERMÁNICO ARTIST
ROMULO FAJARDO JR. COLORIST TOM NAPOLITANO LETTERER
LIAM SHARP & DAVE STEWART COVER HOWARD PORTER & HI-FI VARIANT COVER
ANDREA SHEA ASSOCIATE EDITOR ALEX R. CARR EDITOR
WHAT HAPPENED?
LONG STORY!
THIS SHOULD TAKE CARE OF THEM IN A NONLETHAL WAY.
THOOM
WHAT ELSE IS THIS HELLHOLE GONNA UNLEASH ON US?

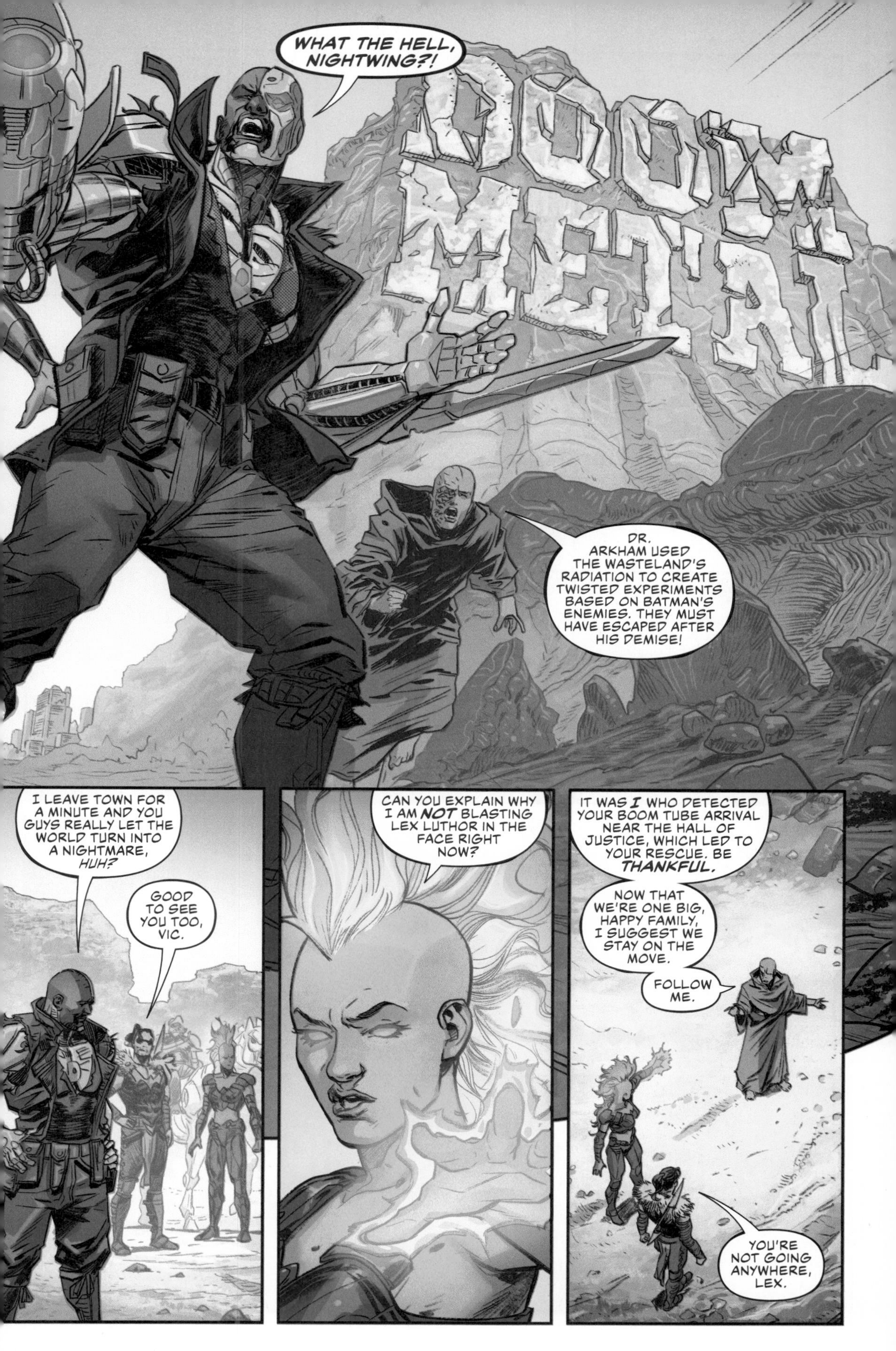
WHAT THE HELL, NIGHTWING?!
DOOM METAL
DR. ARKHAM USED THE WASTELAND'S RADIATION TO CREATE TWISTED EXPERIMENTS BASED ON BATMAN'S ENEMIES. THEY MUST HAVE ESCAPED AFTER HIS DEMISE!
I LEAVE TOWN FOR A MINUTE AND YOU GUYS REALLY LET THE WORLD TURN INTO A NIGHTMARE, *HUH?*
GOOD TO SEE YOU TOO, VIC.
CAN YOU EXPLAIN WHY I AM ***NOT*** BLASTING LEX LUTHOR IN THE FACE RIGHT NOW?
IT WAS ***I*** WHO DETECTED YOUR BOOM TUBE ARRIVAL NEAR THE HALL OF JUSTICE, WHICH LED TO YOUR RESCUE. BE ***THANKFUL.***
NOW THAT WE'RE ONE BIG, HAPPY FAMILY, I SUGGEST WE STAY ON THE MOVE.
FOLLOW ME.
YOU'RE NOT GOING ANYWHERE, LEX.

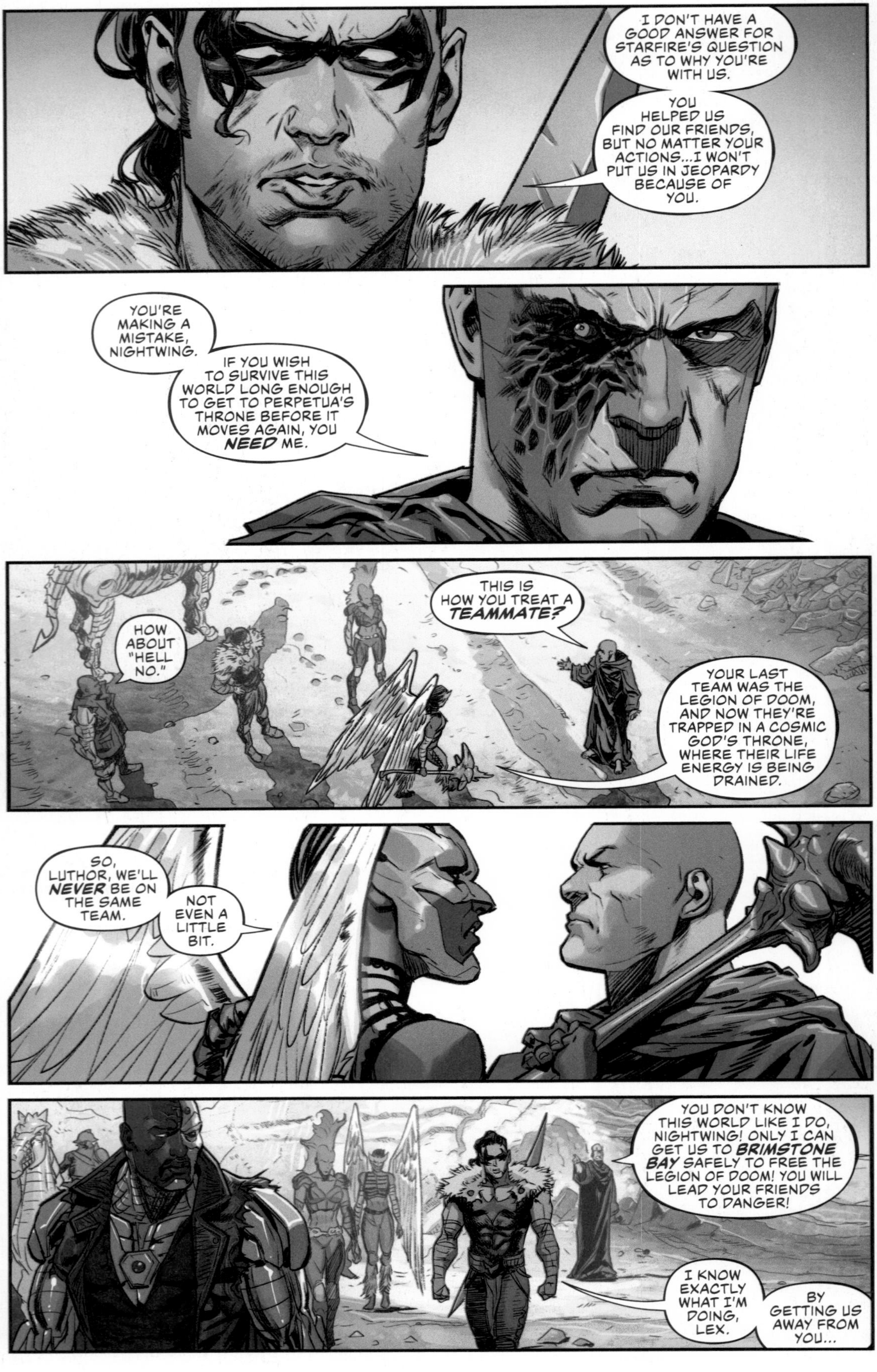
I DON'T HAVE A GOOD ANSWER FOR STARFIRE'S QUESTION AS TO WHY YOU'RE WITH US.
YOU HELPED US FIND OUR FRIENDS, BUT NO MATTER YOUR ACTIONS...I WON'T PUT US IN JEOPARDY BECAUSE OF YOU.
YOU'RE MAKING A MISTAKE, NIGHTWING.
IF YOU WISH TO SURVIVE THIS WORLD LONG ENOUGH TO GET TO PERPETUA'S THRONE BEFORE IT MOVES AGAIN, YOU NEED ME.
HOW ABOUT "HELL NO."
THIS IS HOW YOU TREAT A TEAMMATE?
YOUR LAST TEAM WAS THE LEGION OF DOOM, AND NOW THEY'RE TRAPPED IN A COSMIC GOD'S THRONE, WHERE THEIR LIFE ENERGY IS BEING DRAINED.
SO, LUTHOR, WE'LL NEVER BE ON THE SAME TEAM.
NOT EVEN A LITTLE BIT.
YOU DON'T KNOW THIS WORLD LIKE I DO, NIGHTWING! ONLY I CAN GET US TO BRIMSTONE BAY SAFELY TO FREE THE LEGION OF DOOM! YOU WILL LEAD YOUR FRIENDS TO DANGER!
I KNOW EXACTLY WHAT I'M DOING, LEX.
BY GETTING US AWAY FROM YOU...

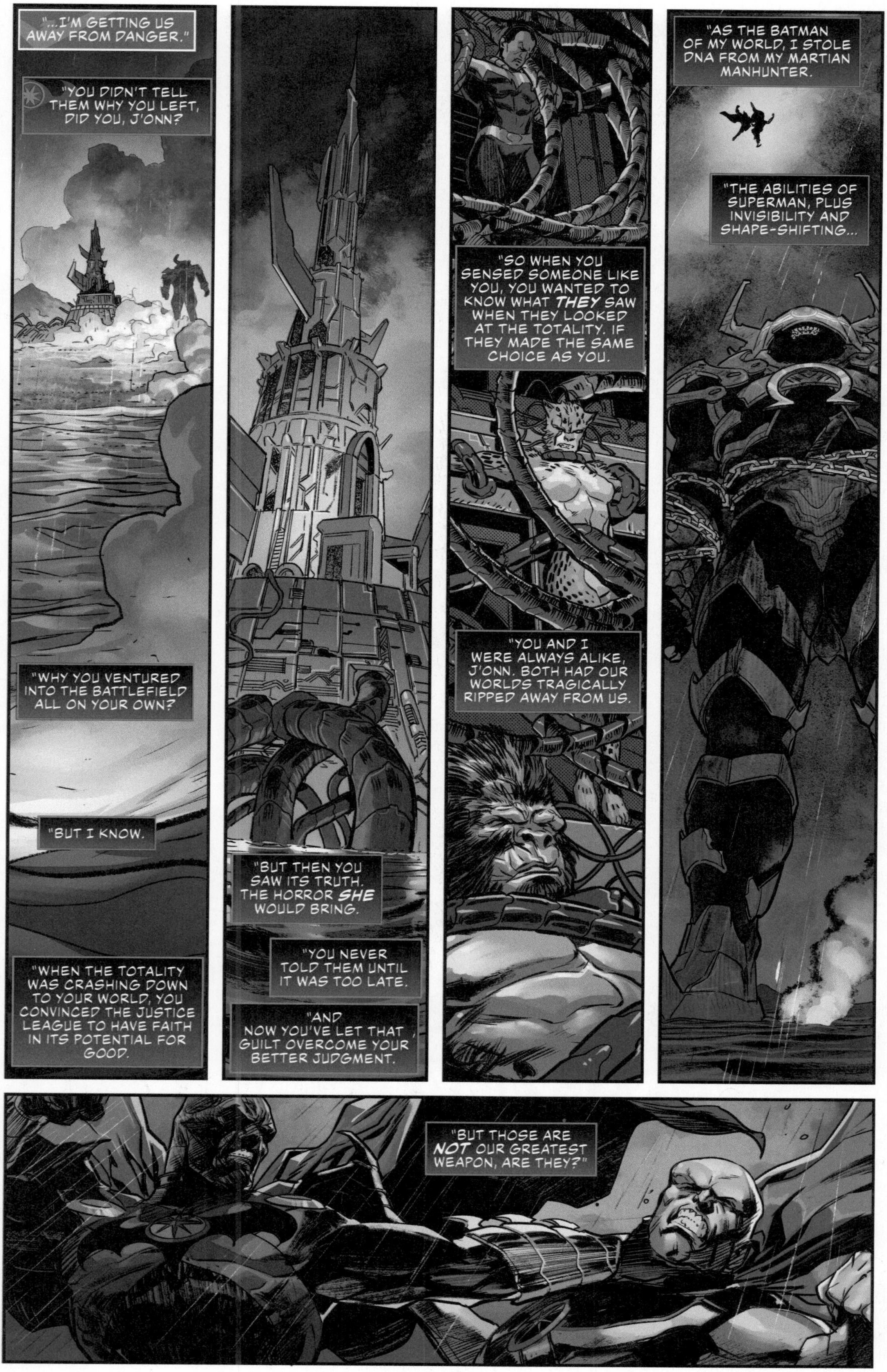
"...I'M GETTING US AWAY FROM DANGER."
"YOU DIDN'T TELL THEM WHY YOU LEFT, DID YOU, J'ONN?
"WHY YOU VENTURED INTO THE BATTLEFIELD ALL ON YOUR OWN?
"BUT I KNOW.
"WHEN THE TOTALITY WAS CRASHING DOWN TO YOUR WORLD, YOU CONVINCED THE JUSTICE LEAGUE TO HAVE FAITH IN ITS POTENTIAL FOR GOOD.
"BUT THEN YOU SAW ITS TRUTH. THE HORROR SHE WOULD BRING.
"YOU NEVER TOLD THEM UNTIL IT WAS TOO LATE.
"AND NOW YOU'VE LET THAT GUILT OVERCOME YOUR BETTER JUDGMENT.
"SO WHEN YOU SENSED SOMEONE LIKE YOU, YOU WANTED TO KNOW WHAT THEY SAW WHEN THEY LOOKED AT THE TOTALITY. IF THEY MADE THE SAME CHOICE AS YOU.
"YOU AND I WERE ALWAYS ALIKE, J'ONN. BOTH HAD OUR WORLDS TRAGICALLY RIPPED AWAY FROM US.
"AS THE BATMAN OF MY WORLD, I STOLE DNA FROM MY MARTIAN MANHUNTER.
"THE ABILITIES OF SUPERMAN, PLUS INVISIBILITY AND SHAPE-SHIFTING...
"BUT THOSE ARE NOT OUR GREATEST WEAPON, ARE THEY?"

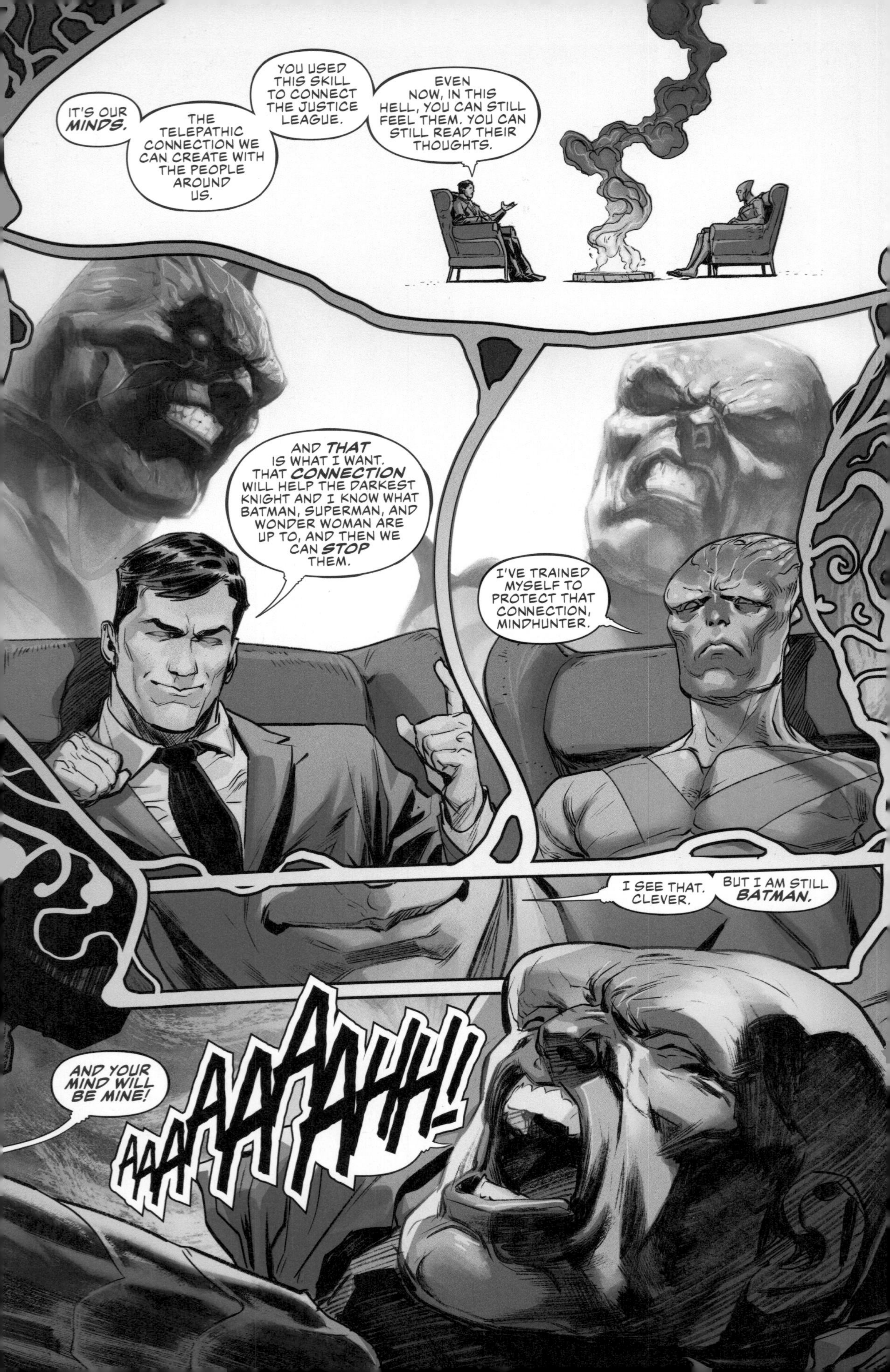
IT'S OUR MINDS.
THE TELEPATHIC CONNECTION WE CAN CREATE WITH THE PEOPLE AROUND US.
YOU USED THIS SKILL TO CONNECT THE JUSTICE LEAGUE.
EVEN NOW, IN THIS HELL, YOU CAN STILL FEEL THEM. YOU CAN STILL READ THEIR THOUGHTS.
AND THAT IS WHAT I WANT. THAT CONNECTION WILL HELP THE DARKEST KNIGHT AND I KNOW WHAT BATMAN, SUPERMAN, AND WONDER WOMAN ARE UP TO, AND THEN WE CAN STOP THEM.
I'VE TRAINED MYSELF TO PROTECT THAT CONNECTION, MINDHUNTER.
I SEE THAT. CLEVER.
BUT I AM STILL BATMAN.
AND YOUR MIND WILL BE MINE!
AAAAAAHH!

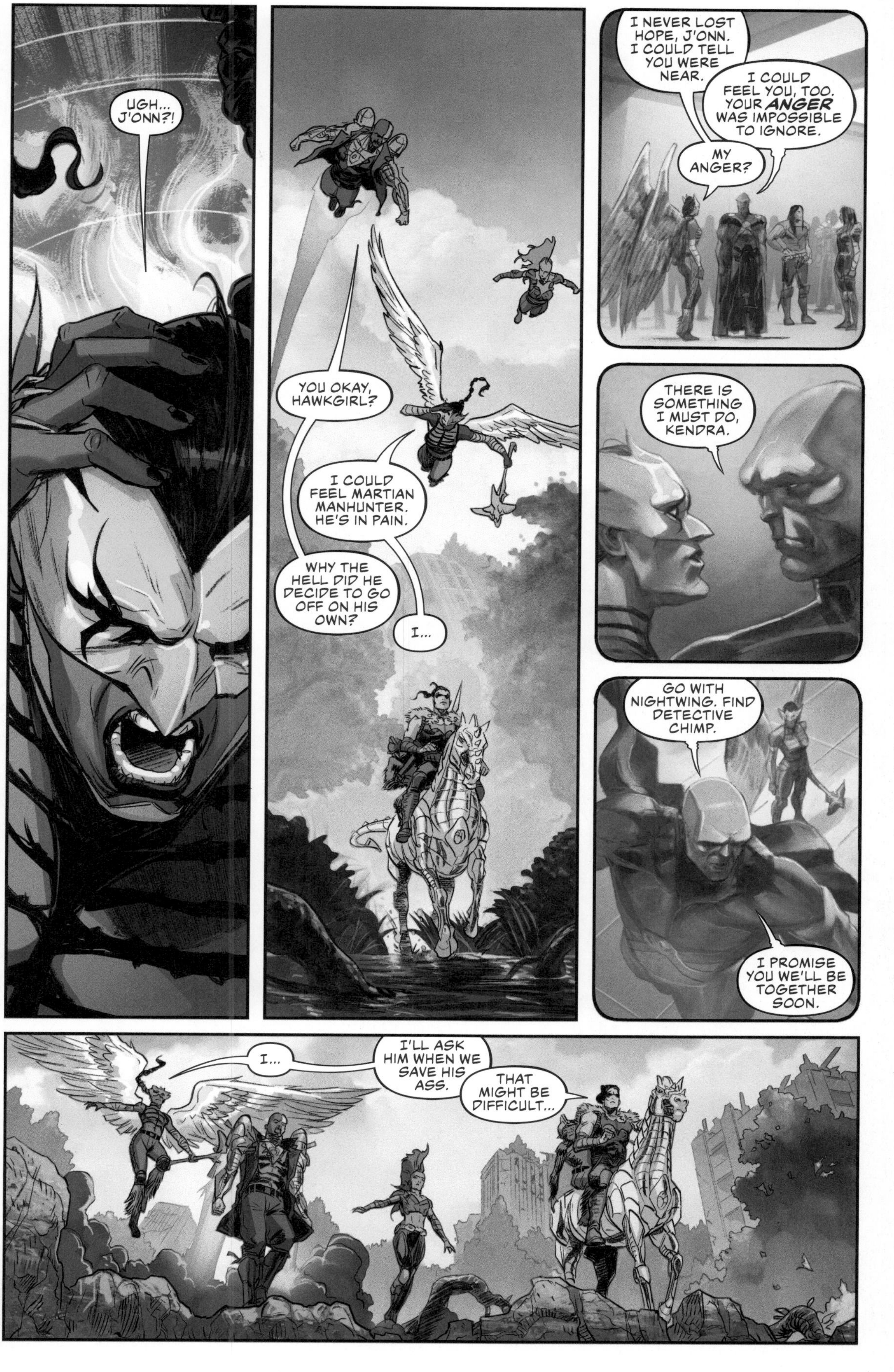
UGH... J'ONN?!
YOU OKAY, HAWKGIRL?
I COULD FEEL MARTIAN MANHUNTER. HE'S IN PAIN.
WHY THE HELL DID HE DECIDE TO GO OFF ON HIS OWN?
I...
I NEVER LOST HOPE, J'ONN. I COULD TELL YOU WERE NEAR.
I COULD FEEL YOU, TOO. YOUR ANGER WAS IMPOSSIBLE TO IGNORE.
MY ANGER?
THERE IS SOMETHING I MUST DO, KENDRA.
GO WITH NIGHTWING. FIND DETECTIVE CHIMP.
I PROMISE YOU WE'LL BE TOGETHER SOON.
I...
I'LL ASK HIM WHEN WE SAVE HIS ASS.
THAT MIGHT BE DIFFICULT...

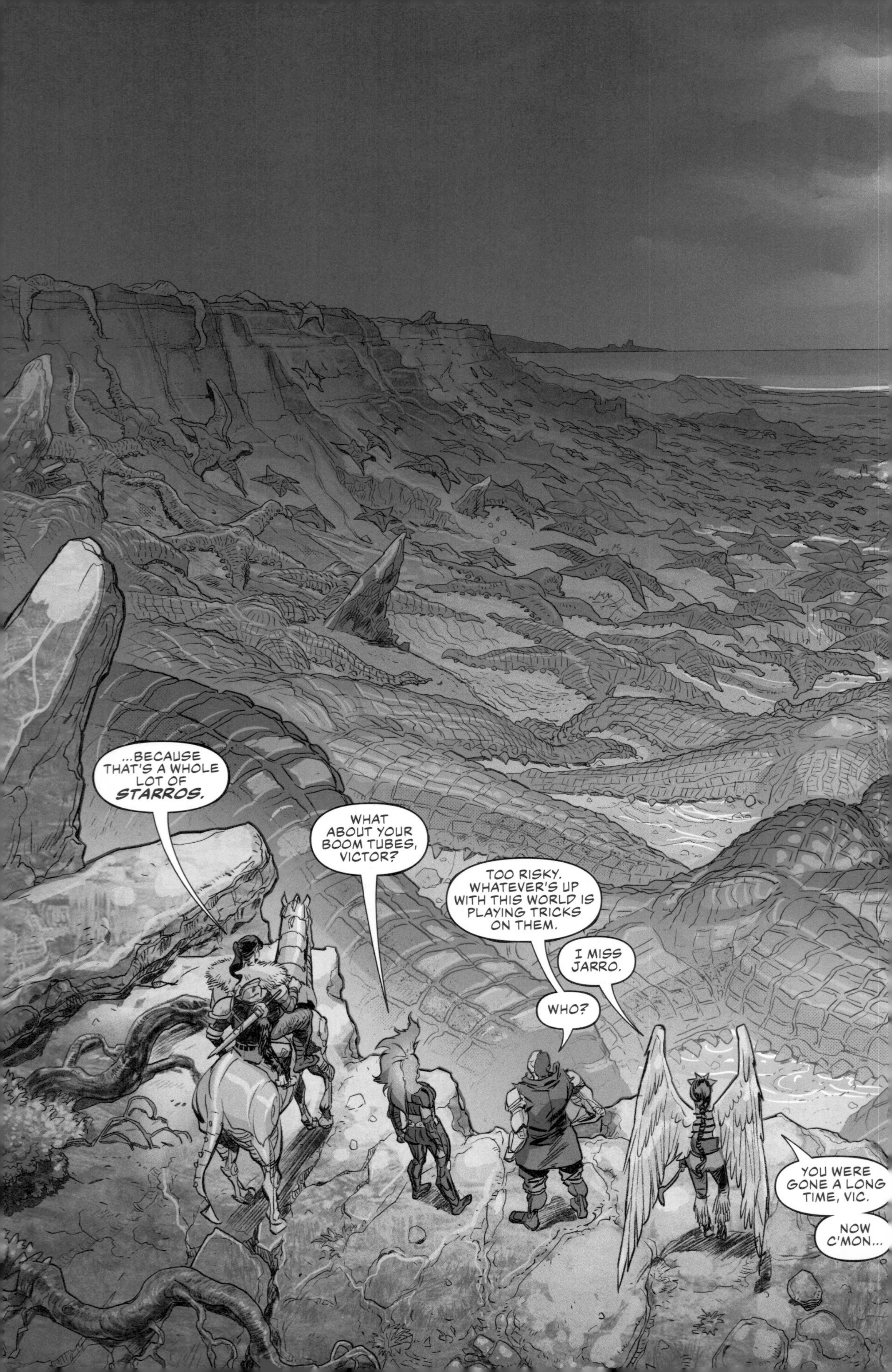
...BECAUSE THAT'S A WHOLE LOT OF STARROS.
WHAT ABOUT YOUR BOOM TUBES, VICTOR?
TOO RISKY. WHATEVER'S UP WITH THIS WORLD IS PLAYING TRICKS ON THEM.
I MISS JARRO.
WHO?
YOU WERE GONE A LONG TIME, VIC.
NOW C'MON...

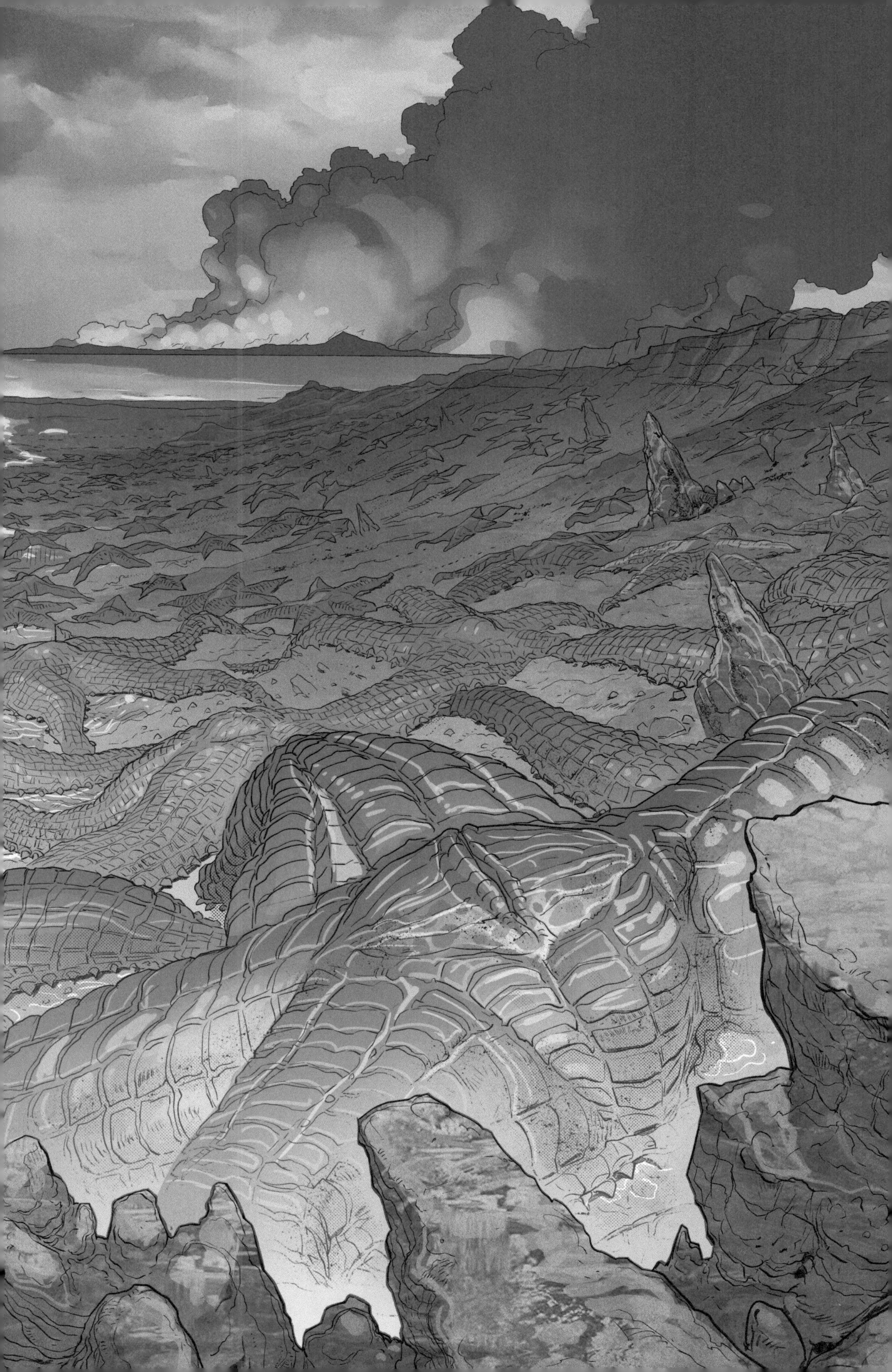

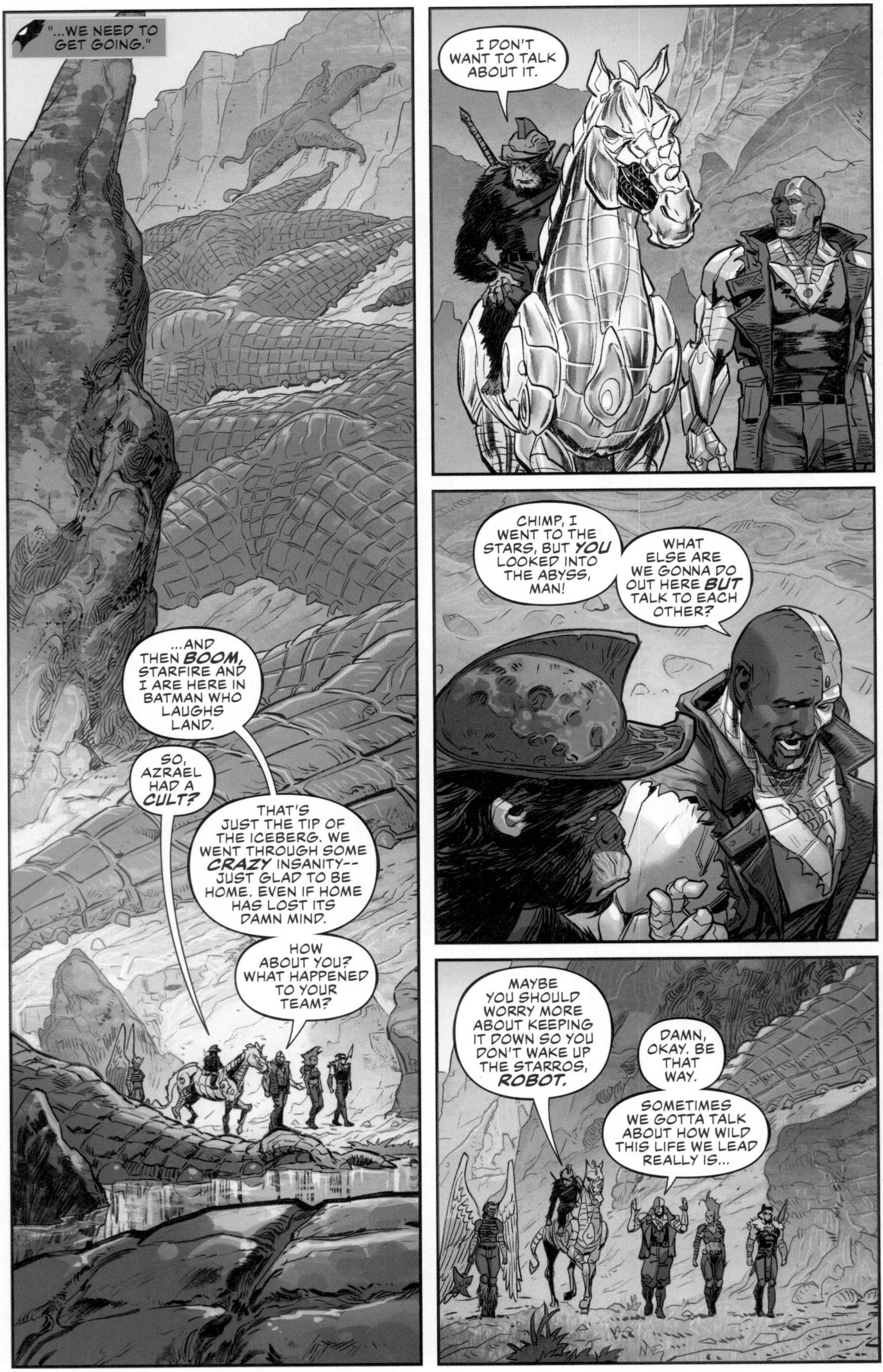
"...WE NEED TO GET GOING."
...AND THEN BOOM, STARFIRE AND I ARE HERE IN BATMAN WHO LAUGHS LAND.
SO, AZRAEL HAD A CULT?
THAT'S JUST THE TIP OF THE ICEBERG. WE WENT THROUGH SOME CRAZY INSANITY--JUST GLAD TO BE HOME. EVEN IF HOME HAS LOST ITS DAMN MIND.
HOW ABOUT YOU? WHAT HAPPENED TO YOUR TEAM?
I DON'T WANT TO TALK ABOUT IT.
CHIMP, I WENT TO THE STARS, BUT YOU LOOKED INTO THE ABYSS, MAN!
WHAT ELSE ARE WE GONNA DO OUT HERE BUT TALK TO EACH OTHER?
MAYBE YOU SHOULD WORRY MORE ABOUT KEEPING IT DOWN SO YOU DON'T WAKE UP THE STARROS, ROBOT.
DAMN, OKAY. BE THAT WAY.
SOMETIMES WE GOTTA TALK ABOUT HOW WILD THIS LIFE WE LEAD REALLY IS...

GOLDIE KNOWS WHAT I'M TALKING ABOUT.

GHOST SECTOR FOR LIFE, RIGHT?

PRAISE X'HAL.

HOW CAN YOU BE SO POSITIVE AROUND ALL OF THIS, VIC?

SOMETIMES ALL YOU CAN DO IS LAUGH, MAN.

VICTOR IS WISE.

I FORGOT YOU AND CYBORG WERE CLOSE.

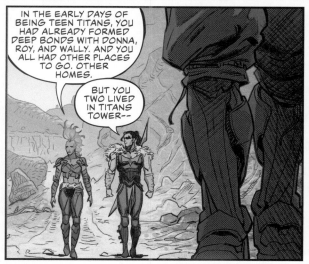

IN THE EARLY DAYS OF BEING TEEN TITANS, YOU HAD ALREADY FORMED DEEP BONDS WITH DONNA, ROY, AND WALLY. AND YOU ALL HAD OTHER PLACES TO GO. OTHER HOMES.

BUT YOU TWO LIVED IN TITANS TOWER--

AND OUR EXPERIENCE IN THE GHOST SECTOR WAS UNIQUE. IT *CHANGED* US.

IT APPEARS YOU ALSO WENT THROUGH SOME CHANGES.

YOU HAVE A NEW SCAR, RICHARD.

OH YEAH, *THAT.*

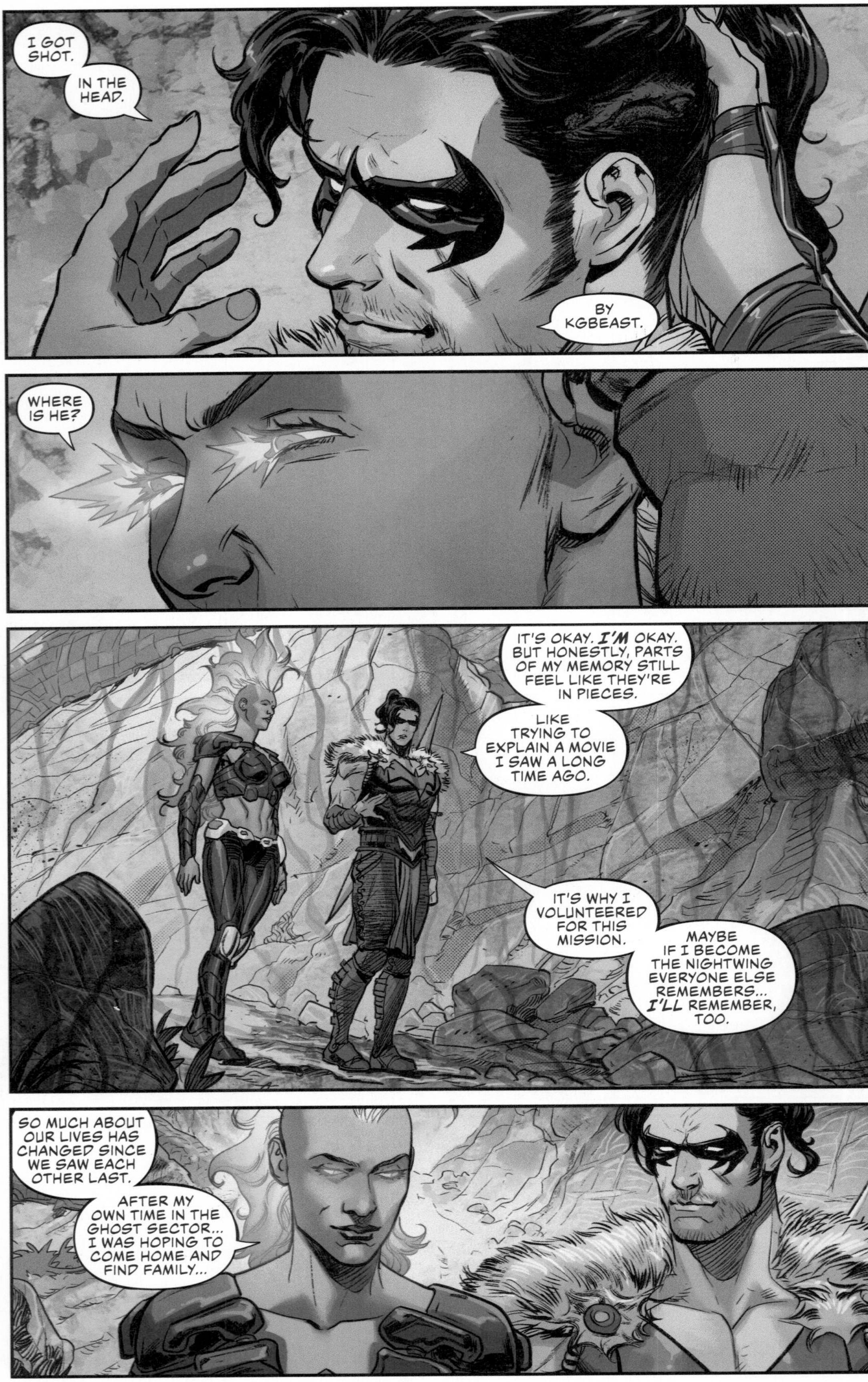
I GOT SHOT.
IN THE HEAD.
BY KGBEAST.
WHERE IS HE?
IT'S OKAY. I'M OKAY. BUT HONESTLY, PARTS OF MY MEMORY STILL FEEL LIKE THEY'RE IN PIECES.
LIKE TRYING TO EXPLAIN A MOVIE I SAW A LONG TIME AGO.
IT'S WHY I VOLUNTEERED FOR THIS MISSION.
MAYBE IF I BECOME THE NIGHTWING EVERYONE ELSE REMEMBERS... I'LL REMEMBER, TOO.
SO MUCH ABOUT OUR LIVES HAS CHANGED SINCE WE SAW EACH OTHER LAST.
AFTER MY OWN TIME IN THE GHOST SECTOR... I WAS HOPING TO COME HOME AND FIND FAMILY...

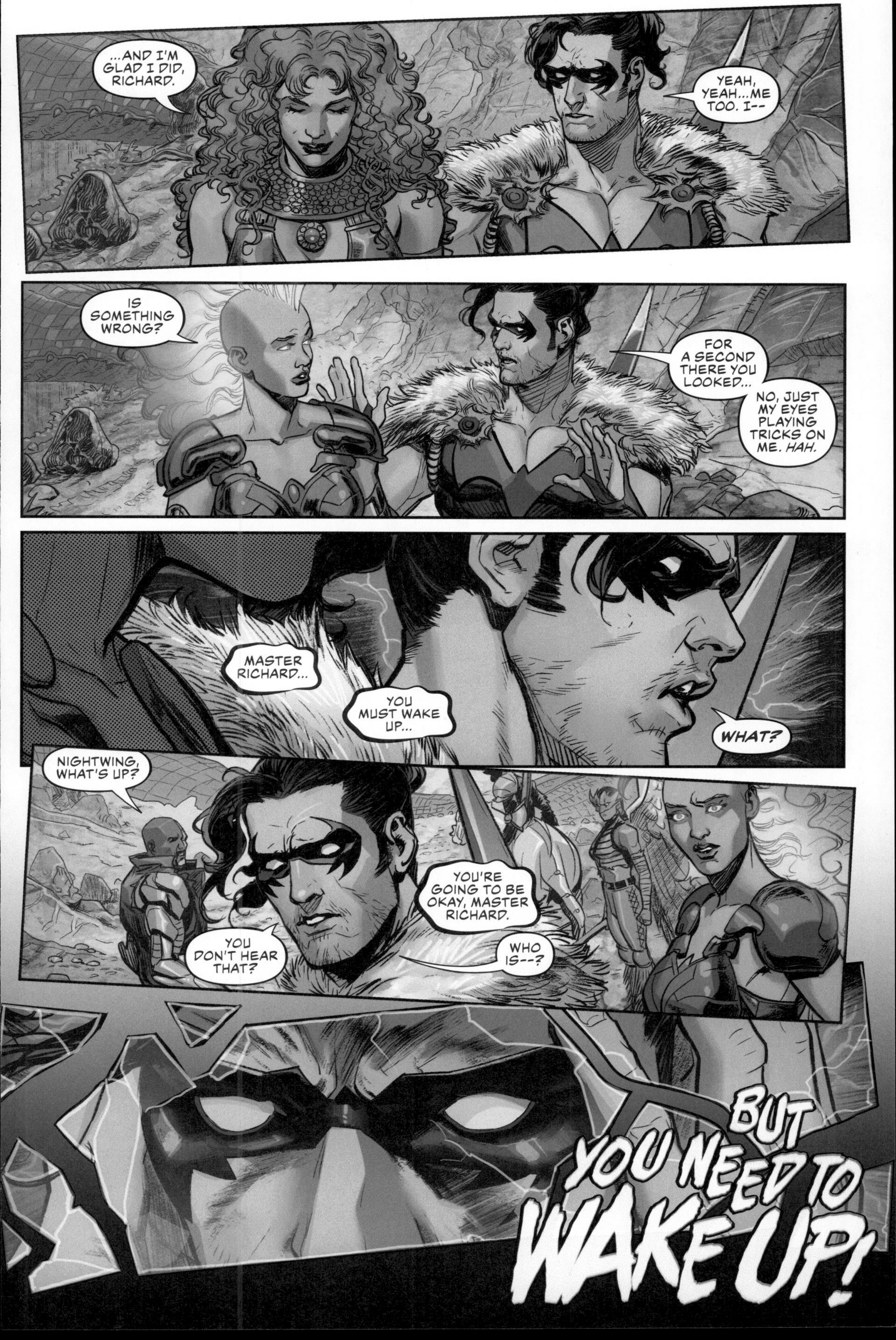
...AND I'M GLAD I DID, RICHARD.
YEAH, YEAH...ME TOO. I--
IS SOMETHING WRONG?
FOR A SECOND THERE YOU LOOKED...
NO, JUST MY EYES PLAYING TRICKS ON ME. *HAH.*
MASTER RICHARD...
YOU MUST WAKE UP...
WHAT?
NIGHTWING, WHAT'S UP?
YOU'RE GOING TO BE OKAY, MASTER RICHARD.
YOU DON'T HEAR THAT?
WHO IS--?
BUT YOU NEED TO WAKE UP!

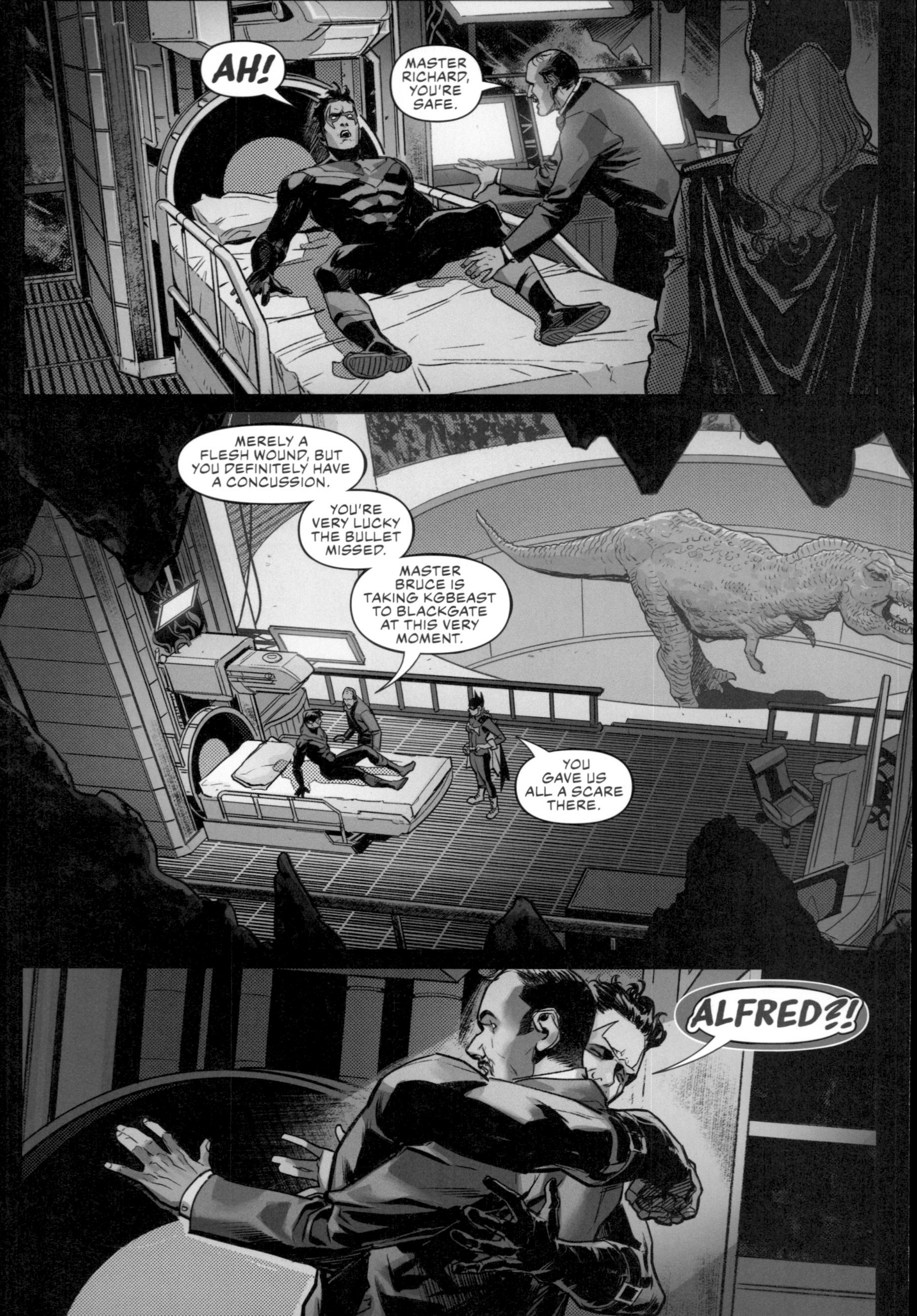
AH!
MASTER RICHARD, YOU'RE SAFE.
MERELY A FLESH WOUND, BUT YOU DEFINITELY HAVE A CONCUSSION.
YOU'RE VERY LUCKY THE BULLET MISSED.
MASTER BRUCE IS TAKING KGBEAST TO BLACKGATE AT THIS VERY MOMENT.
YOU GAVE US ALL A SCARE THERE.
ALFRED?!

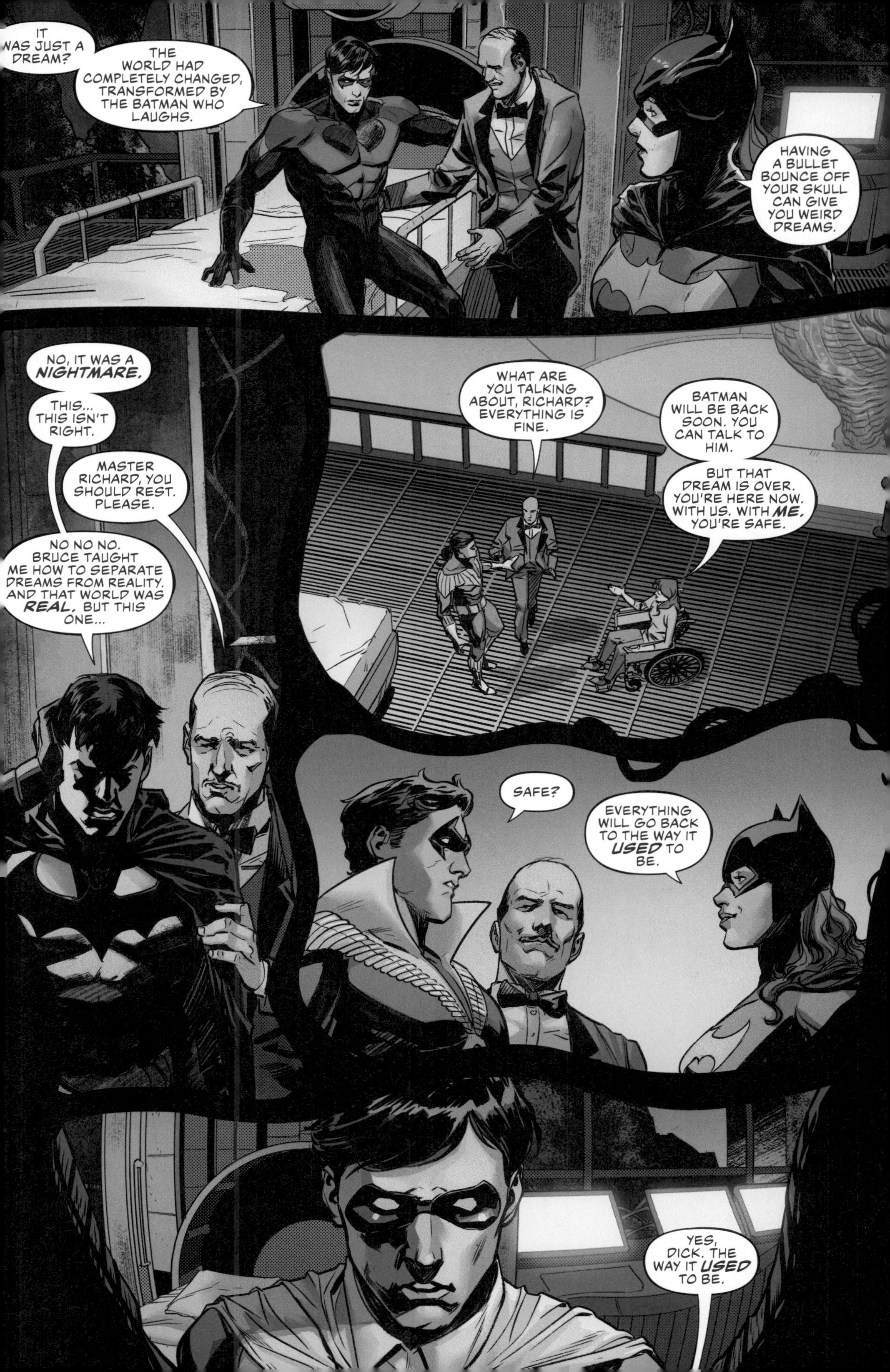

IT WAS JUST A DREAM?
THE WORLD HAD COMPLETELY CHANGED, TRANSFORMED BY THE BATMAN WHO LAUGHS.
HAVING A BULLET BOUNCE OFF YOUR SKULL CAN GIVE YOU WEIRD DREAMS.
NO, IT WAS A *NIGHTMARE.*
THIS... THIS ISN'T RIGHT.
MASTER RICHARD, YOU SHOULD REST. PLEASE.
NO NO NO. BRUCE TAUGHT ME HOW TO SEPARATE DREAMS FROM REALITY. AND THAT WORLD WAS *REAL.* BUT THIS ONE...
WHAT ARE YOU TALKING ABOUT, RICHARD? EVERYTHING IS FINE.
BATMAN WILL BE BACK SOON. YOU CAN TALK TO HIM.
BUT THAT DREAM IS OVER. YOU'RE HERE NOW. WITH US. WITH *ME.* YOU'RE SAFE.
SAFE?
EVERYTHING WILL GO BACK TO THE WAY IT *USED* TO BE.
YES, DICK. THE WAY IT *USED* TO BE.

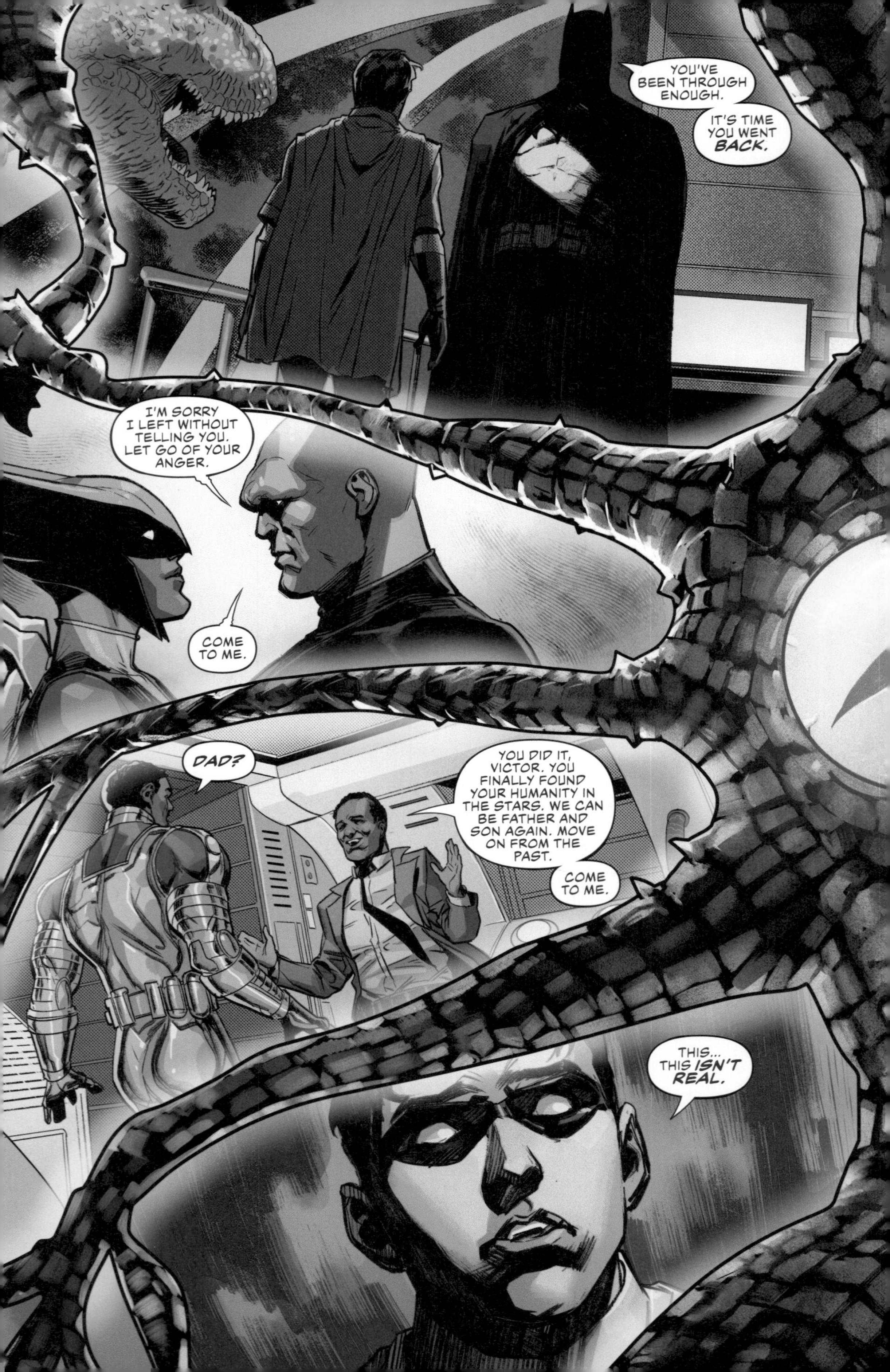
YOU'VE BEEN THROUGH ENOUGH.
IT'S TIME YOU WENT BACK.
I'M SORRY I LEFT WITHOUT TELLING YOU. LET GO OF YOUR ANGER.
COME TO ME.
DAD?
YOU DID IT, VICTOR. YOU FINALLY FOUND YOUR HUMANITY IN THE STARS. WE CAN BE FATHER AND SON AGAIN. MOVE ON FROM THE PAST.
COME TO ME.
THIS... THIS ISN'T REAL.

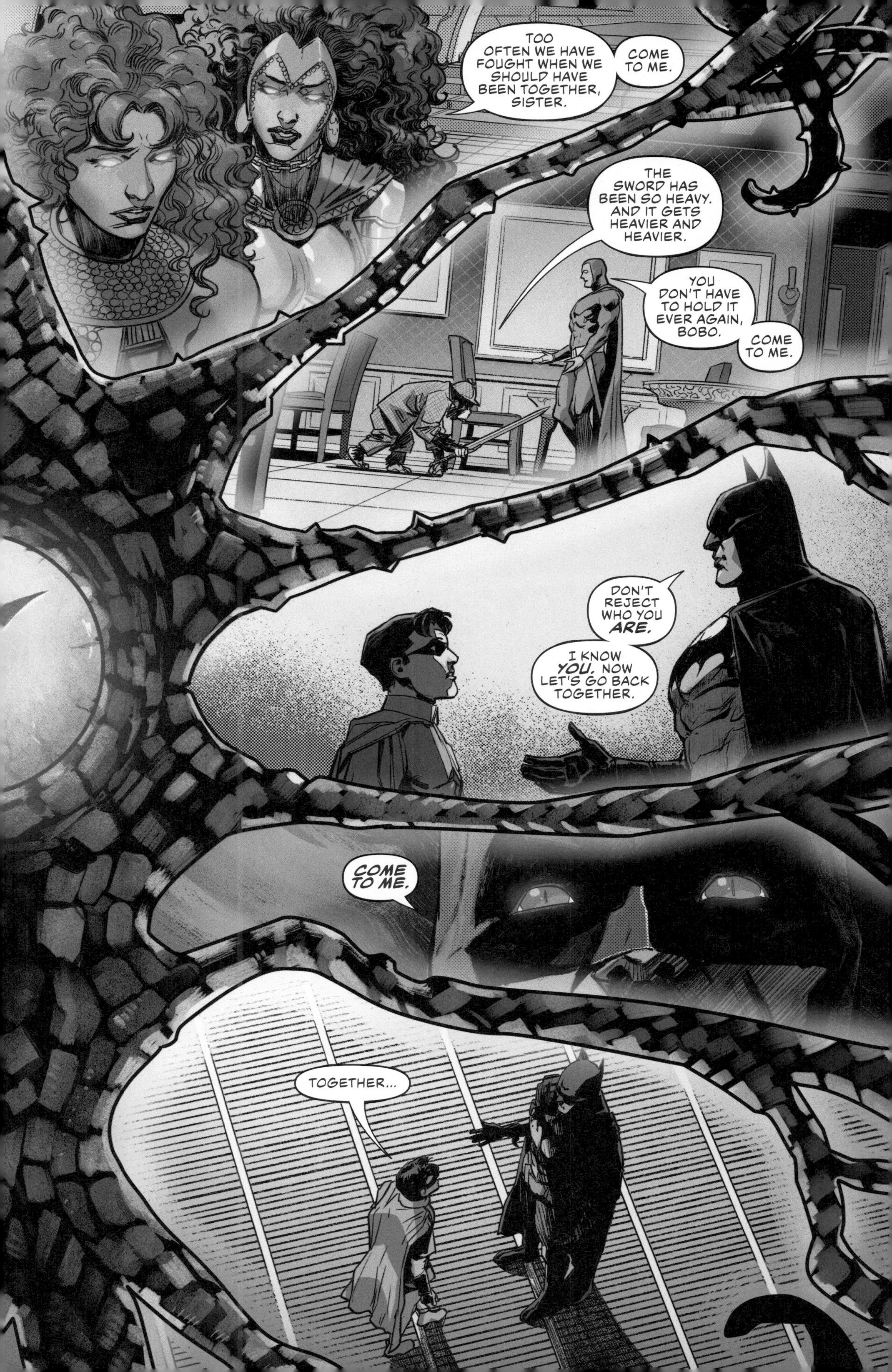
TOO OFTEN WE HAVE FOUGHT WHEN WE SHOULD HAVE BEEN TOGETHER, SISTER.
COME TO ME.
THE SWORD HAS BEEN SO HEAVY. AND IT GETS HEAVIER AND HEAVIER.
YOU DON'T HAVE TO HOLD IT EVER AGAIN, BOBO.
COME TO ME.
DON'T REJECT WHO YOU ARE.
I KNOW YOU. NOW LET'S GO BACK TOGETHER.
COME TO ME.
TOGETHER...

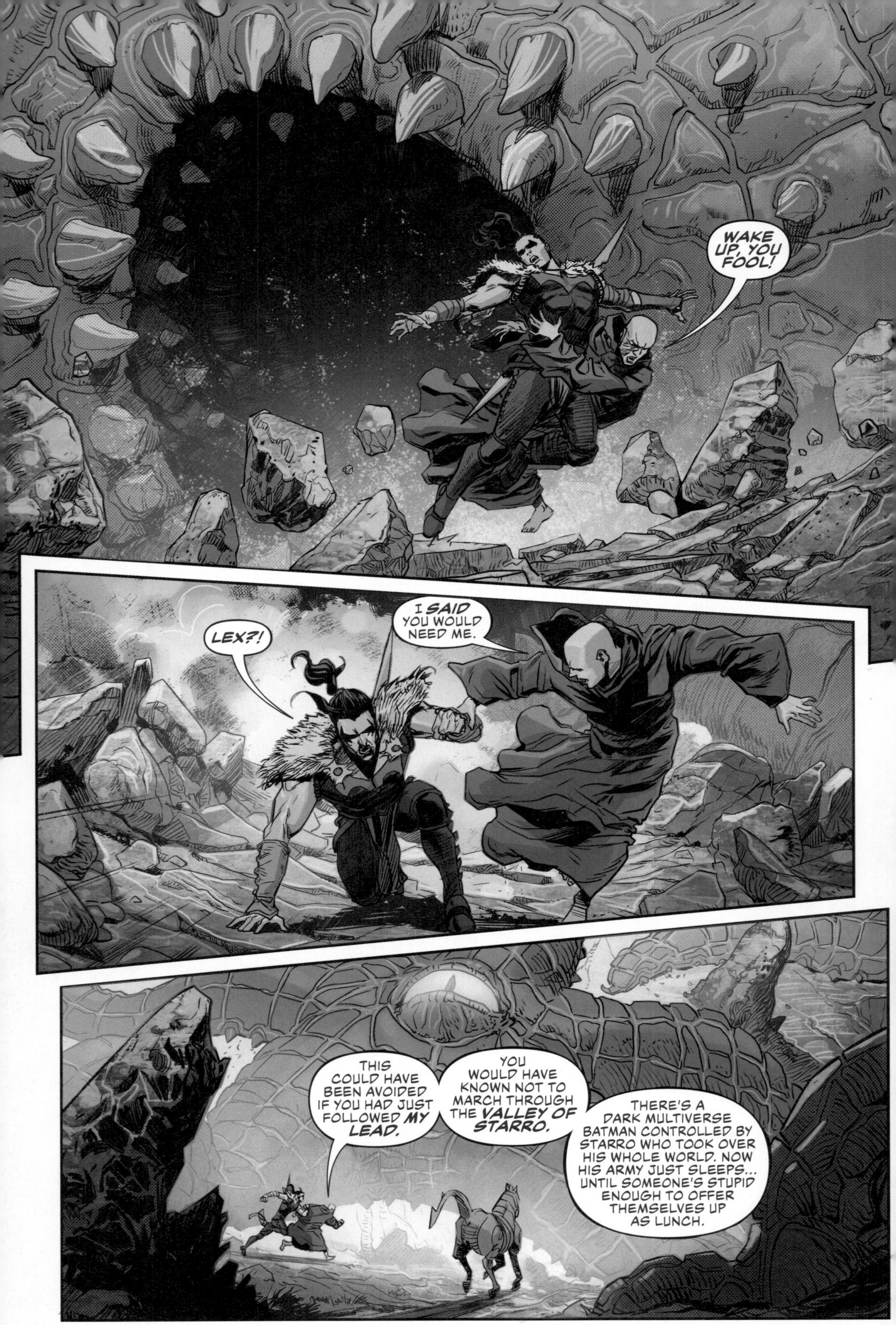
WAKE UP, YOU FOOL!
LEX?!
I SAID YOU WOULD NEED ME.
THIS COULD HAVE BEEN AVOIDED IF YOU HAD JUST FOLLOWED MY LEAD.
YOU WOULD HAVE KNOWN NOT TO MARCH THROUGH THE VALLEY OF STARRO.
THERE'S A DARK MULTIVERSE BATMAN CONTROLLED BY STARRO WHO TOOK OVER HIS WHOLE WORLD. NOW HIS ARMY JUST SLEEPS... UNTIL SOMEONE'S STUPID ENOUGH TO OFFER THEMSELVES UP AS LUNCH.

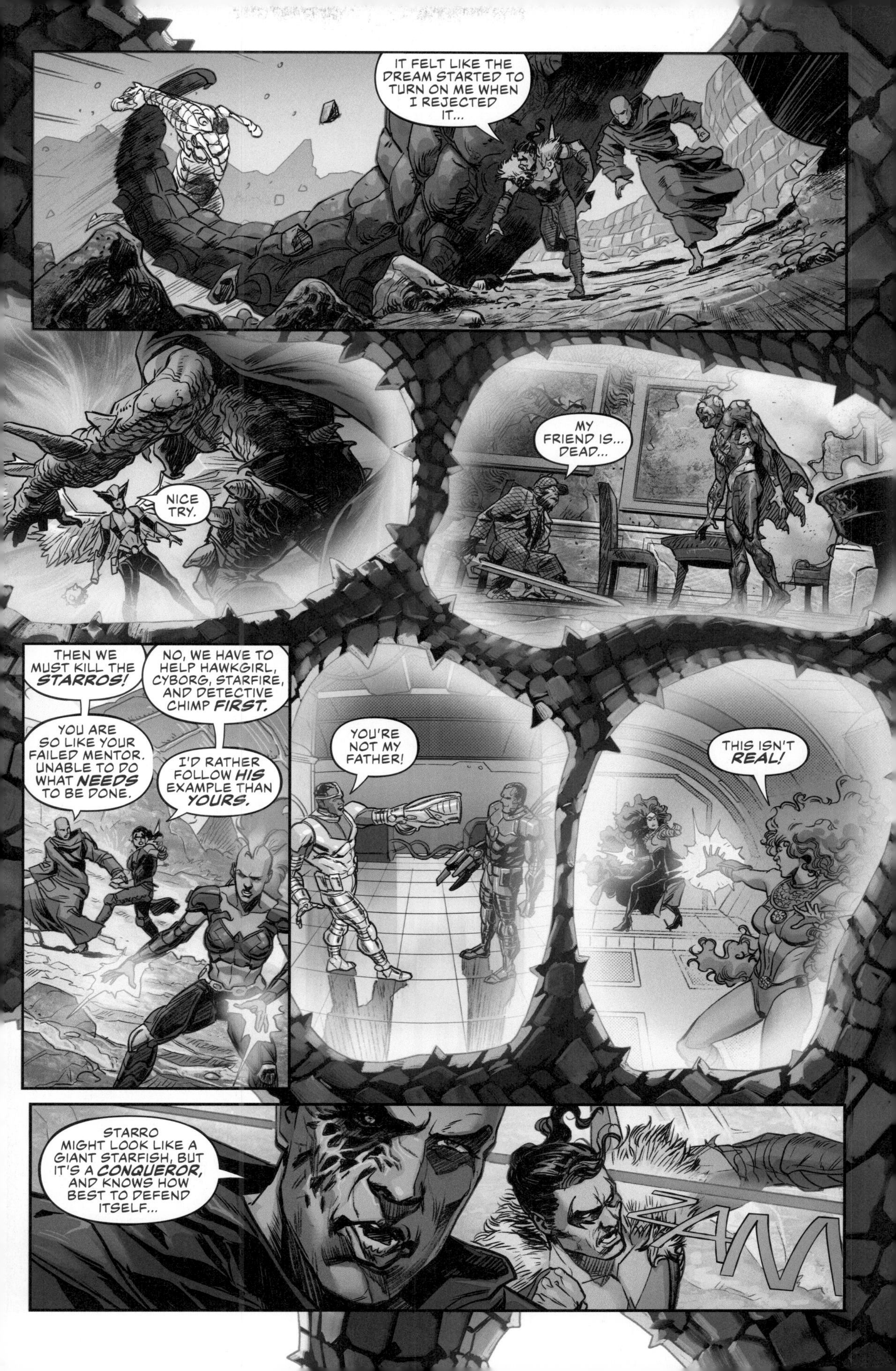
IT FELT LIKE THE DREAM STARTED TO TURN ON ME WHEN I REJECTED IT...
NICE TRY.
MY FRIEND IS... DEAD...
THEN WE MUST KILL THE STARROS!
NO, WE HAVE TO HELP HAWKGIRL, CYBORG, STARFIRE, AND DETECTIVE CHIMP FIRST.
YOU ARE SO LIKE YOUR FAILED MENTOR. UNABLE TO DO WHAT NEEDS TO BE DONE.
I'D RATHER FOLLOW HIS EXAMPLE THAN YOURS.
YOU'RE NOT MY FATHER!
THIS ISN'T REAL!
STARRO MIGHT LOOK LIKE A GIANT STARFISH, BUT IT'S A CONQUEROR, AND KNOWS HOW BEST TO DEFEND ITSELF...
ZAM

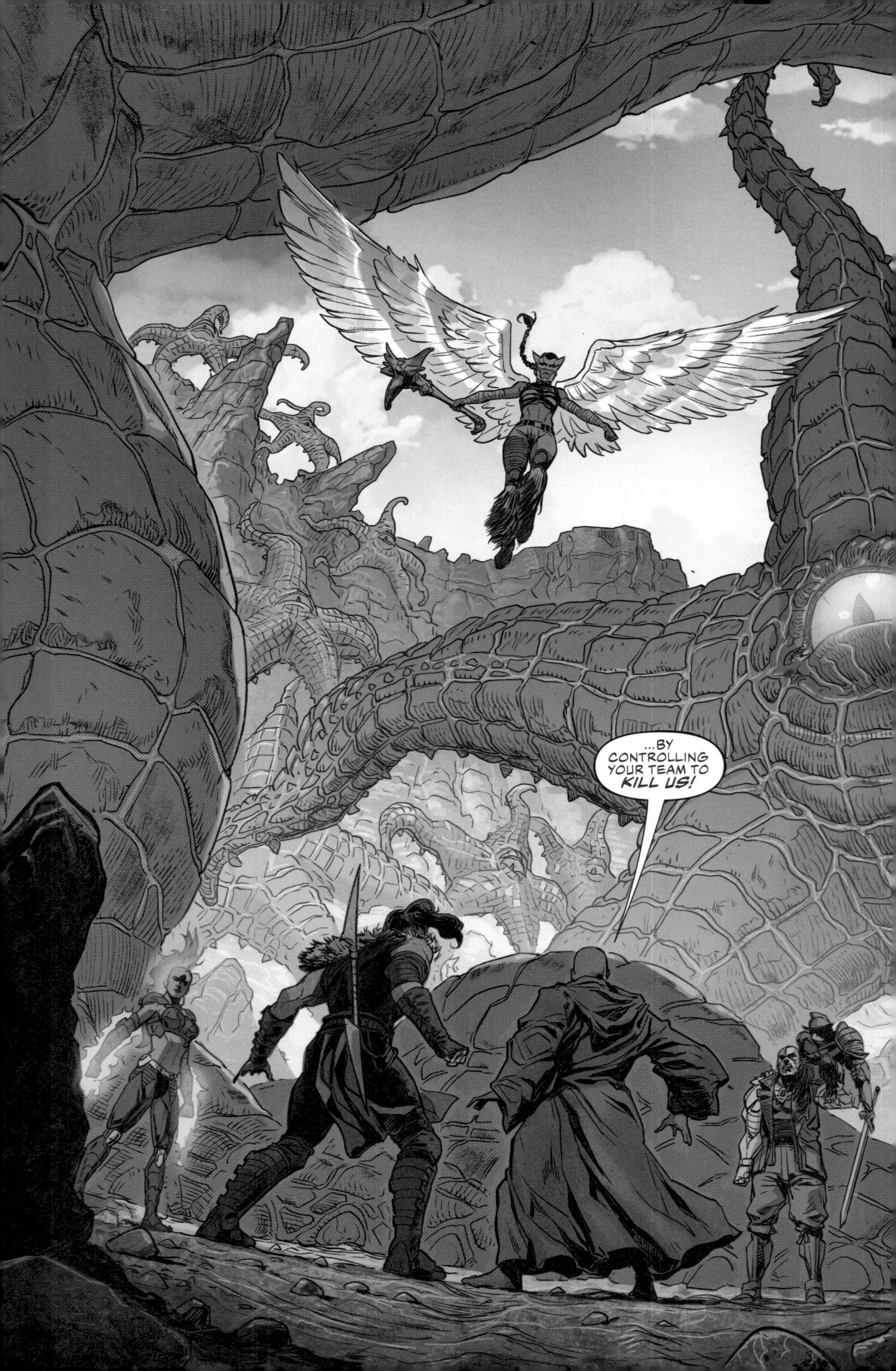
...BY CONTROLLING YOUR TEAM TO KILL US!

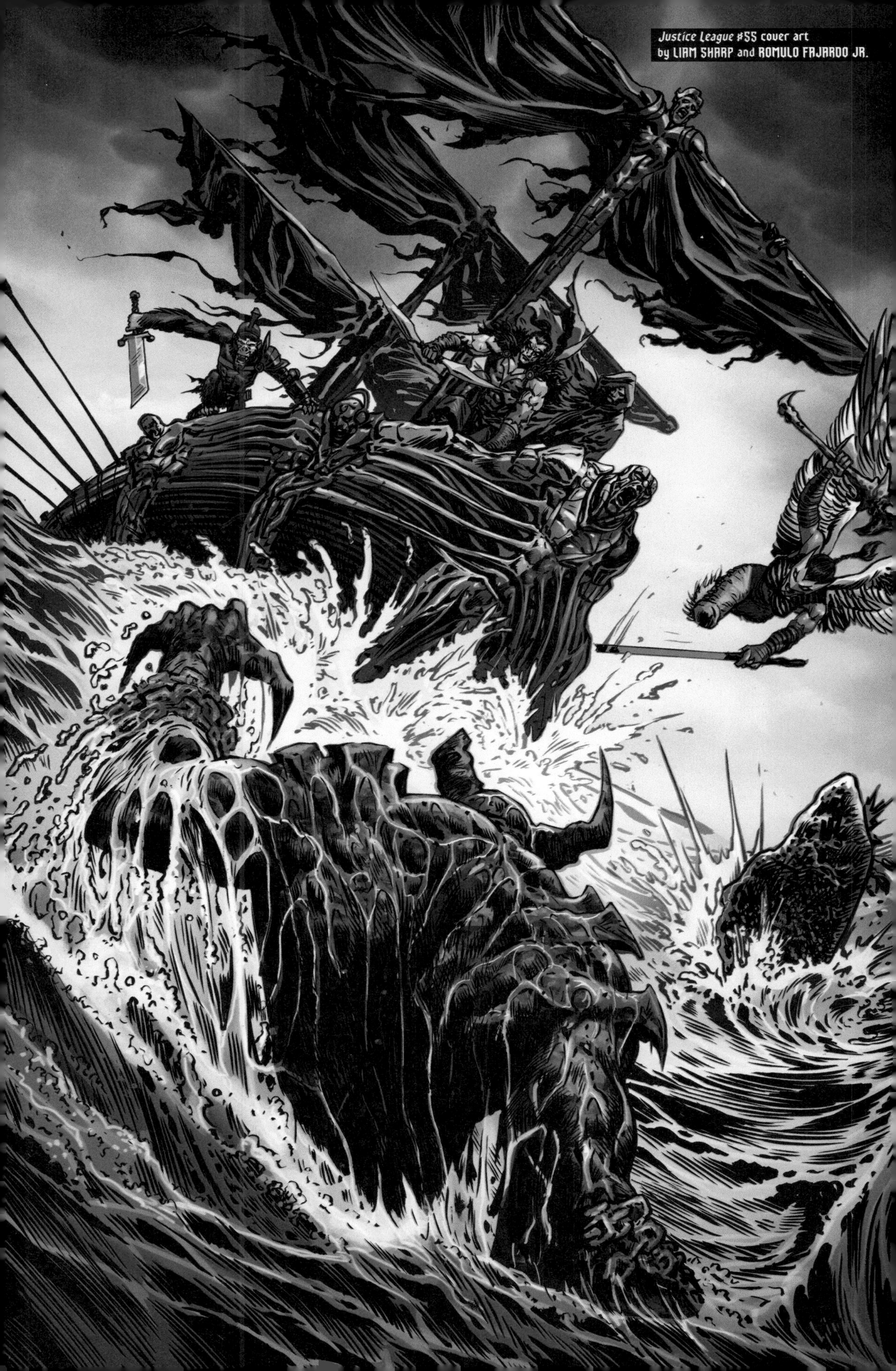

Justice League #55 cover art
by LIAM SHARP and ROMULO FAJARDO JR.

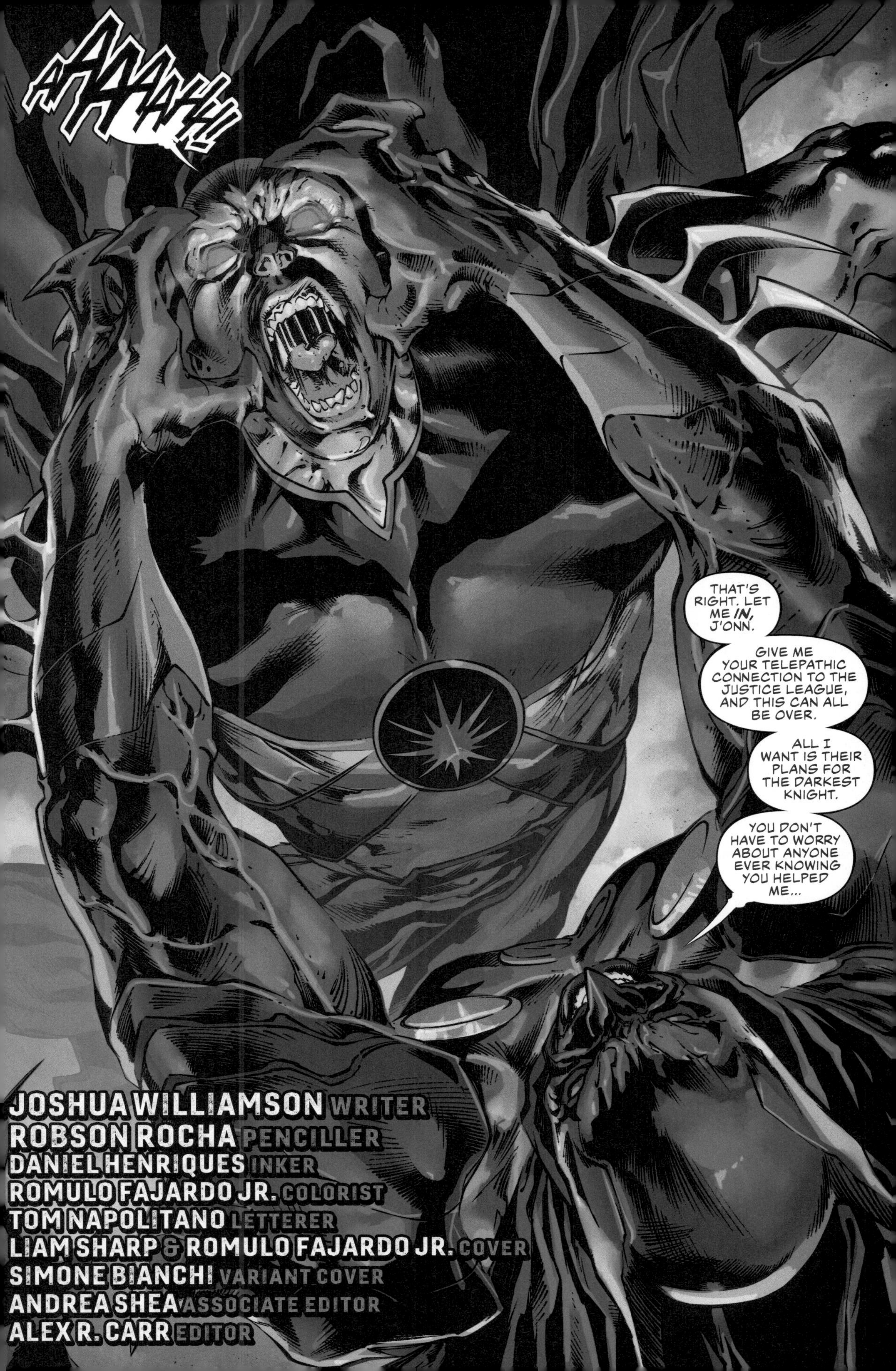
AAAAAKH!!
THAT'S RIGHT. LET ME *IN*, J'ONN.
GIVE ME YOUR TELEPATHIC CONNECTION TO THE JUSTICE LEAGUE, AND THIS CAN ALL BE OVER.
ALL I WANT IS THEIR PLANS FOR THE DARKEST KNIGHT.
YOU DON'T HAVE TO WORRY ABOUT ANYONE EVER KNOWING YOU HELPED ME...
JOSHUA WILLIAMSON WRITER
ROBSON ROCHA PENCILLER
DANIEL HENRIQUES INKER
ROMULO FAJARDO JR. COLORIST
TOM NAPOLITANO LETTERER
LIAM SHARP & ROMULO FAJARDO JR. COVER
SIMONE BIANCHI VARIANT COVER
ANDREA SHEA ASSOCIATE EDITOR
ALEX R. CARR EDITOR

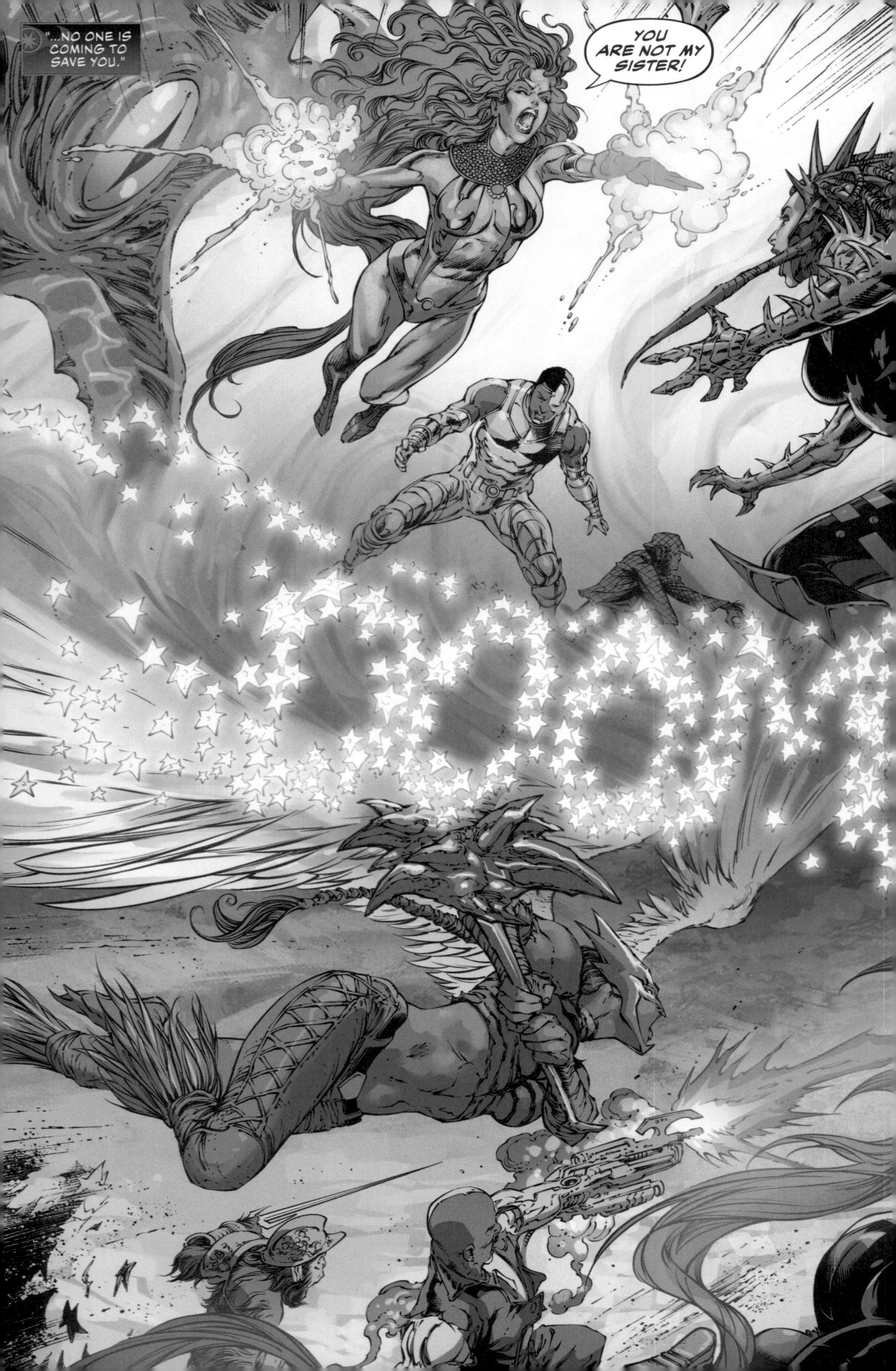
"...NO ONE IS COMING TO SAVE YOU."
YOU ARE NOT MY SISTER!

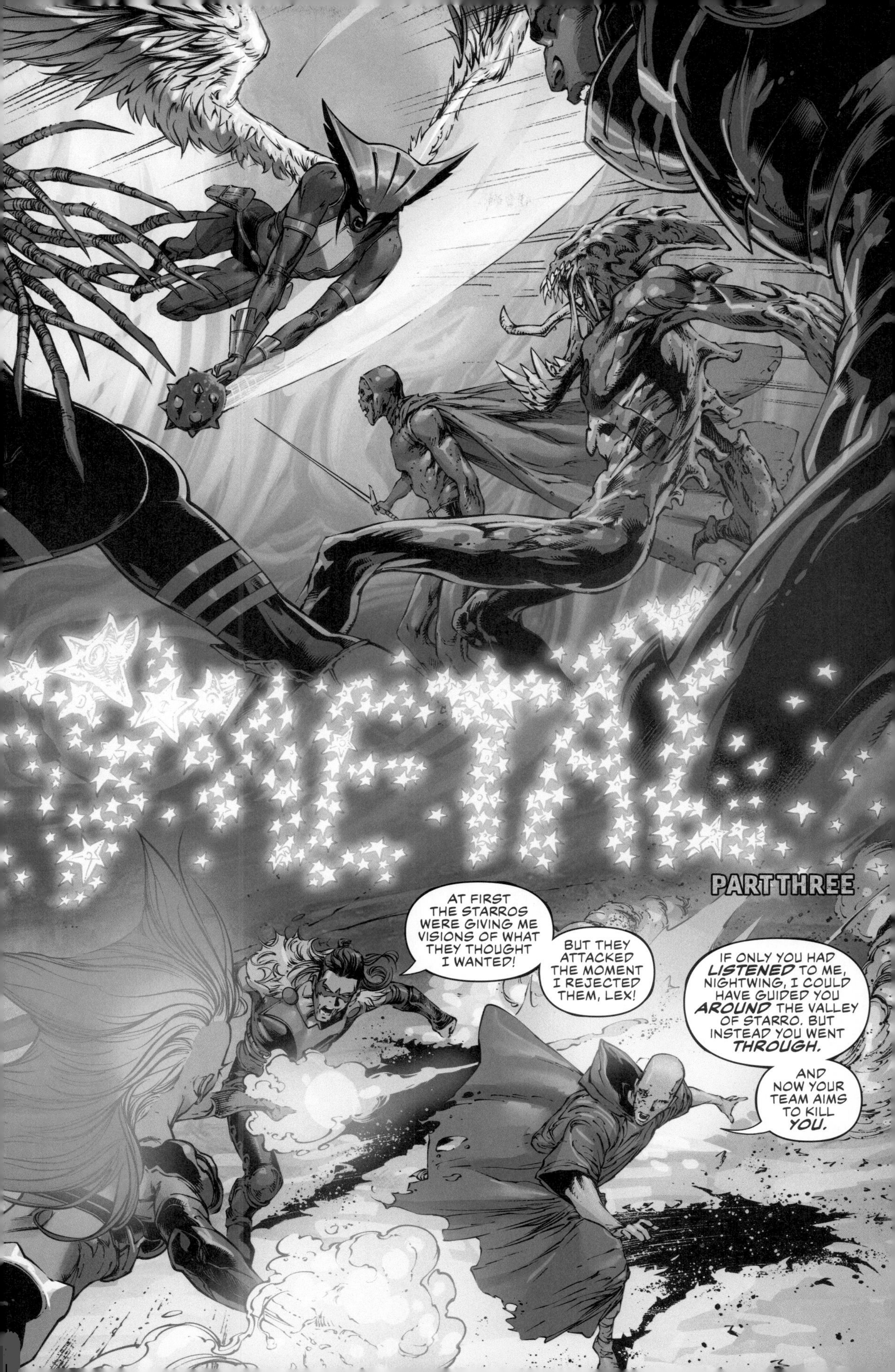
PART THREE
AT FIRST THE STARROS WERE GIVING ME VISIONS OF WHAT THEY THOUGHT I WANTED!
BUT THEY ATTACKED THE MOMENT I REJECTED THEM, LEX!
IF ONLY YOU HAD LISTENED TO ME, NIGHTWING, I COULD HAVE GUIDED YOU AROUND THE VALLEY OF STARRO. BUT INSTEAD YOU WENT THROUGH.
AND NOW YOUR TEAM AIMS TO KILL YOU.

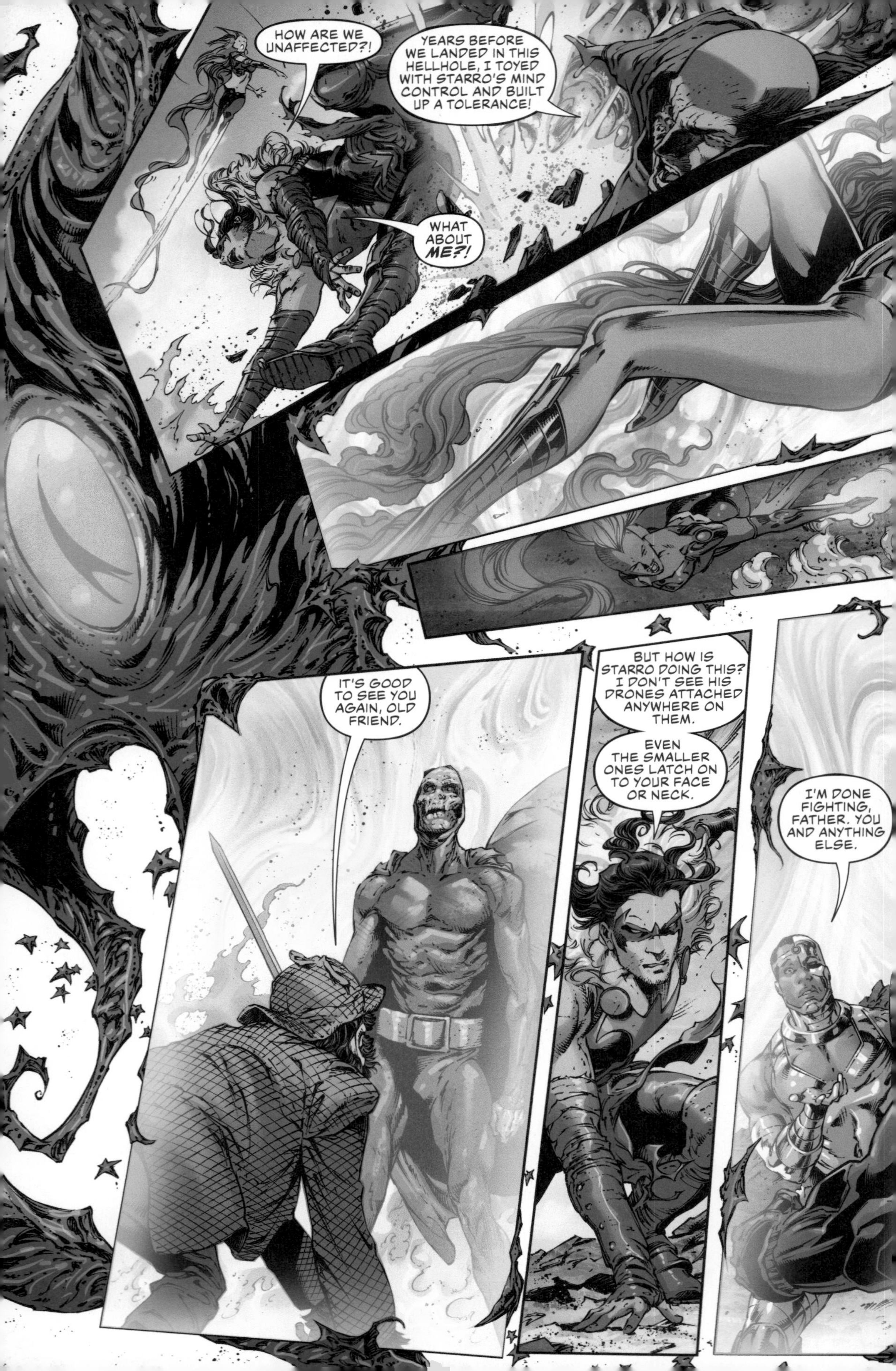
HOW ARE WE UNAFFECTED?!
YEARS BEFORE WE LANDED IN THIS HELLHOLE, I TOYED WITH STARRO'S MIND CONTROL AND BUILT UP A TOLERANCE!
WHAT ABOUT ME?!
IT'S GOOD TO SEE YOU AGAIN, OLD FRIEND.
BUT HOW IS STARRO DOING THIS? I DON'T SEE HIS DRONES ATTACHED ANYWHERE ON THEM.
EVEN THE SMALLER ONES LATCH ON TO YOUR FACE OR NECK.
I'M DONE FIGHTING, FATHER. YOU AND ANYTHING ELSE.

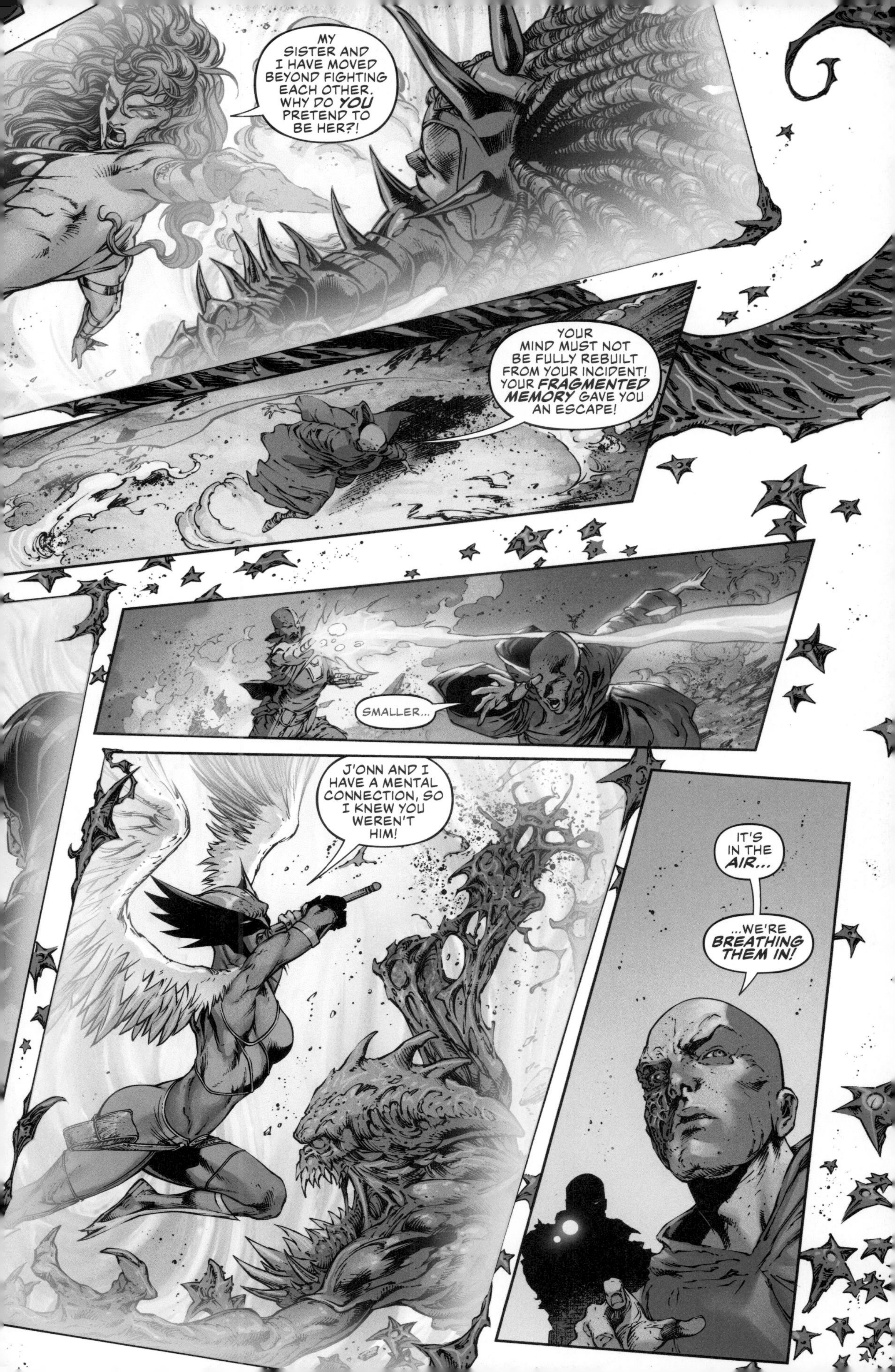

MY SISTER AND I HAVE MOVED BEYOND FIGHTING EACH OTHER. WHY DO YOU PRETEND TO BE HER?!
YOUR MIND MUST NOT BE FULLY REBUILT FROM YOUR INCIDENT! YOUR FRAGMENTED MEMORY GAVE YOU AN ESCAPE!
SMALLER...
J'ONN AND I HAVE A MENTAL CONNECTION, SO I KNEW YOU WEREN'T HIM!
IT'S IN THE AIR...
...WE'RE BREATHING THEM IN!

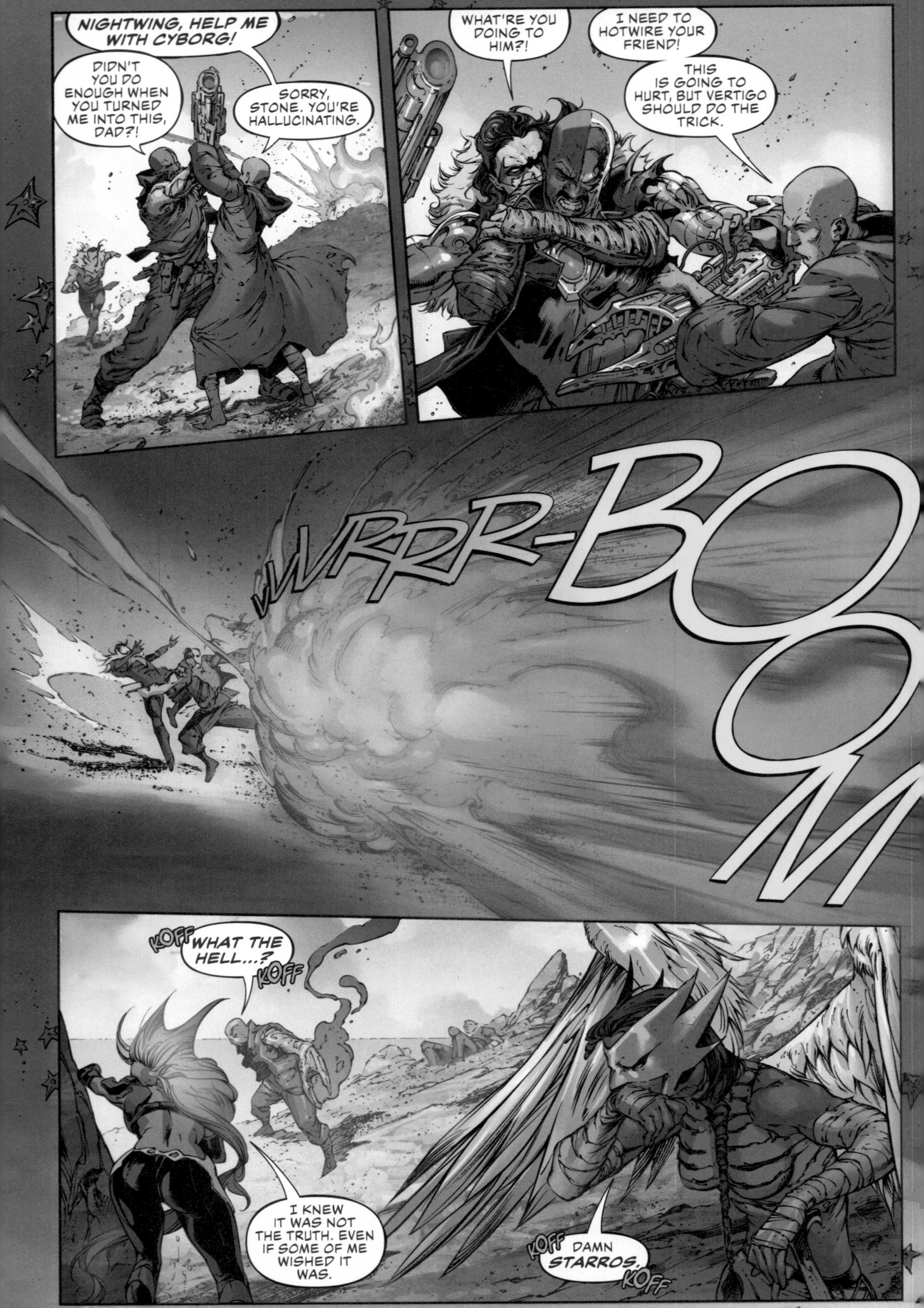
NIGHTWING, HELP ME WITH CYBORG!
DIDN'T YOU DO ENOUGH WHEN YOU TURNED ME INTO THIS, DAD?!
SORRY, STONE. YOU'RE HALLUCINATING.
WHAT'RE YOU DOING TO HIM?!
I NEED TO HOTWIRE YOUR FRIEND!
THIS IS GOING TO HURT, BUT VERTIGO SHOULD DO THE TRICK.
VVVRRR-BOOM
KOFF
WHAT THE HELL...?
KOFF
I KNEW IT WAS NOT THE TRUTH. EVEN IF SOME OF ME WISHED IT WAS.
KOFF
DAMN STARROS.
KOFF

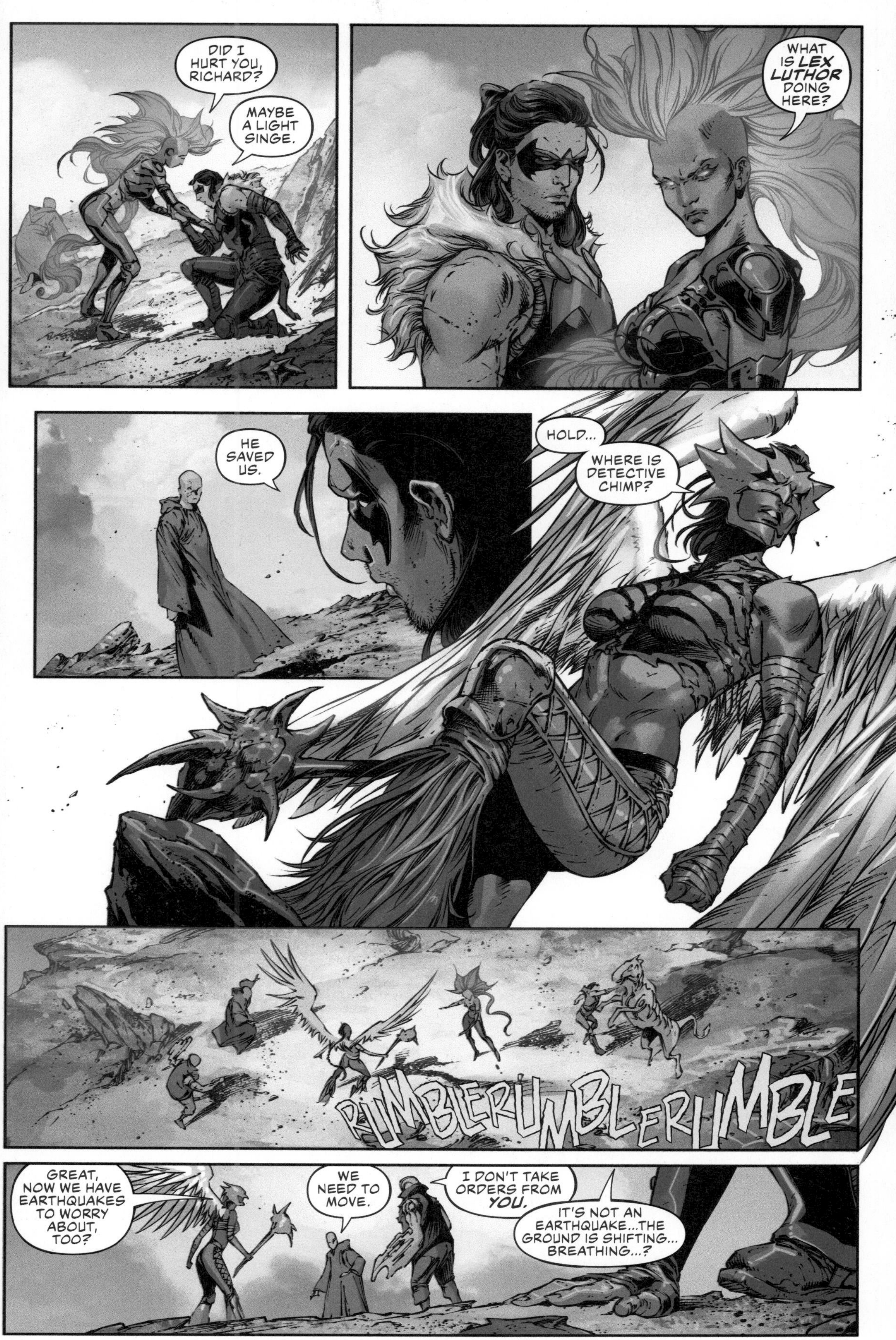
DID I HURT YOU, RICHARD?
MAYBE A LIGHT SINGE.
WHAT IS LEX LUTHOR DOING HERE?
HE SAVED US.
HOLD...
WHERE IS DETECTIVE CHIMP?
RUMBLERUMBLERUMBLE
GREAT, NOW WE HAVE EARTHQUAKES TO WORRY ABOUT, TOO?
WE NEED TO MOVE.
I DON'T TAKE ORDERS FROM YOU.
IT'S NOT AN EARTHQUAKE...THE GROUND IS SHIFTING... BREATHING...?

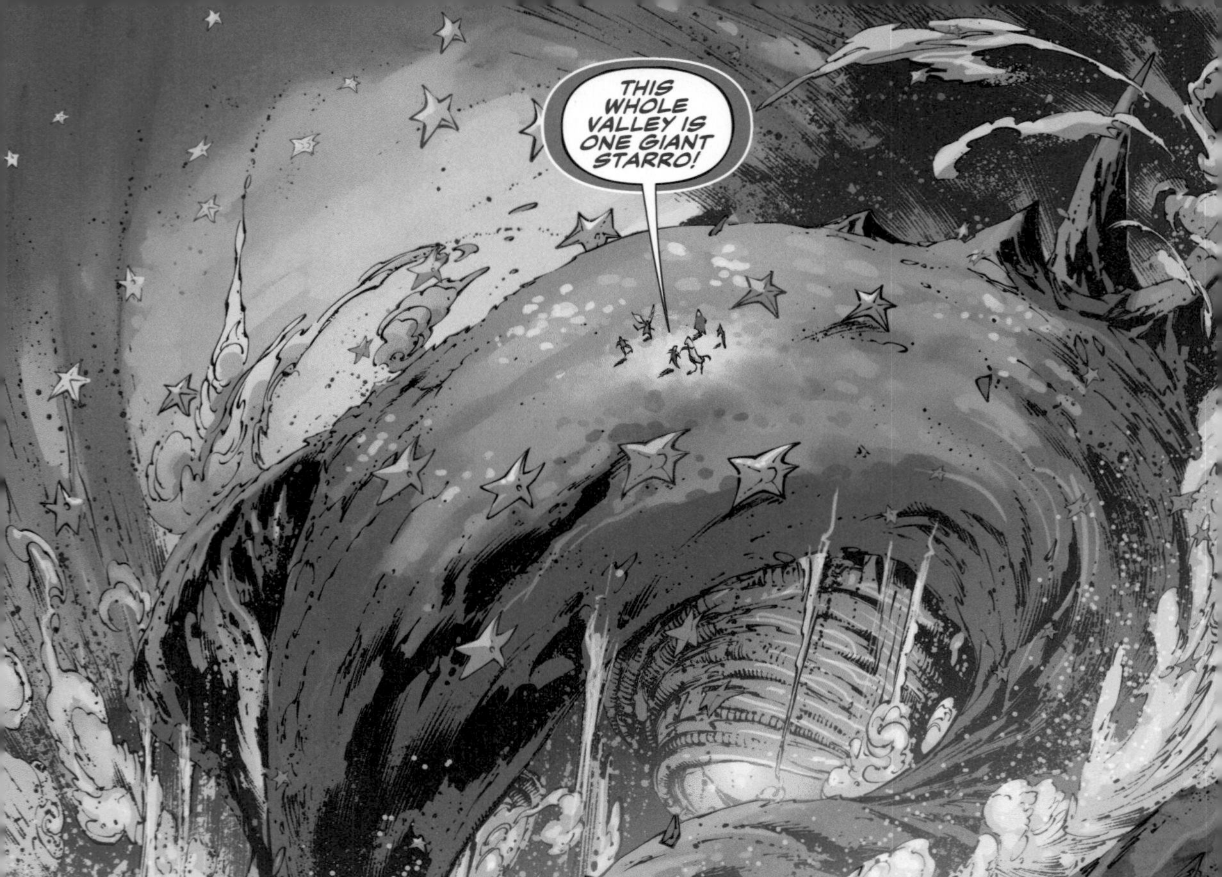
THIS WHOLE VALLEY IS ONE GIANT STARRO!

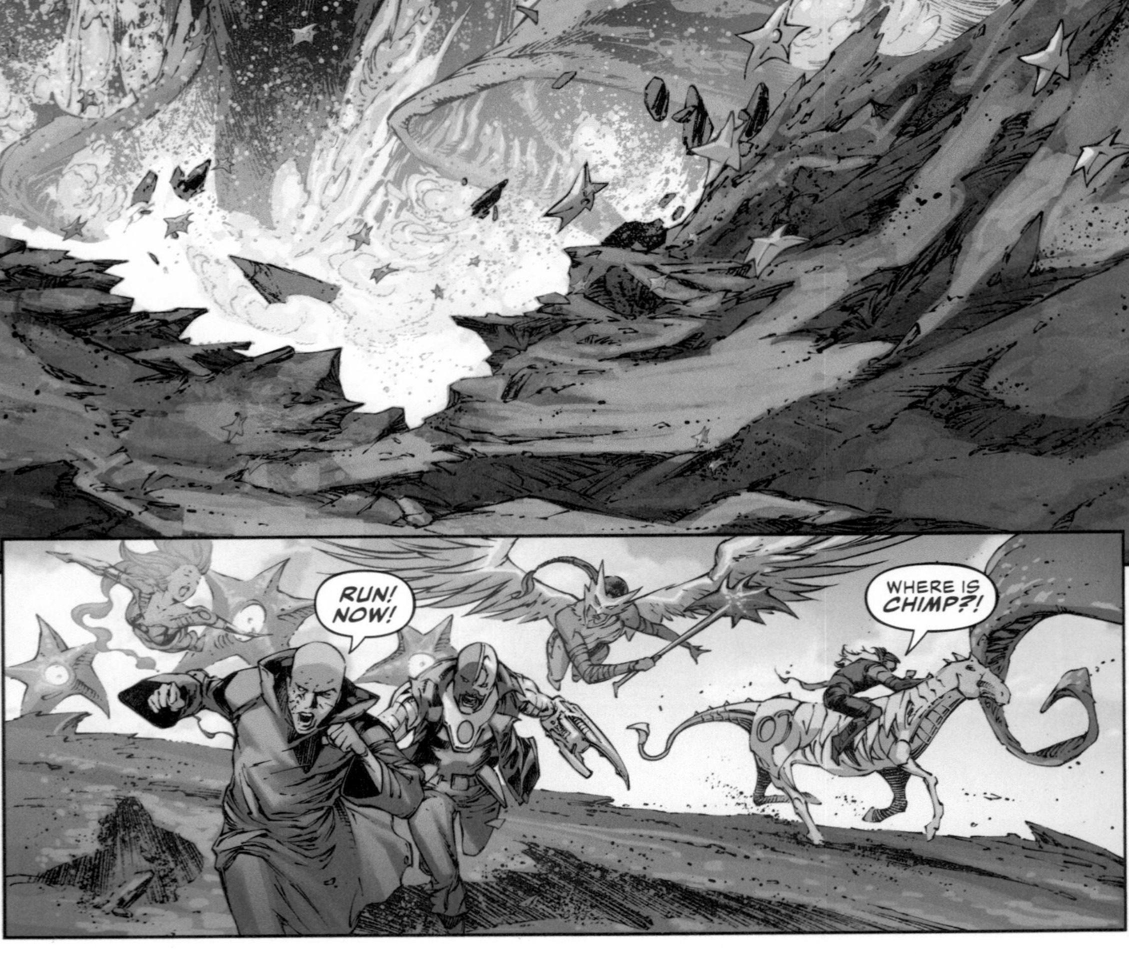
RUN! NOW!
WHERE IS CHIMP?!

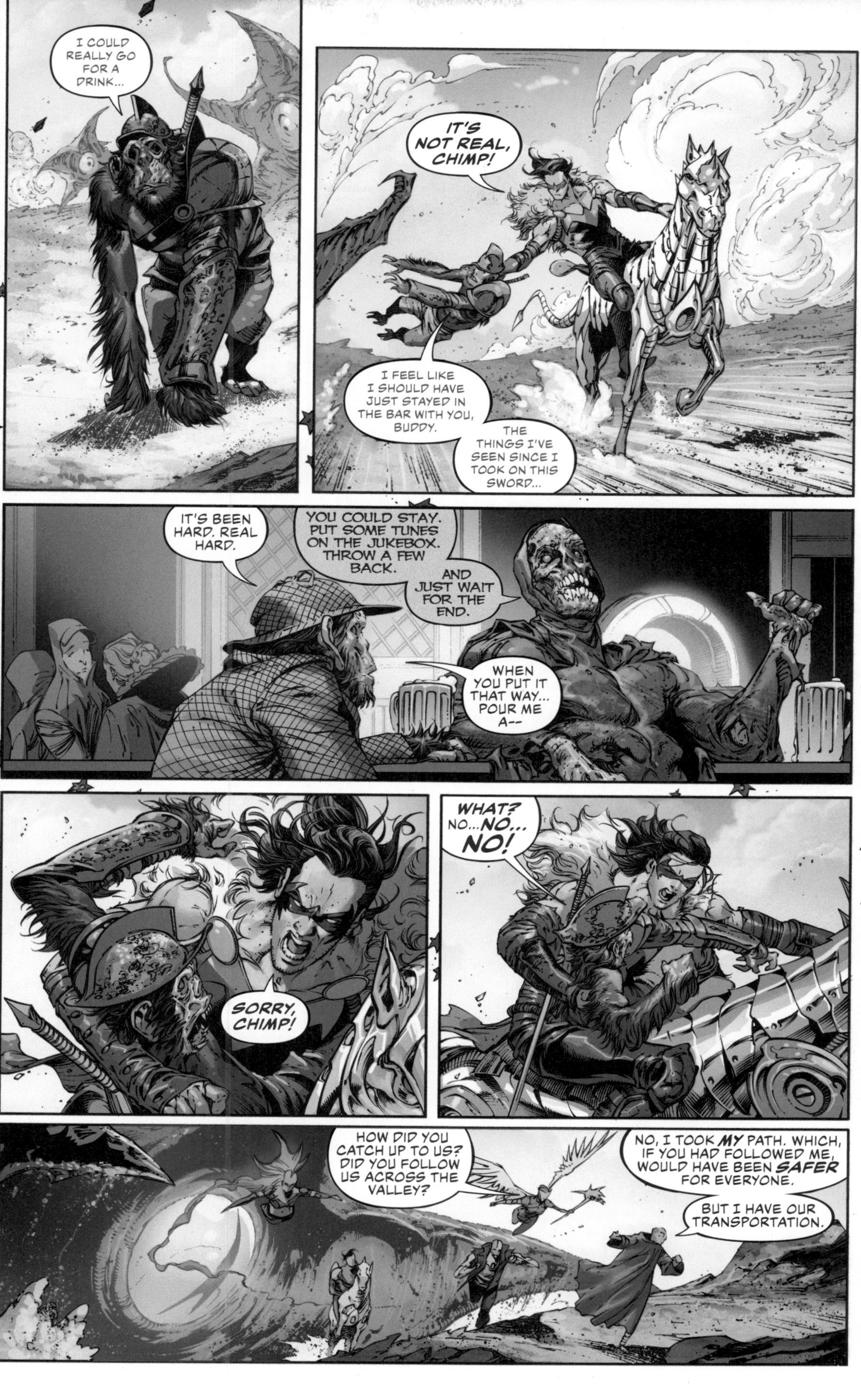
I COULD REALLY GO FOR A DRINK...
IT'S NOT REAL, CHIMP!
I FEEL LIKE I SHOULD HAVE JUST STAYED IN THE BAR WITH YOU, BUDDY.
THE THINGS I'VE SEEN SINCE I TOOK ON THIS SWORD...
IT'S BEEN HARD. REAL HARD.
YOU COULD STAY. PUT SOME TUNES ON THE JUKEBOX. THROW A FEW BACK.
AND JUST WAIT FOR THE END.
WHEN YOU PUT IT THAT WAY... POUR ME A--
SORRY, CHIMP!
WHAT? NO...NO... NO!
HOW DID YOU CATCH UP TO US? DID YOU FOLLOW US ACROSS THE VALLEY?
NO, I TOOK MY PATH. WHICH, IF YOU HAD FOLLOWED ME, WOULD HAVE BEEN SAFER FOR EVERYONE.
BUT I HAVE OUR TRANSPORTATION.

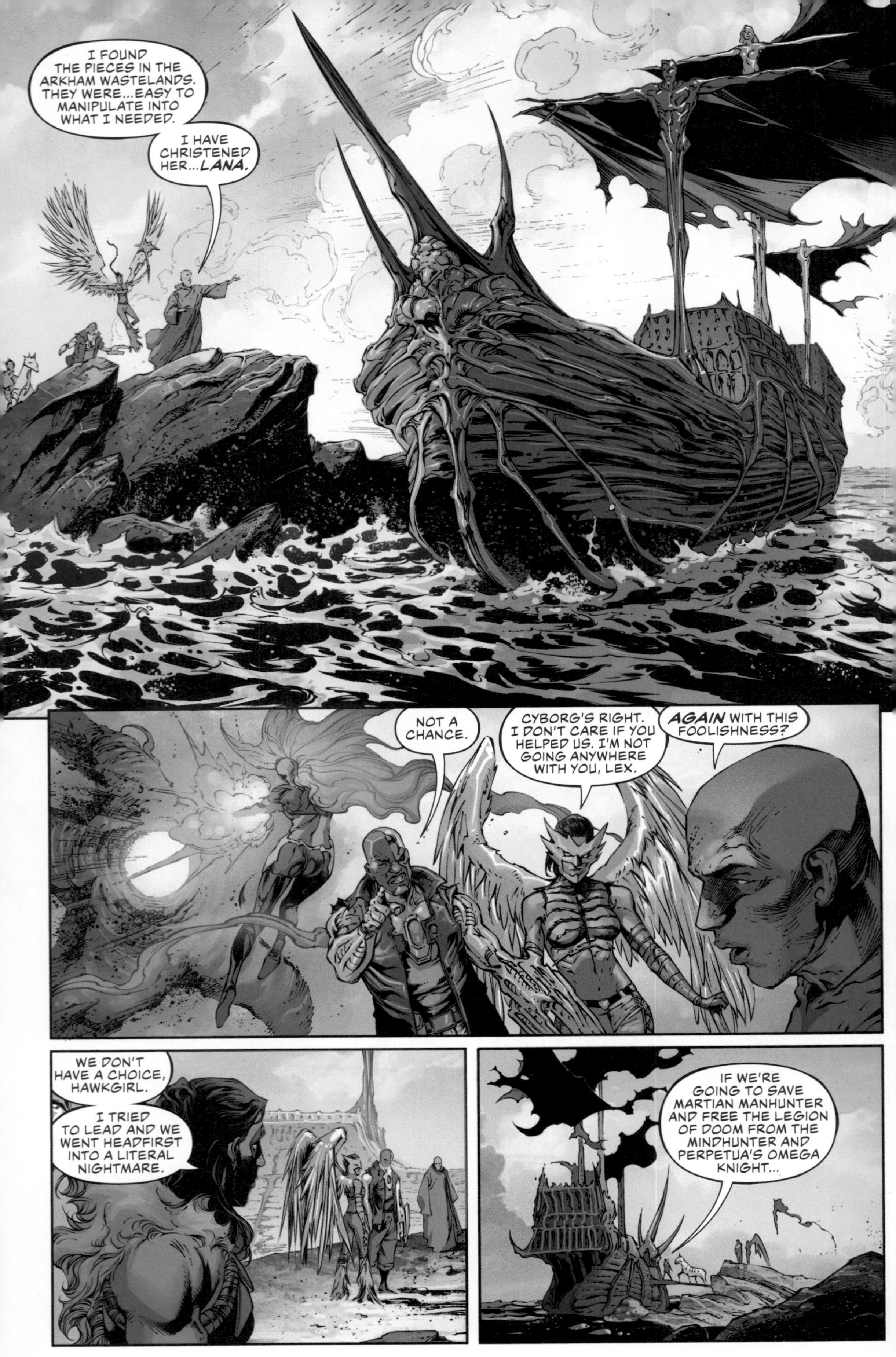
I FOUND THE PIECES IN THE ARKHAM WASTELANDS. THEY WERE...EASY TO MANIPULATE INTO WHAT I NEEDED.
I HAVE CHRISTENED HER...*LANA.*
NOT A CHANCE.
CYBORG'S RIGHT. I DON'T CARE IF YOU HELPED US. I'M NOT GOING ANYWHERE WITH YOU, LEX.
AGAIN WITH THIS FOOLISHNESS?
WE DON'T HAVE A CHOICE, HAWKGIRL.
I TRIED TO LEAD AND WE WENT HEADFIRST INTO A LITERAL NIGHTMARE.
IF WE'RE GOING TO SAVE MARTIAN MANHUNTER AND FREE THE LEGION OF DOOM FROM THE MINDHUNTER AND PERPETUA'S OMEGA KNIGHT...

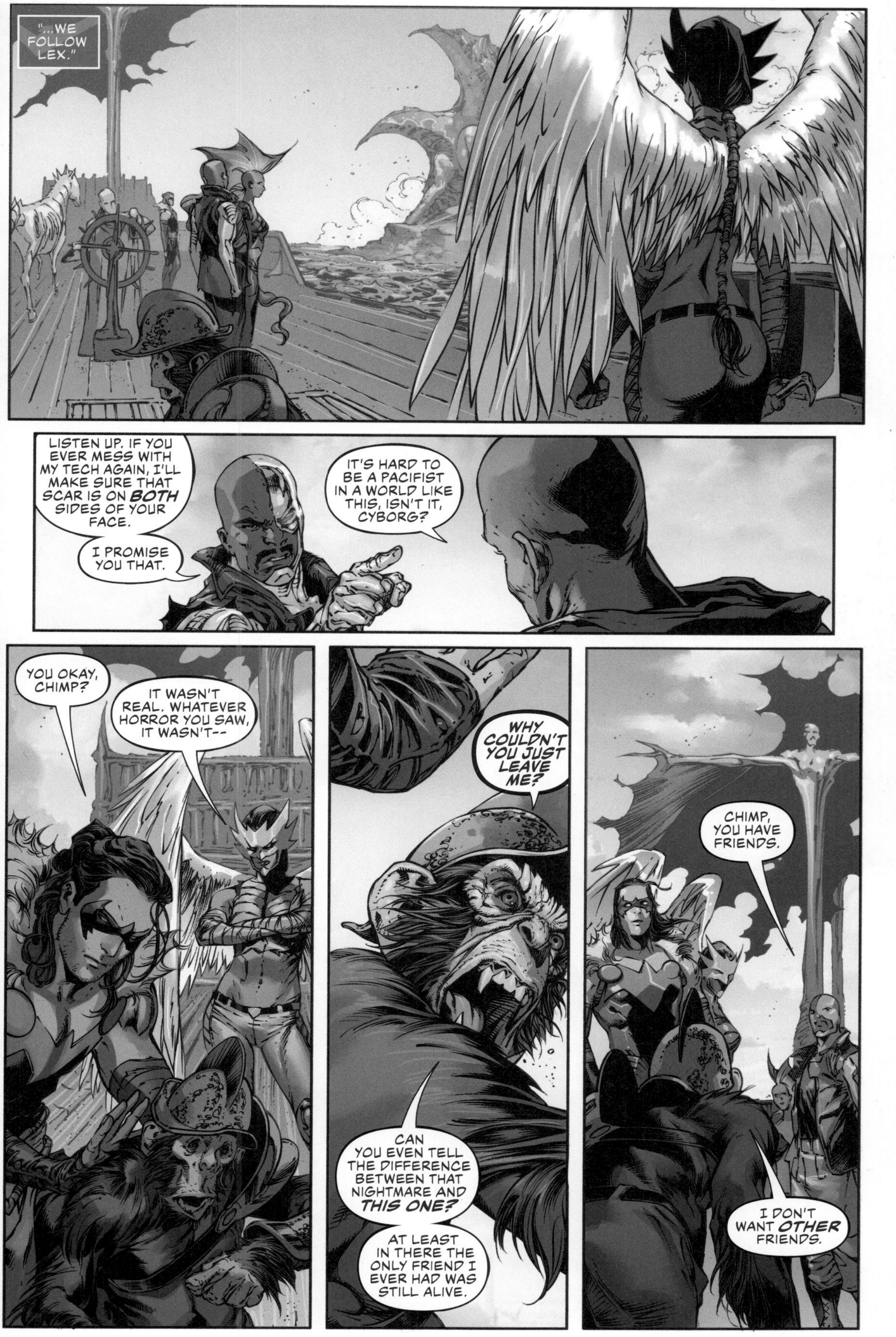
"...WE FOLLOW LEX."
LISTEN UP. IF YOU EVER MESS WITH MY TECH AGAIN, I'LL MAKE SURE THAT SCAR IS ON BOTH SIDES OF YOUR FACE.
I PROMISE YOU THAT.
IT'S HARD TO BE A PACIFIST IN A WORLD LIKE THIS, ISN'T IT, CYBORG?
YOU OKAY, CHIMP?
IT WASN'T REAL. WHATEVER HORROR YOU SAW, IT WASN'T--
WHY COULDN'T YOU JUST LEAVE ME?
CAN YOU EVEN TELL THE DIFFERENCE BETWEEN THAT NIGHTMARE AND THIS ONE?
AT LEAST IN THERE THE ONLY FRIEND I EVER HAD WAS STILL ALIVE.
CHIMP, YOU HAVE FRIENDS.
I DON'T WANT OTHER FRIENDS.

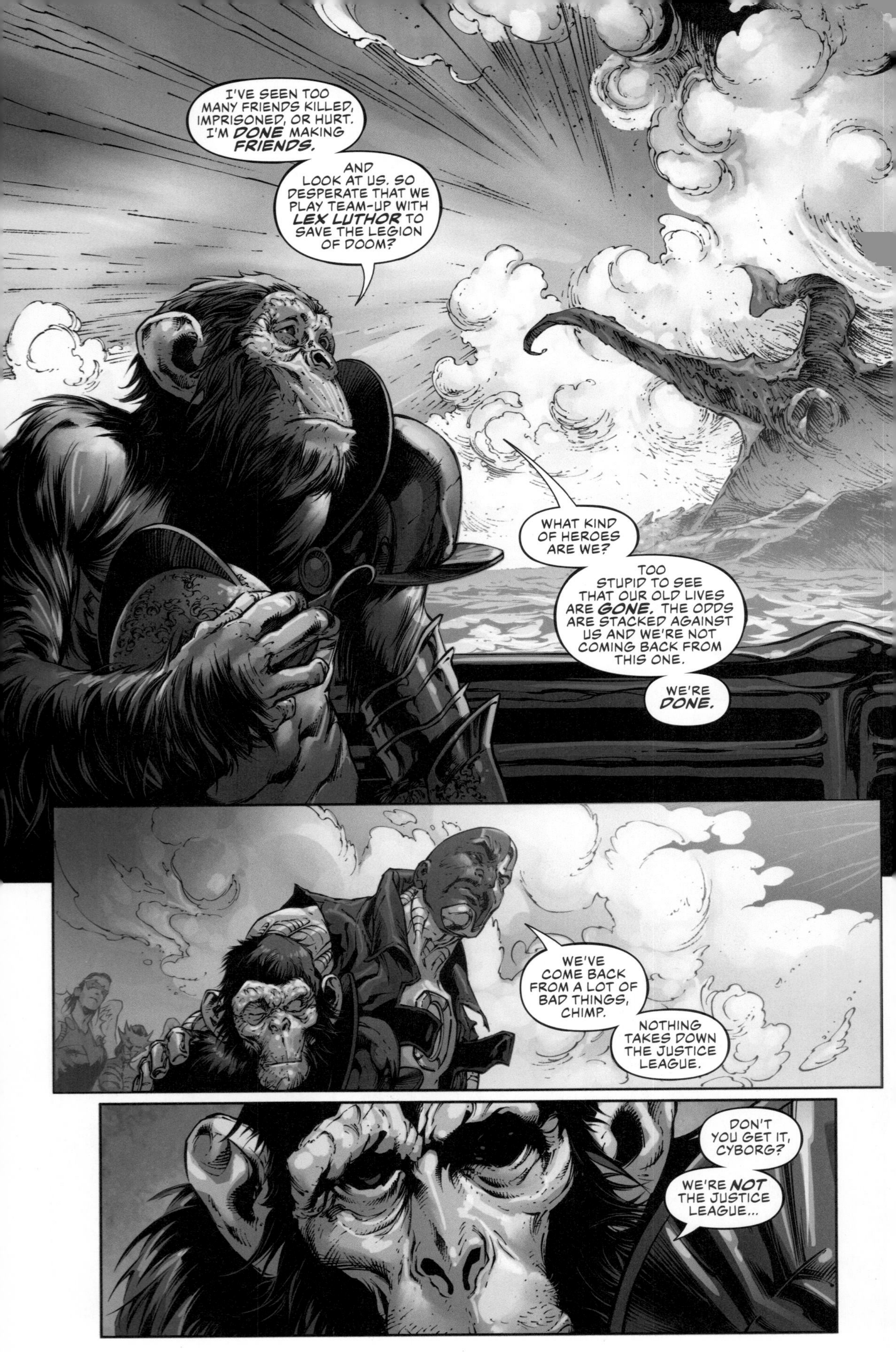

I'VE SEEN TOO MANY FRIENDS KILLED, IMPRISONED, OR HURT. I'M DONE MAKING FRIENDS.
AND LOOK AT US. SO DESPERATE THAT WE PLAY TEAM-UP WITH LEX LUTHOR TO SAVE THE LEGION OF DOOM?
WHAT KIND OF HEROES ARE WE?
TOO STUPID TO SEE THAT OUR OLD LIVES ARE GONE. THE ODDS ARE STACKED AGAINST US AND WE'RE NOT COMING BACK FROM THIS ONE.
WE'RE DONE.
WE'VE COME BACK FROM A LOT OF BAD THINGS, CHIMP.
NOTHING TAKES DOWN THE JUSTICE LEAGUE.
DON'T YOU GET IT, CYBORG?
WE'RE NOT THE JUSTICE LEAGUE...

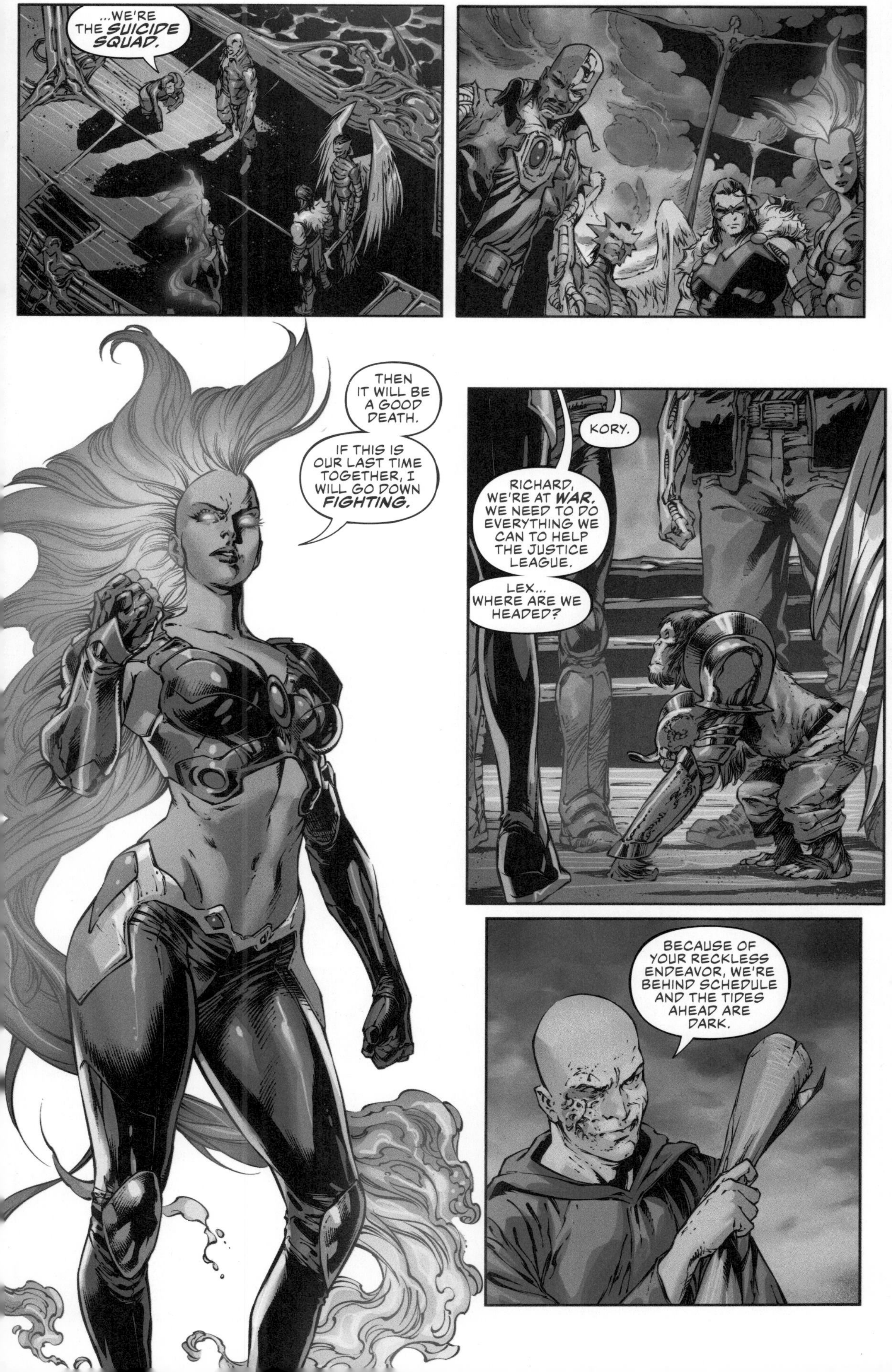
...WE'RE THE SUICIDE SQUAD.
THEN IT WILL BE A GOOD DEATH.
IF THIS IS OUR LAST TIME TOGETHER, I WILL GO DOWN FIGHTING.
KORY.
RICHARD, WE'RE AT WAR. WE NEED TO DO EVERYTHING WE CAN TO HELP THE JUSTICE LEAGUE.
LEX... WHERE ARE WE HEADED?
BECAUSE OF YOUR RECKLESS ENDEAVOR, WE'RE BEHIND SCHEDULE AND THE TIDES AHEAD ARE DARK.

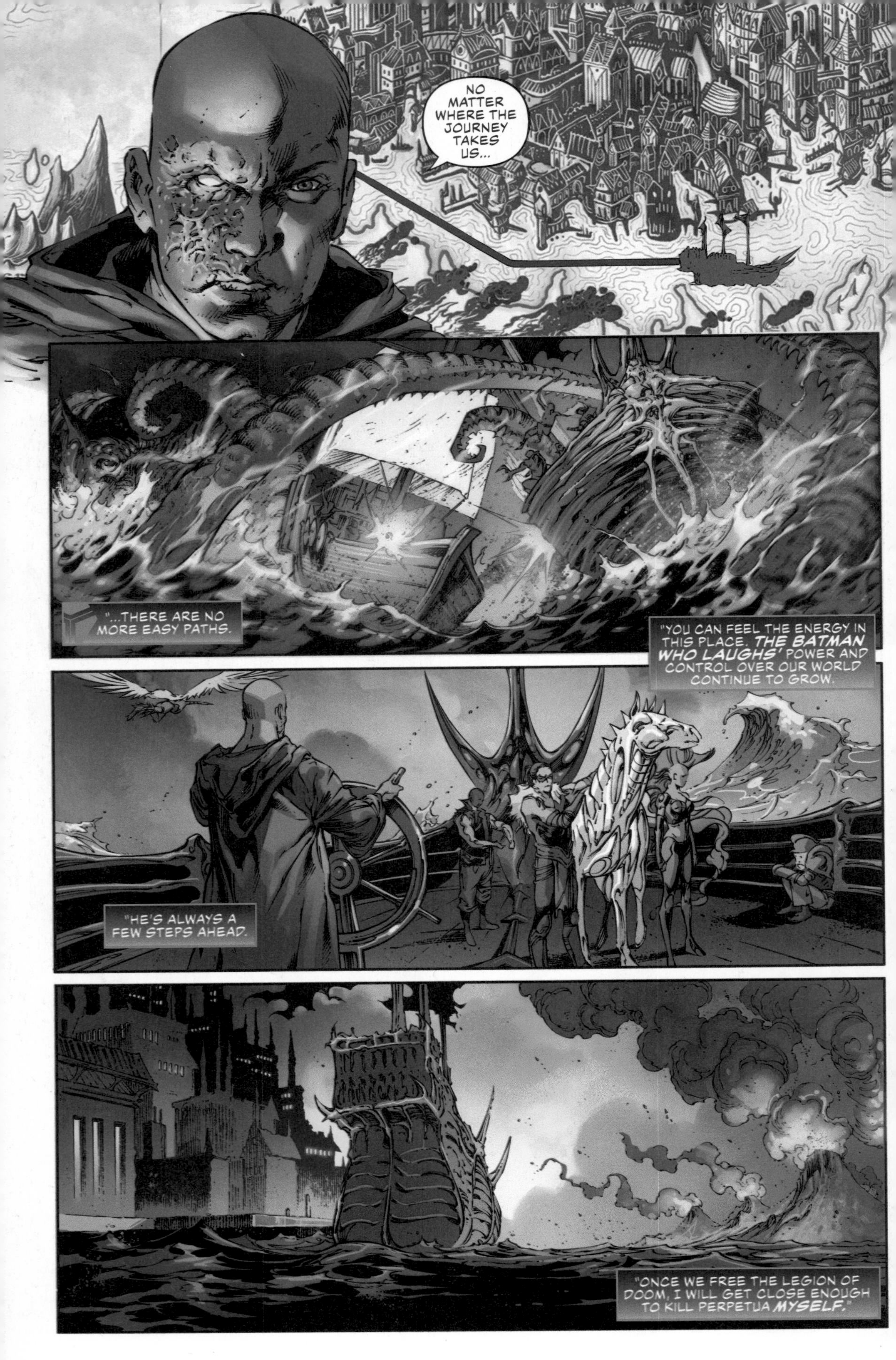
NO MATTER WHERE THE JOURNEY TAKES US...
"...THERE ARE NO MORE EASY PATHS.
"YOU CAN FEEL THE ENERGY IN THIS PLACE. THE BATMAN WHO LAUGHS' POWER AND CONTROL OVER OUR WORLD CONTINUE TO GROW.
"HE'S ALWAYS A FEW STEPS AHEAD.
"ONCE WE FREE THE LEGION OF DOOM, I WILL GET CLOSE ENOUGH TO KILL PERPETUA MYSELF."

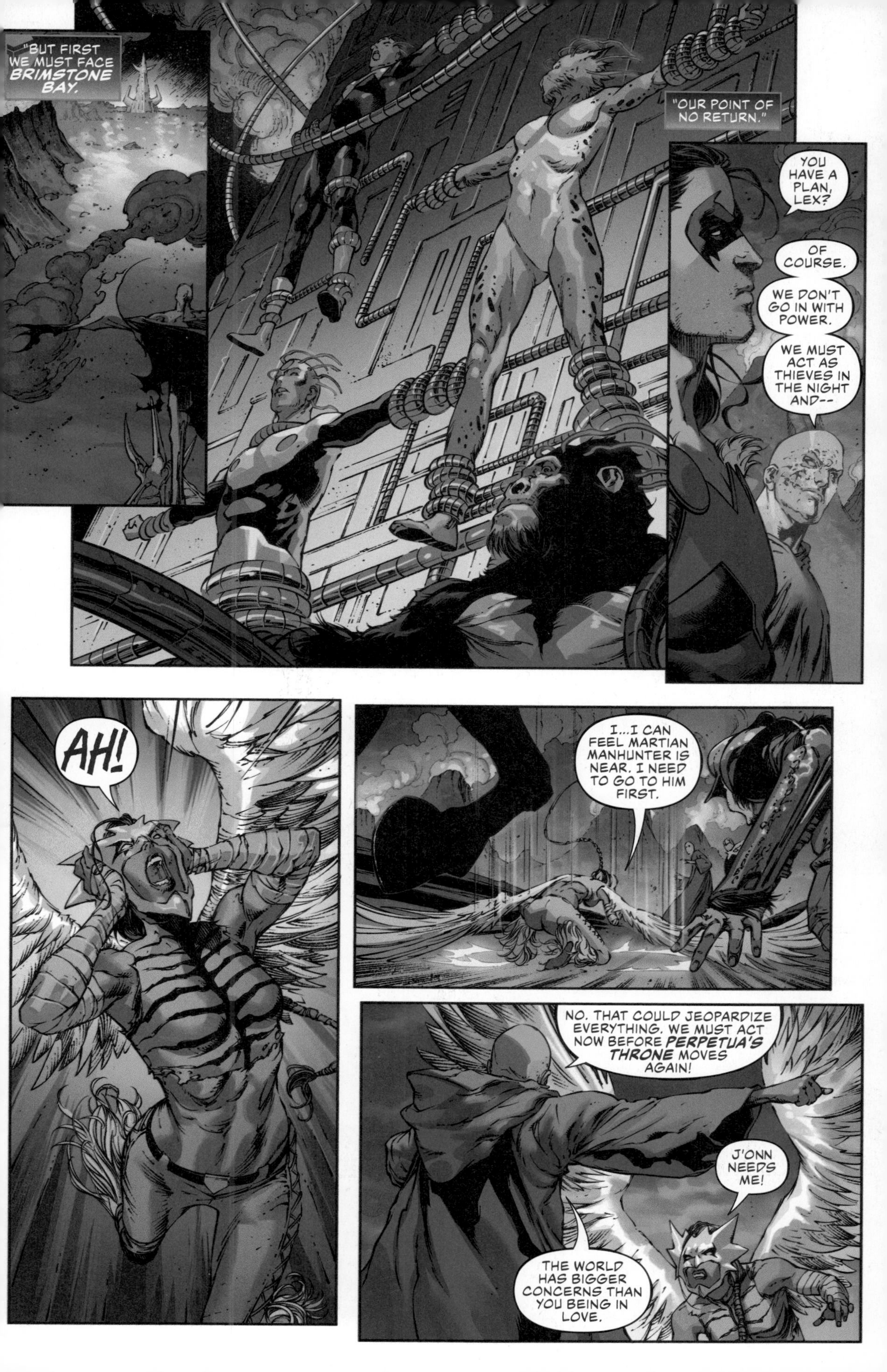

"BUT FIRST WE MUST FACE BRIMSTONE BAY.
"OUR POINT OF NO RETURN."
YOU HAVE A PLAN, LEX?
OF COURSE.
WE DON'T GO IN WITH POWER.
WE MUST ACT AS THIEVES IN THE NIGHT AND--
AH!
I...I CAN FEEL MARTIAN MANHUNTER IS NEAR. I NEED TO GO TO HIM FIRST.
NO. THAT COULD JEOPARDIZE EVERYTHING. WE MUST ACT NOW BEFORE PERPETUA'S THRONE MOVES AGAIN!
J'ONN NEEDS ME!
THE WORLD HAS BIGGER CONCERNS THAN YOU BEING IN LOVE.

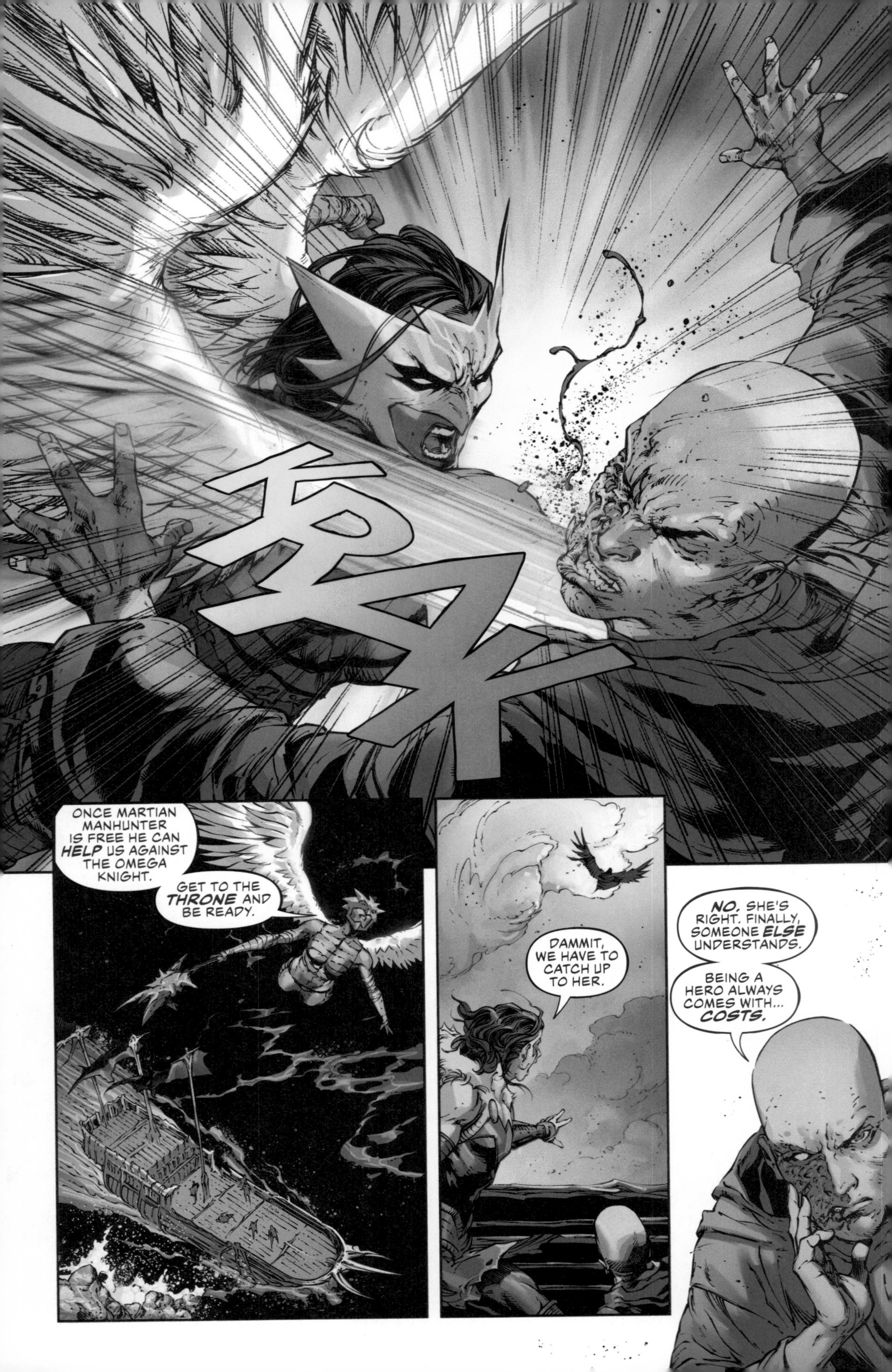
KRAK
ONCE MARTIAN MANHUNTER IS FREE HE CAN HELP US AGAINST THE OMEGA KNIGHT.
GET TO THE THRONE AND BE READY.
DAMMIT, WE HAVE TO CATCH UP TO HER.
NO. SHE'S RIGHT. FINALLY, SOMEONE ELSE UNDERSTANDS.
BEING A HERO ALWAYS COMES WITH... COSTS.

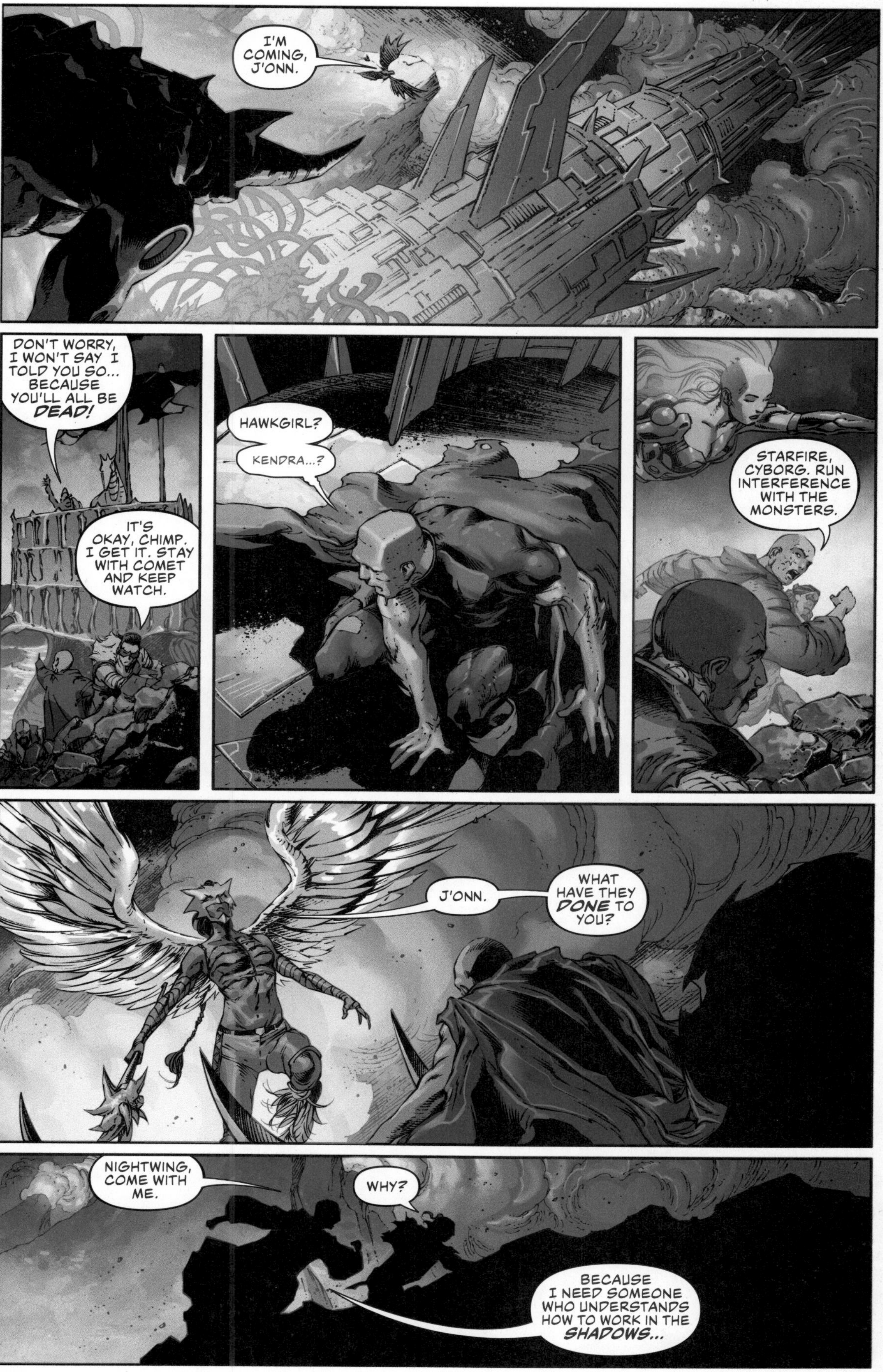
I'M COMING, J'ONN.
DON'T WORRY, I WON'T SAY I TOLD YOU SO... BECAUSE YOU'LL ALL BE DEAD!
IT'S OKAY, CHIMP. I GET IT. STAY WITH COMET AND KEEP WATCH.
HAWKGIRL?
KENDRA...?
STARFIRE, CYBORG. RUN INTERFERENCE WITH THE MONSTERS.
J'ONN.
WHAT HAVE THEY DONE TO YOU?
NIGHTWING, COME WITH ME.
WHY?
BECAUSE I NEED SOMEONE WHO UNDERSTANDS HOW TO WORK IN THE SHADOWS...

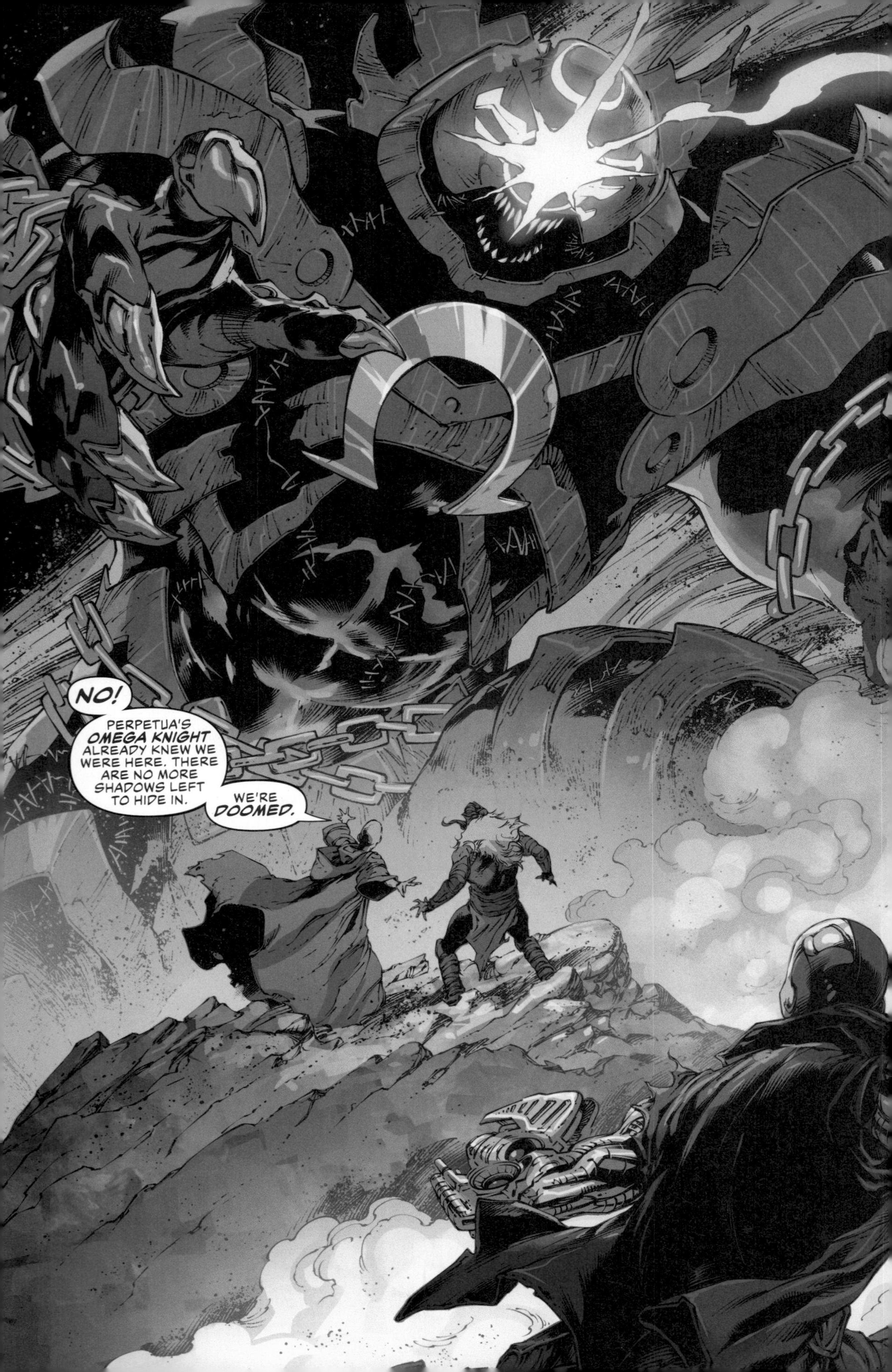
NO!
PERPETUA'S OMEGA KNIGHT ALREADY KNEW WE WERE HERE. THERE ARE NO MORE SHADOWS LEFT TO HIDE IN.
WE'RE DOOMED.

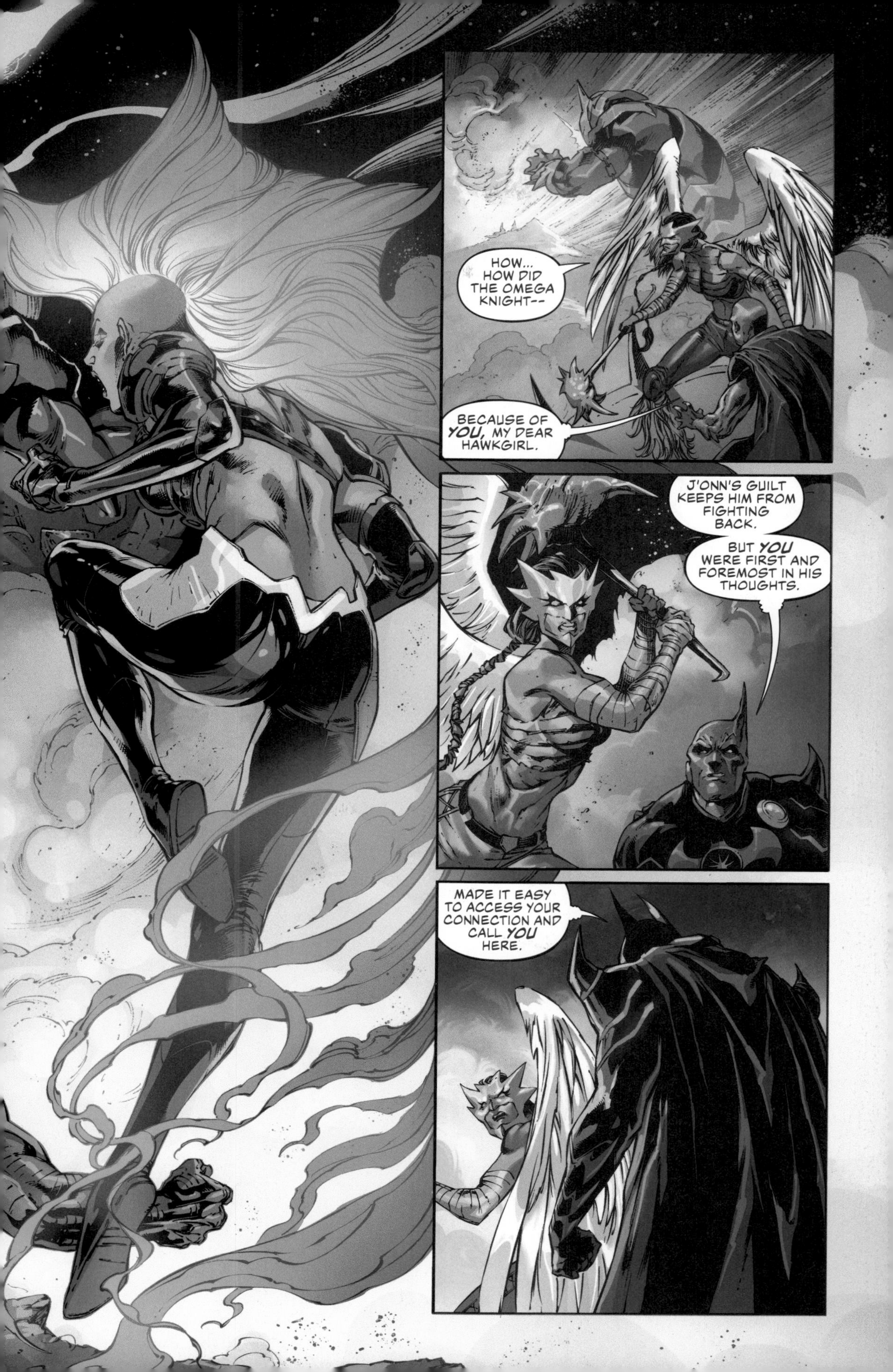
HOW... HOW DID THE OMEGA KNIGHT--
BECAUSE OF YOU, MY DEAR HAWKGIRL.
J'ONN'S GUILT KEEPS HIM FROM FIGHTING BACK.
BUT YOU WERE FIRST AND FOREMOST IN HIS THOUGHTS.
MADE IT EASY TO ACCESS YOUR CONNECTION AND CALL YOU HERE.

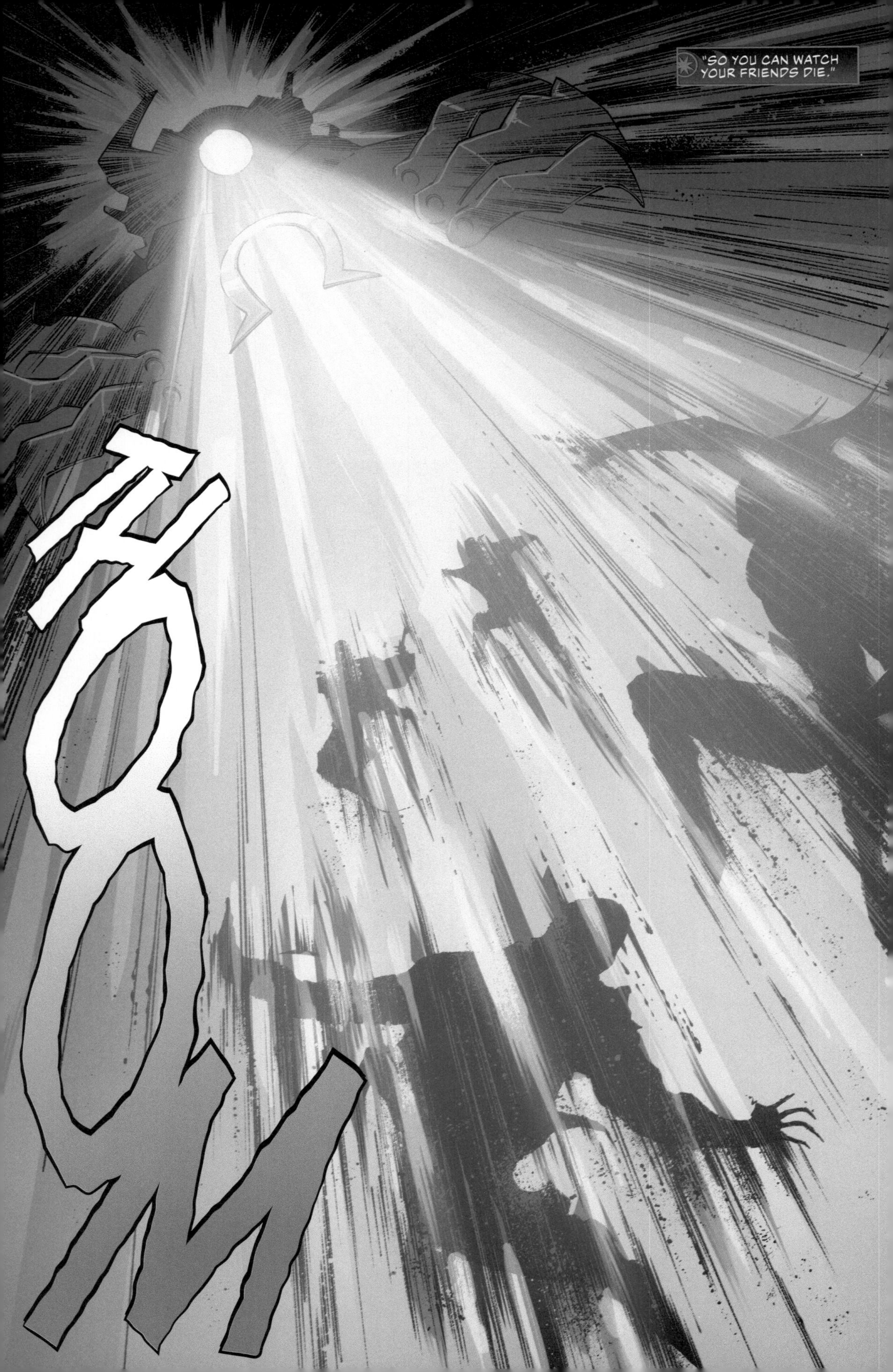
"SO YOU CAN WATCH YOUR FRIENDS DIE."
THOOM

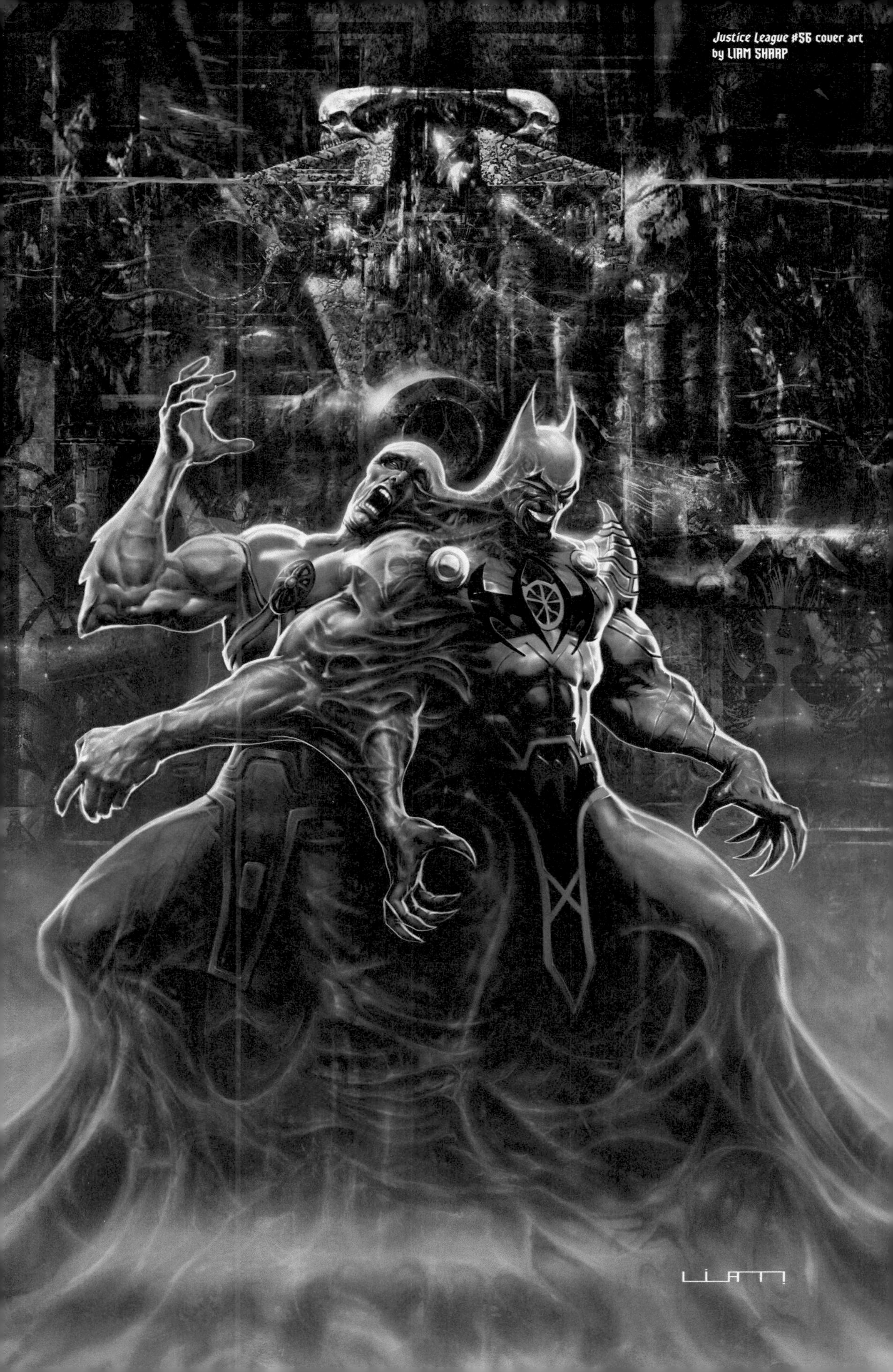

Justice League #56 cover art
by LIAM SHARP

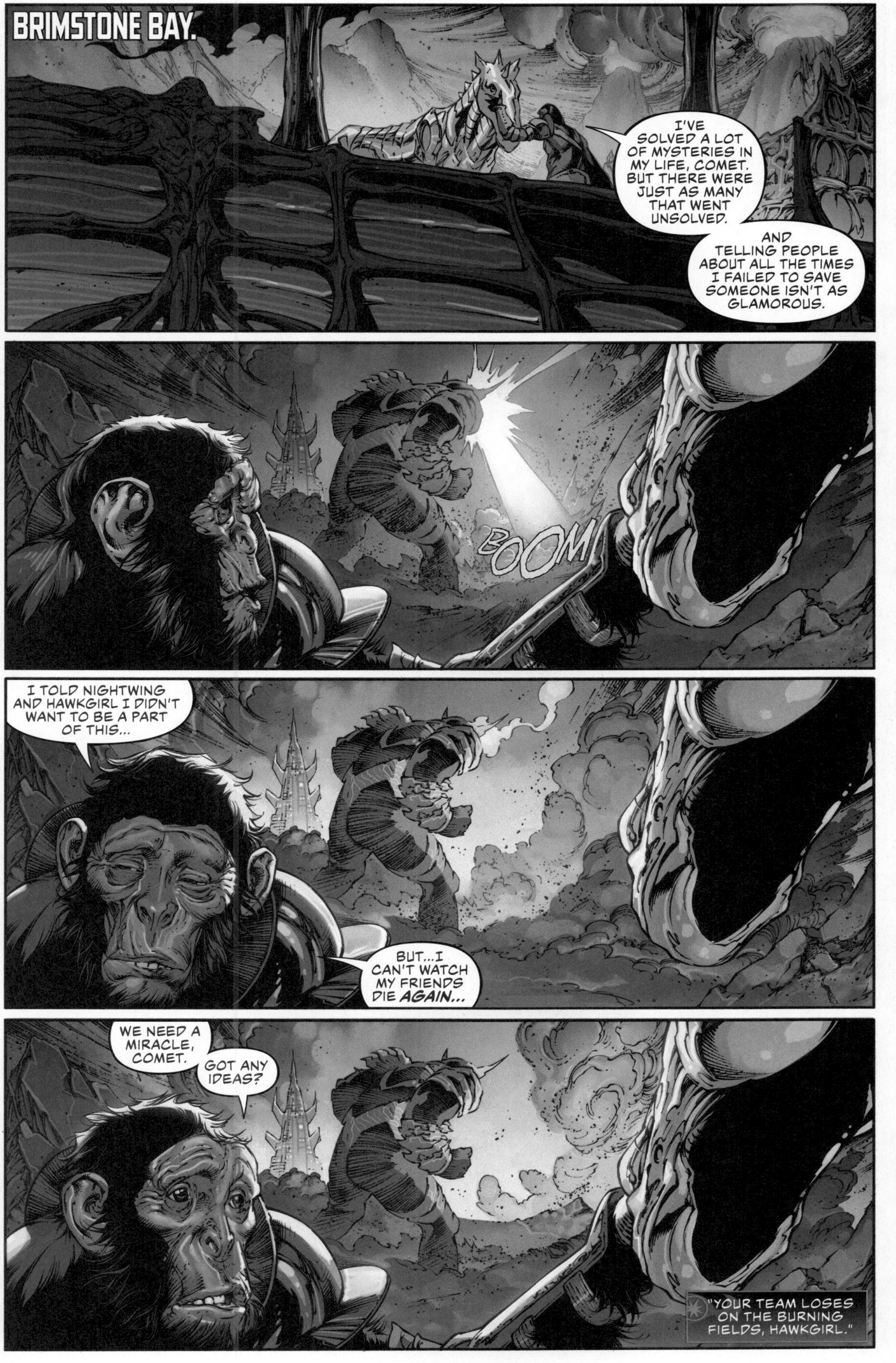
BRIMSTONE BAY.
I'VE SOLVED A LOT OF MYSTERIES IN MY LIFE, COMET. BUT THERE WERE JUST AS MANY THAT WENT UNSOLVED.
AND TELLING PEOPLE ABOUT ALL THE TIMES I FAILED TO SAVE SOMEONE ISN'T AS GLAMOROUS.
BOOM
I TOLD NIGHTWING AND HAWKGIRL I DIDN'T WANT TO BE A PART OF THIS...
BUT...I CAN'T WATCH MY FRIENDS DIE *AGAIN*...
WE NEED A MIRACLE, COMET.
GOT ANY IDEAS?
"YOUR TEAM LOSES ON THE BURNING FIELDS, HAWKGIRL."

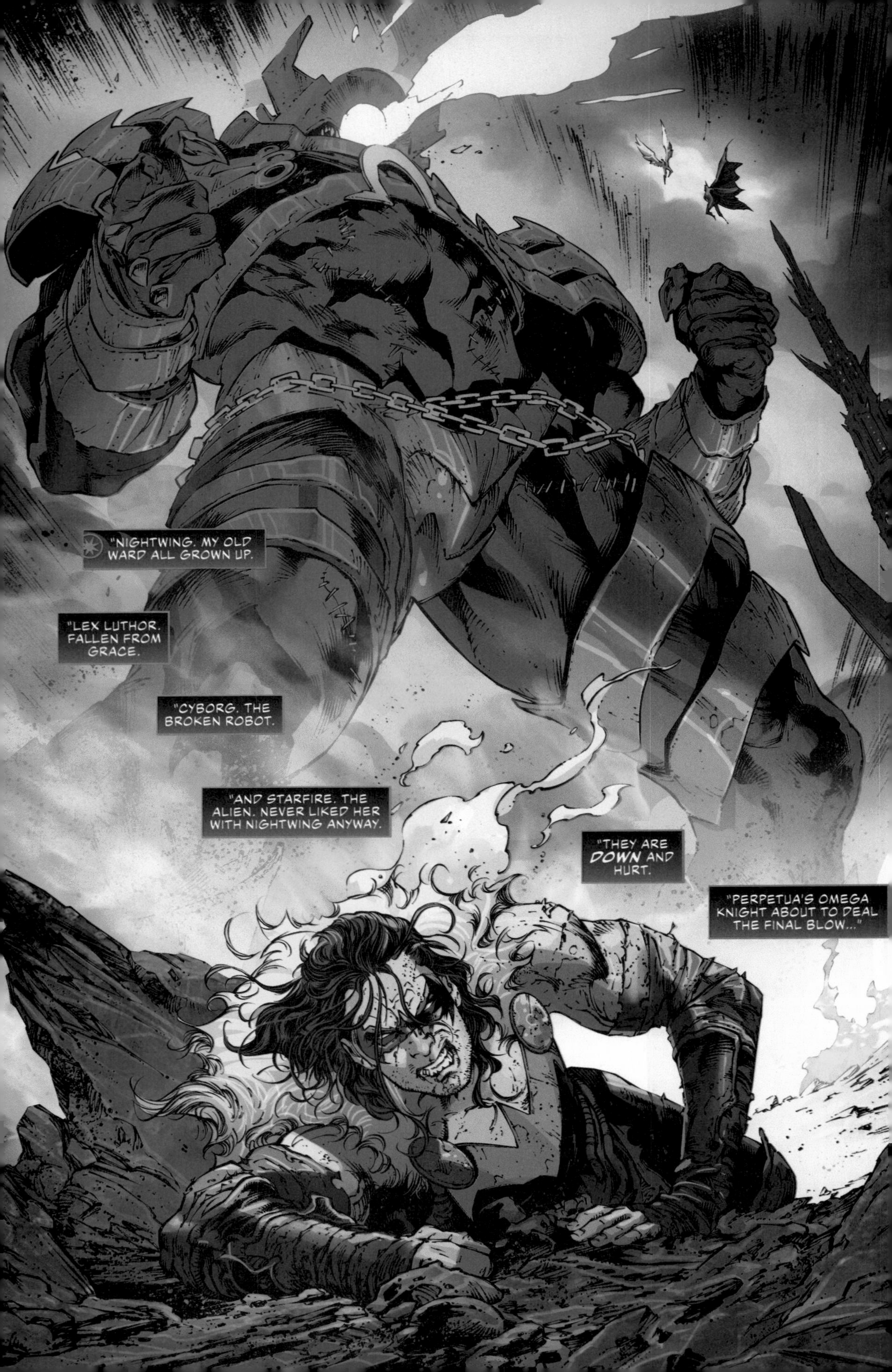
"NIGHTWING. MY OLD WARD ALL GROWN UP.
"LEX LUTHOR. FALLEN FROM GRACE.
"CYBORG. THE BROKEN ROBOT.
"AND STARFIRE. THE ALIEN. NEVER LIKED HER WITH NIGHTWING ANYWAY.
"THEY ARE *DOWN* AND HURT.
"PERPETUA'S OMEGA KNIGHT ABOUT TO DEAL THE FINAL BLOW..."

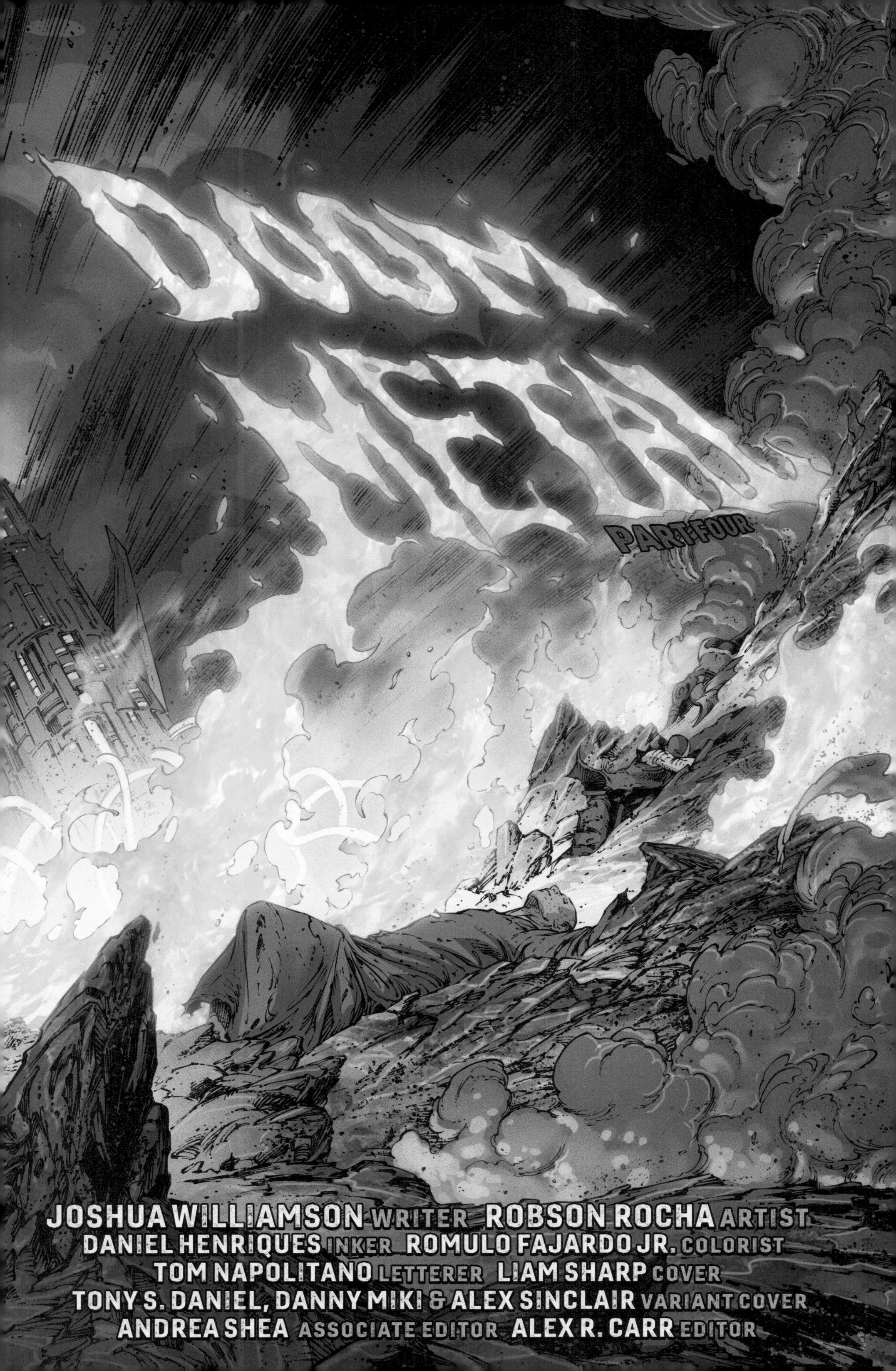
DOOM WAR
PART FOUR
JOSHUA WILLIAMSON WRITER ROBSON ROCHA ARTIST
DANIEL HENRIQUES INKER ROMULO FAJARDO JR. COLORIST
TOM NAPOLITANO LETTERER LIAM SHARP COVER
TONY S. DANIEL, DANNY MIKI & ALEX SINCLAIR VARIANT COVER
ANDREA SHEA ASSOCIATE EDITOR ALEX R. CARR EDITOR

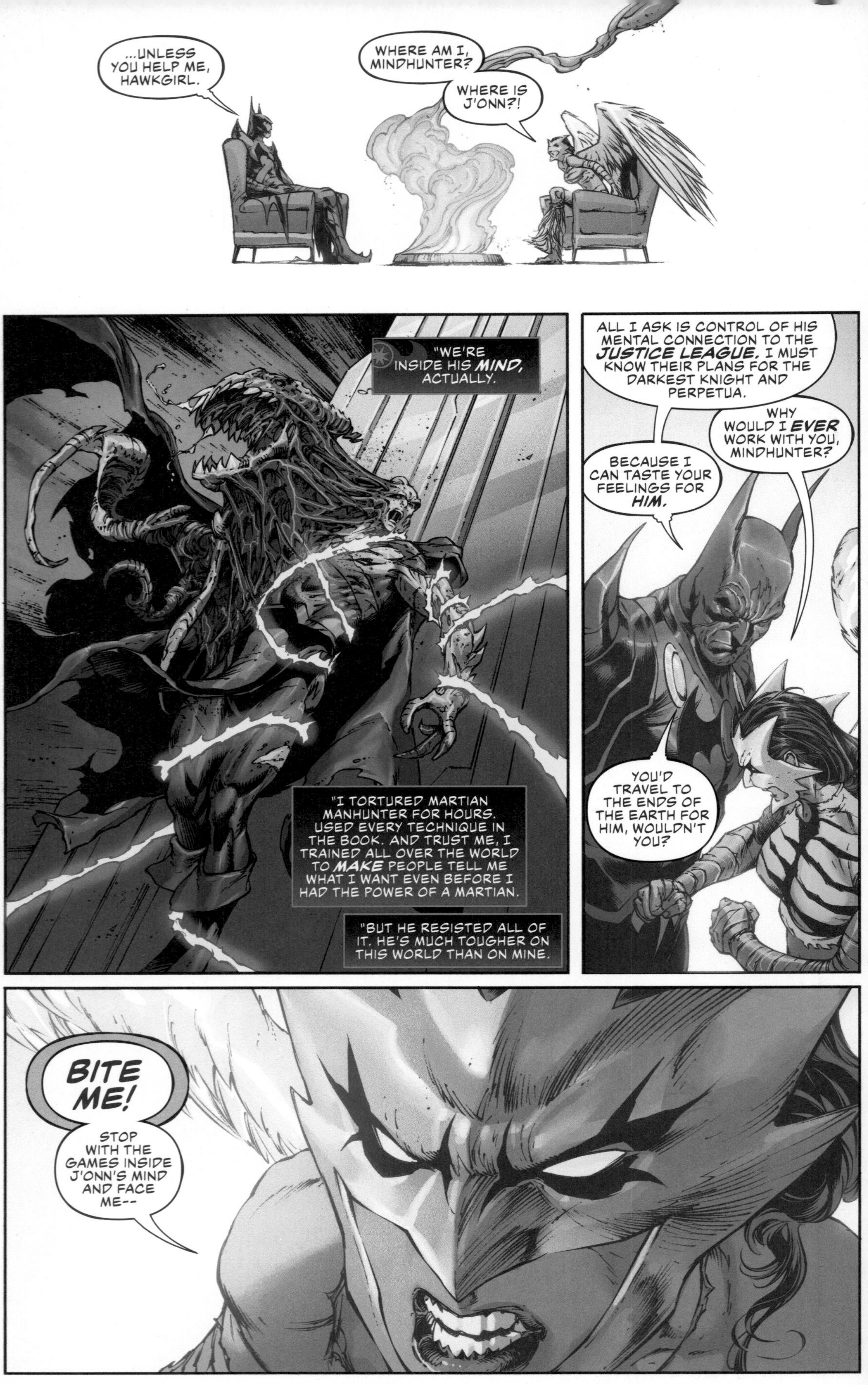
...UNLESS YOU HELP ME, HAWKGIRL.
WHERE AM I, MINDHUNTER?
WHERE IS J'ONN?!
"WE'RE INSIDE HIS MIND, ACTUALLY.
"I TORTURED MARTIAN MANHUNTER FOR HOURS. USED EVERY TECHNIQUE IN THE BOOK. AND TRUST ME, I TRAINED ALL OVER THE WORLD TO MAKE PEOPLE TELL ME WHAT I WANT EVEN BEFORE I HAD THE POWER OF A MARTIAN.
"BUT HE RESISTED ALL OF IT. HE'S MUCH TOUGHER ON THIS WORLD THAN ON MINE.
ALL I ASK IS CONTROL OF HIS MENTAL CONNECTION TO THE JUSTICE LEAGUE. I MUST KNOW THEIR PLANS FOR THE DARKEST KNIGHT AND PERPETUA.
WHY WOULD I EVER WORK WITH YOU, MINDHUNTER?
BECAUSE I CAN TASTE YOUR FEELINGS FOR HIM.
YOU'D TRAVEL TO THE ENDS OF THE EARTH FOR HIM, WOULDN'T YOU?
BITE ME!
STOP WITH THE GAMES INSIDE J'ONN'S MIND AND FACE ME--

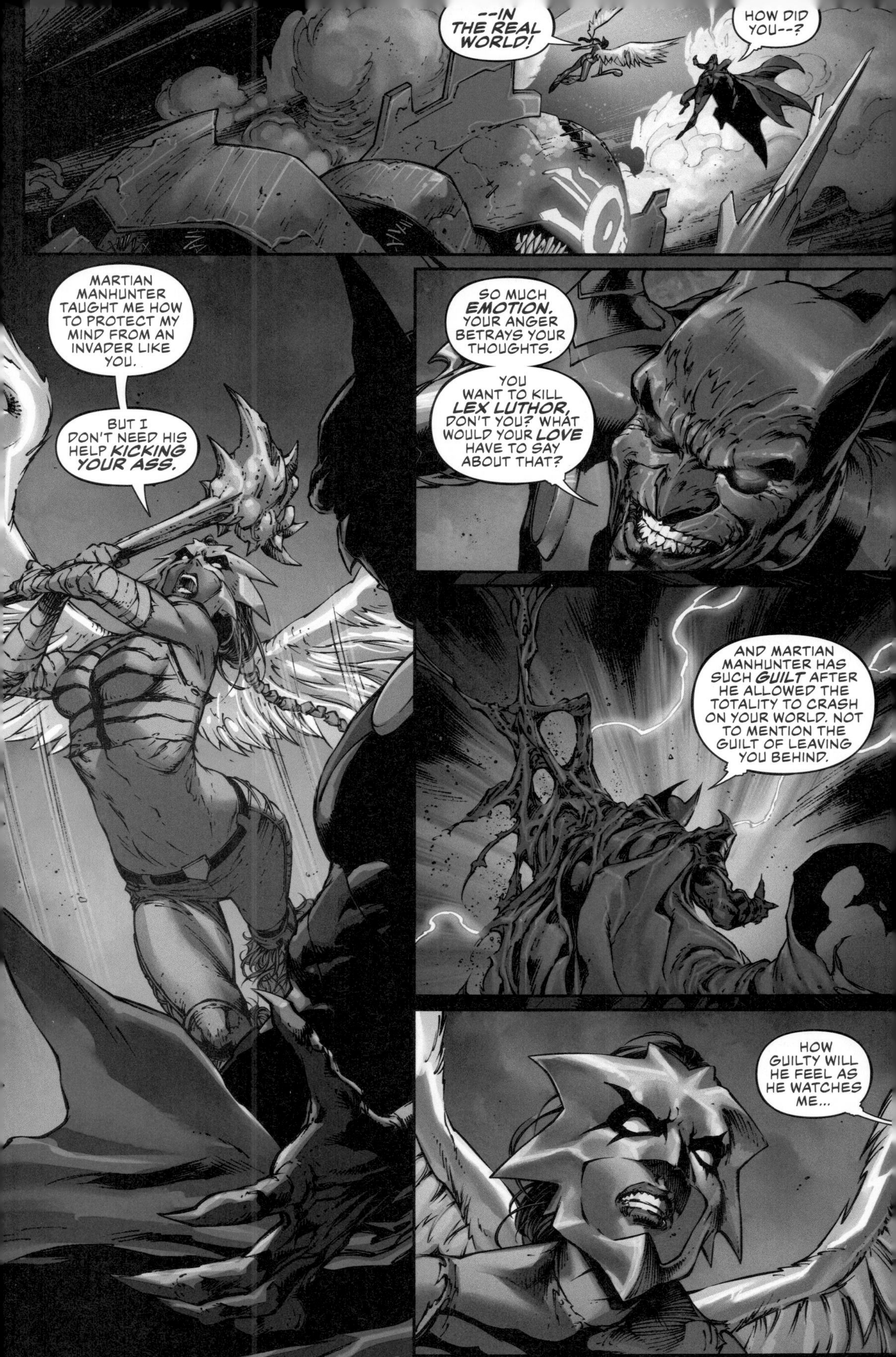
--IN THE REAL WORLD!
HOW DID YOU--?
MARTIAN MANHUNTER TAUGHT ME HOW TO PROTECT MY MIND FROM AN INVADER LIKE YOU.
BUT I DON'T NEED HIS HELP KICKING YOUR ASS.
SO MUCH EMOTION. YOUR ANGER BETRAYS YOUR THOUGHTS.
YOU WANT TO KILL LEX LUTHOR, DON'T YOU? WHAT WOULD YOUR LOVE HAVE TO SAY ABOUT THAT?
AND MARTIAN MANHUNTER HAS SUCH GUILT AFTER HE ALLOWED THE TOTALITY TO CRASH ON YOUR WORLD. NOT TO MENTION THE GUILT OF LEAVING YOU BEHIND.
HOW GUILTY WILL HE FEEL AS HE WATCHES ME...

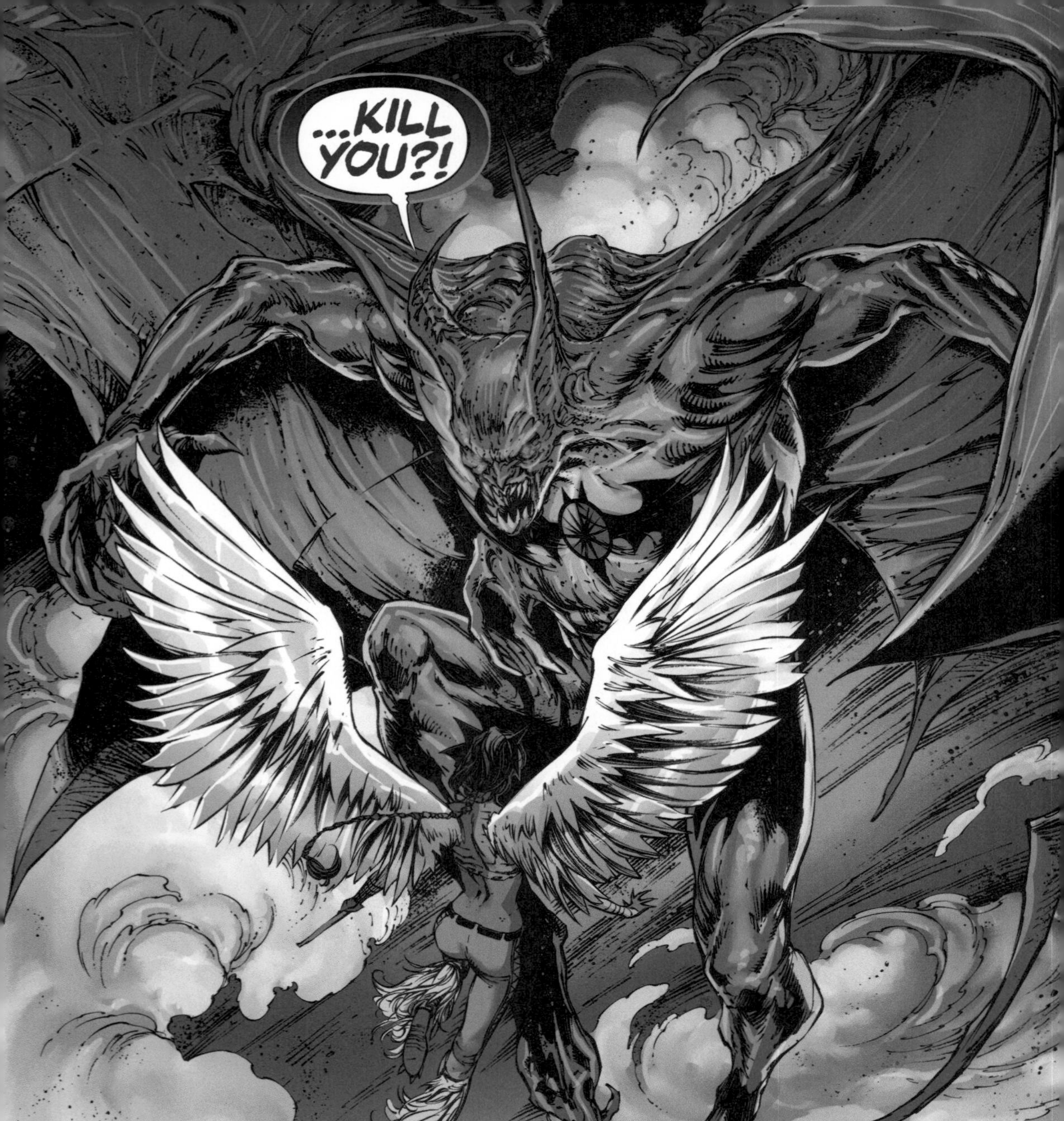
...KILL YOU?!

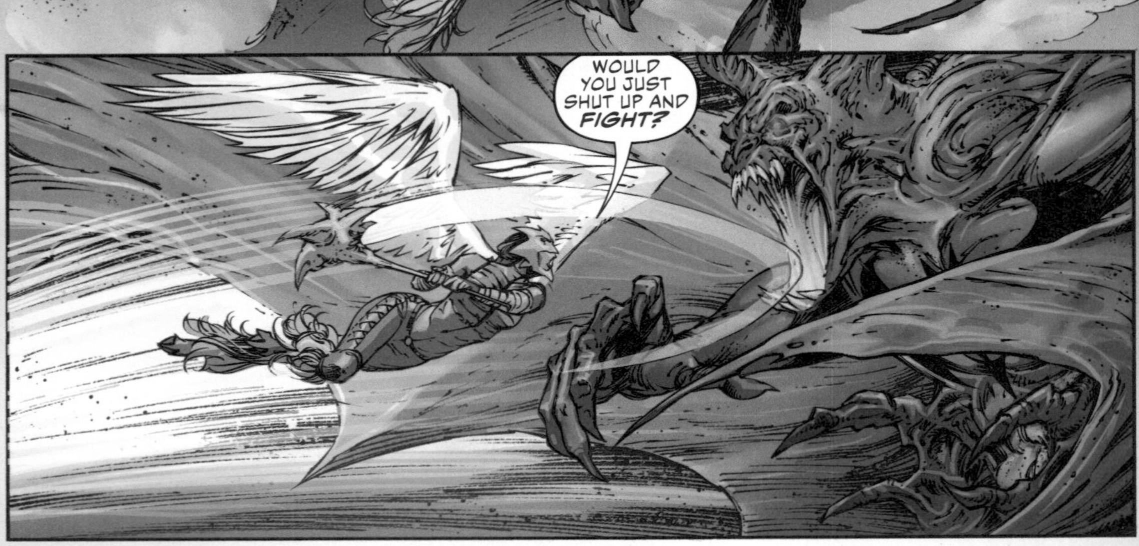
WOULD YOU JUST SHUT UP AND FIGHT?

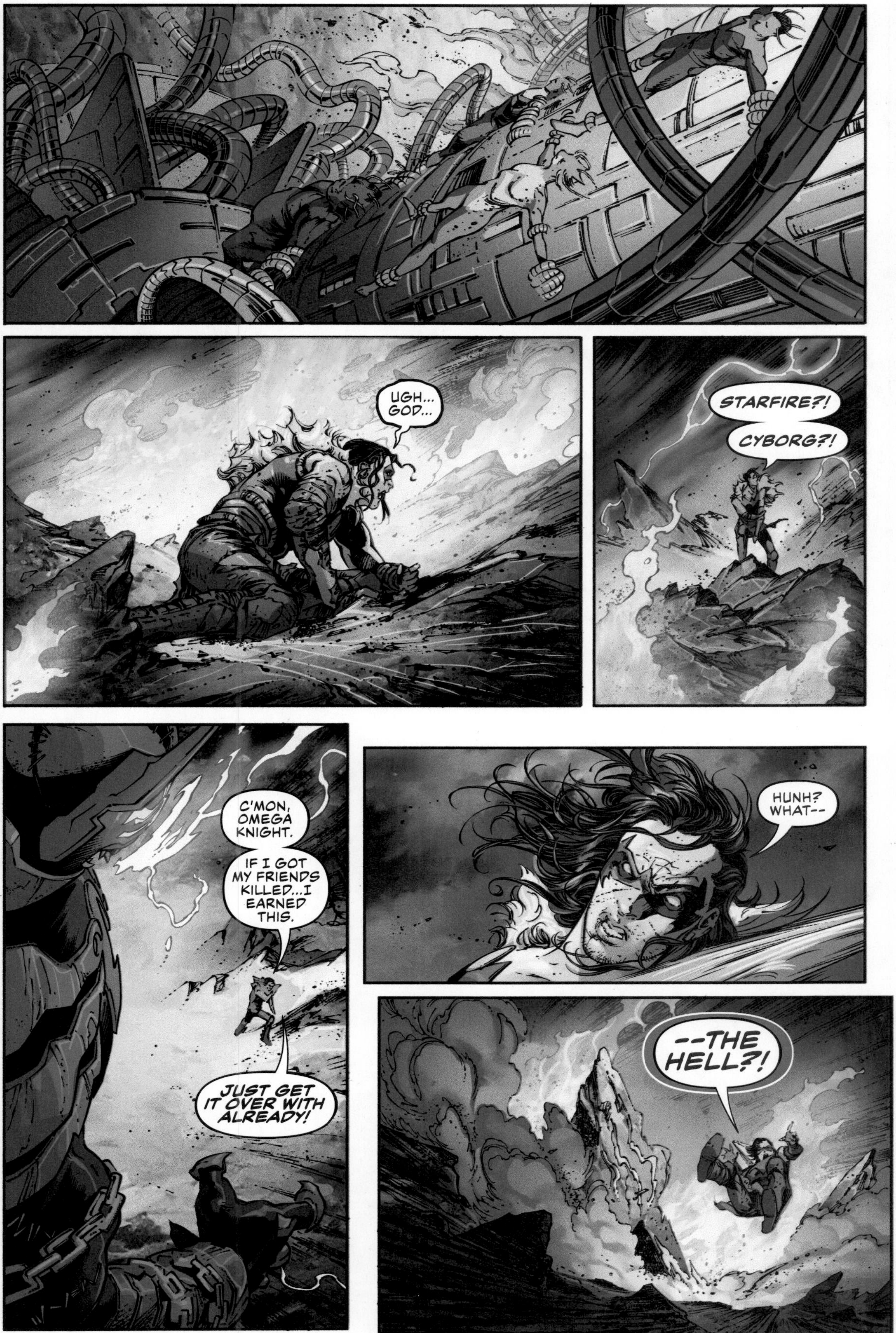
UGH... GOD...
STARFIRE?!
CYBORG?!
C'MON, OMEGA KNIGHT.
IF I GOT MY FRIENDS KILLED...I EARNED THIS.
JUST GET IT OVER WITH ALREADY!
HUNH? WHAT--
--THE HELL?!

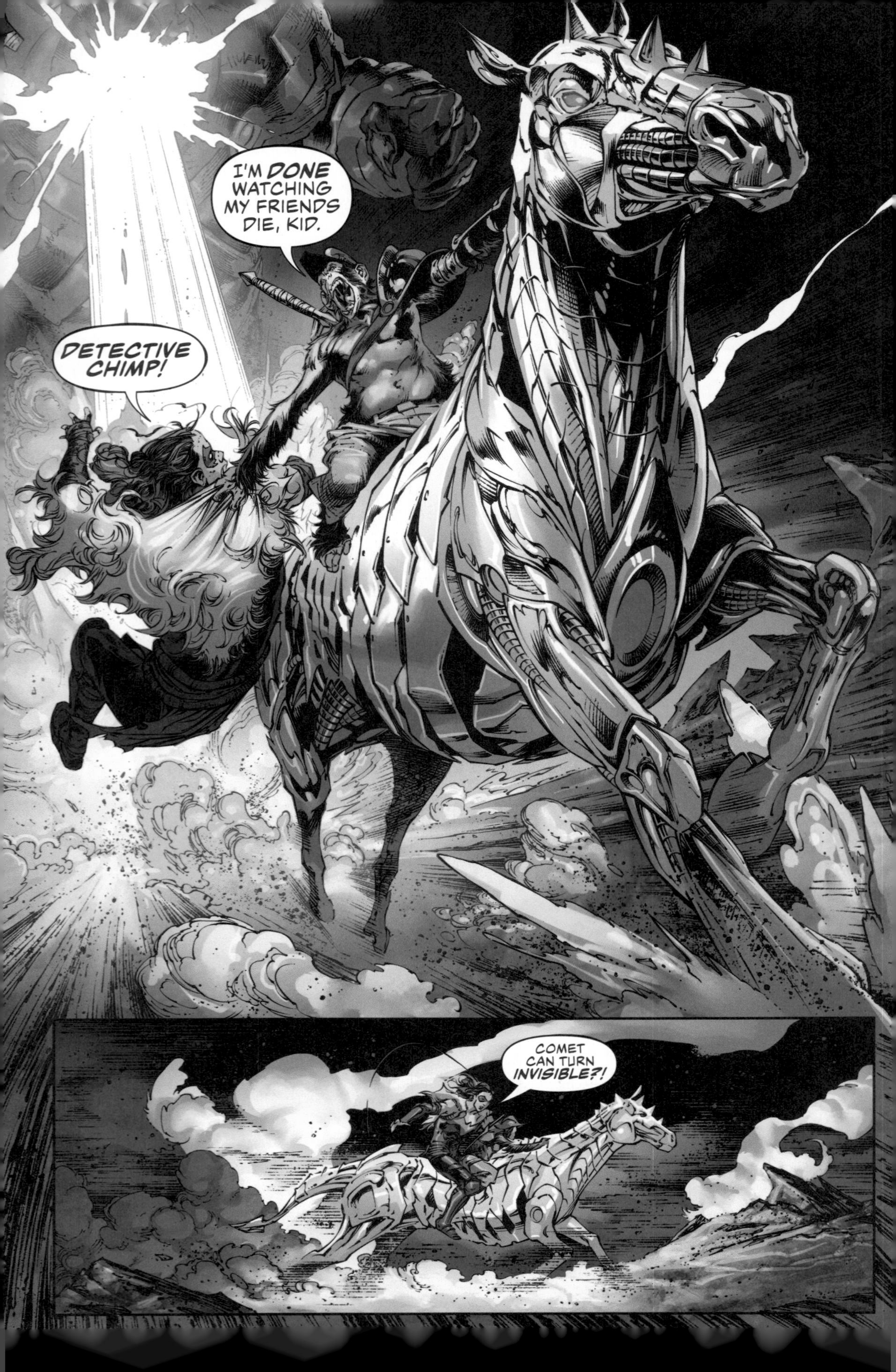
I'M DONE WATCHING MY FRIENDS DIE, KID.
DETECTIVE CHIMP!
COMET CAN TURN INVISIBLE?!

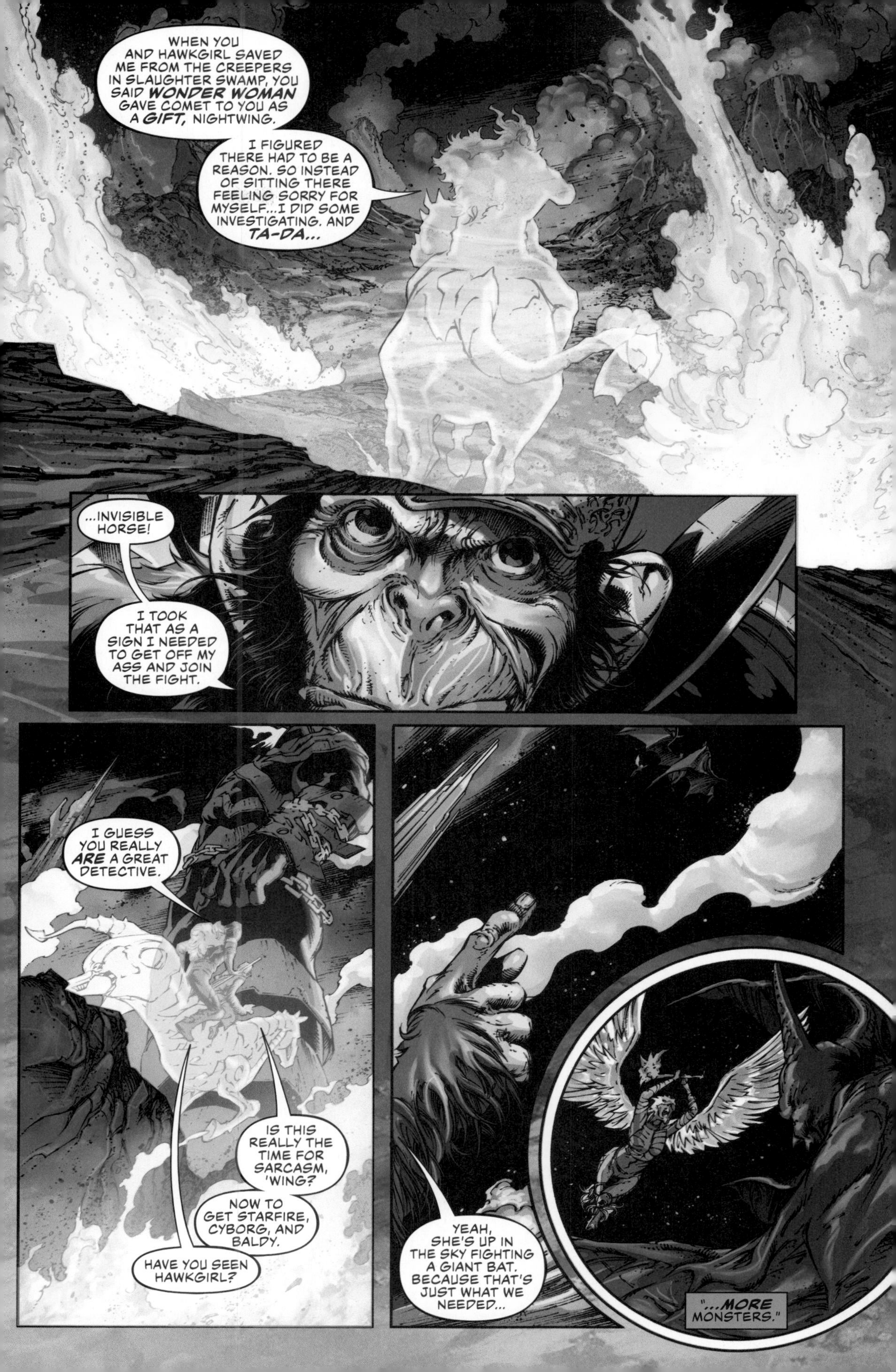
WHEN YOU AND HAWKGIRL SAVED ME FROM THE CREEPERS IN SLAUGHTER SWAMP, YOU SAID WONDER WOMAN GAVE COMET TO YOU AS A GIFT, NIGHTWING.
I FIGURED THERE HAD TO BE A REASON. SO INSTEAD OF SITTING THERE FEELING SORRY FOR MYSELF...I DID SOME INVESTIGATING. AND TA-DA...
...INVISIBLE HORSE!
I TOOK THAT AS A SIGN I NEEDED TO GET OFF MY ASS AND JOIN THE FIGHT.
I GUESS YOU REALLY ARE A GREAT DETECTIVE.
IS THIS REALLY THE TIME FOR SARCASM, 'WING?
NOW TO GET STARFIRE, CYBORG, AND BALDY.
HAVE YOU SEEN HAWKGIRL?
YEAH, SHE'S UP IN THE SKY FIGHTING A GIANT BAT. BECAUSE THAT'S JUST WHAT WE NEEDED...
"...MORE MONSTERS."

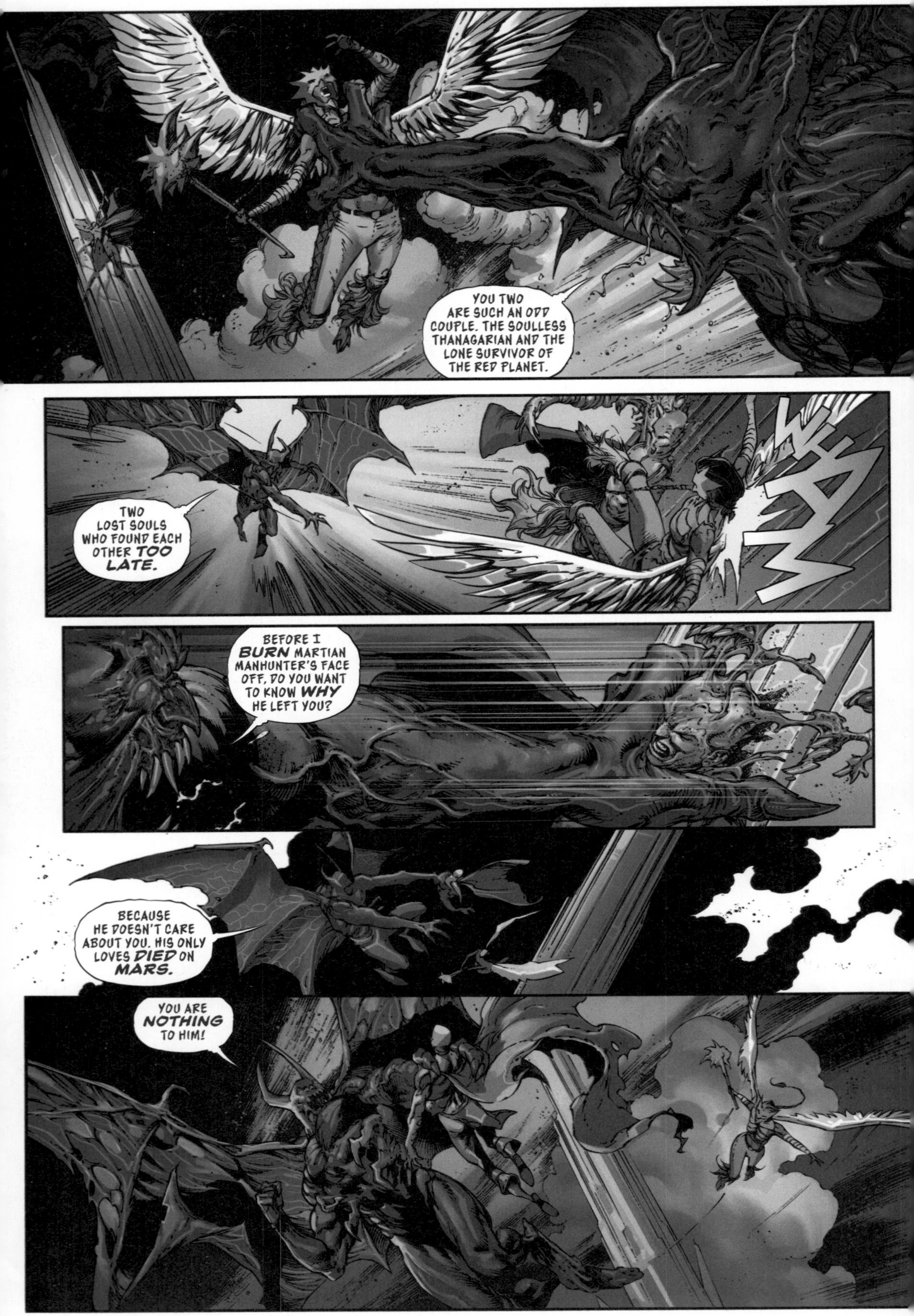
YOU TWO ARE SUCH AN ODD COUPLE. THE SOULLESS THANAGARIAN AND THE LONE SURVIVOR OF THE RED PLANET.
TWO LOST SOULS WHO FOUND EACH OTHER TOO LATE.
WHAM
BEFORE I BURN MARTIAN MANHUNTER'S FACE OFF, DO YOU WANT TO KNOW WHY HE LEFT YOU?
BECAUSE HE DOESN'T CARE ABOUT YOU. HIS ONLY LOVES DIED ON MARS.
YOU ARE NOTHING TO HIM!

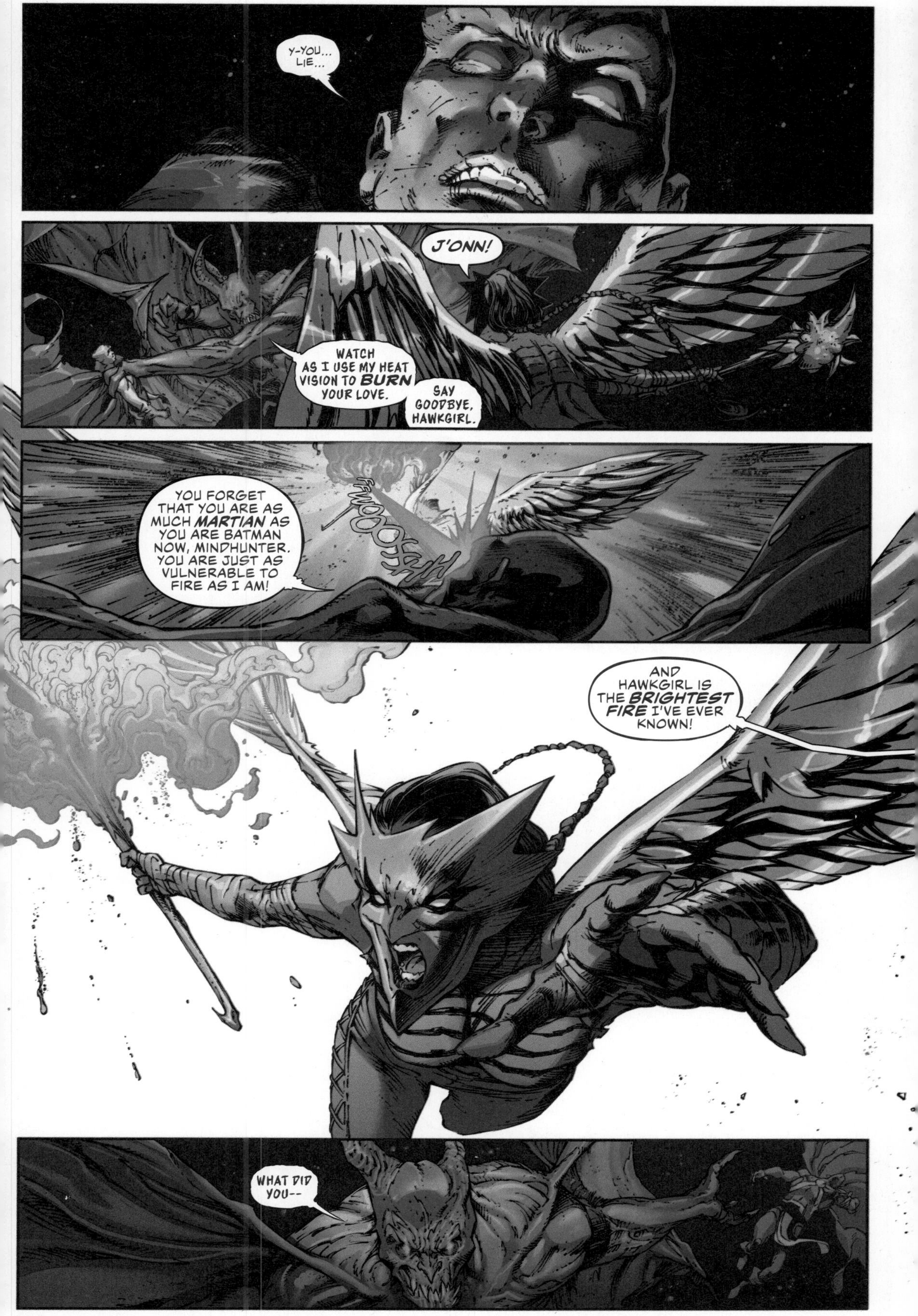
Y-YOU... LIE...
J'ONN!
WATCH AS I USE MY HEAT VISION TO BURN YOUR LOVE.
SAY GOODBYE, HAWKGIRL.
YOU FORGET THAT YOU ARE AS MUCH MARTIAN AS YOU ARE BATMAN NOW, MINDHUNTER. YOU ARE JUST AS VULNERABLE TO FIRE AS I AM!
FWOOOSHH
AND HAWKGIRL IS THE BRIGHTEST FIRE I'VE EVER KNOWN!
WHAT DID YOU--

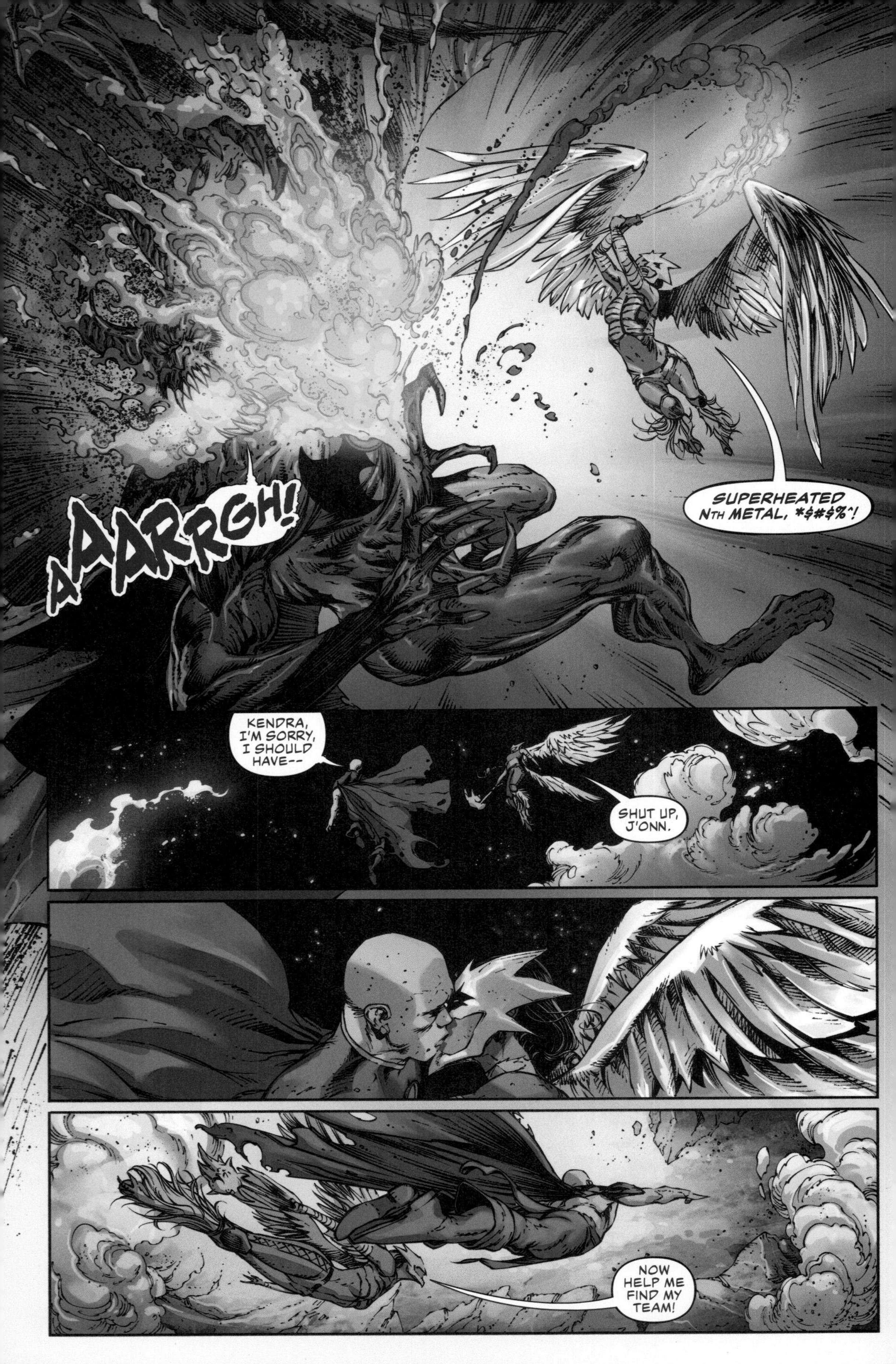

AARRGH!
SUPERHEATED NTH METAL, *$#$%^!
KENDRA, I'M SORRY, I SHOULD HAVE--
SHUT UP, J'ONN.
NOW HELP ME FIND MY TEAM!

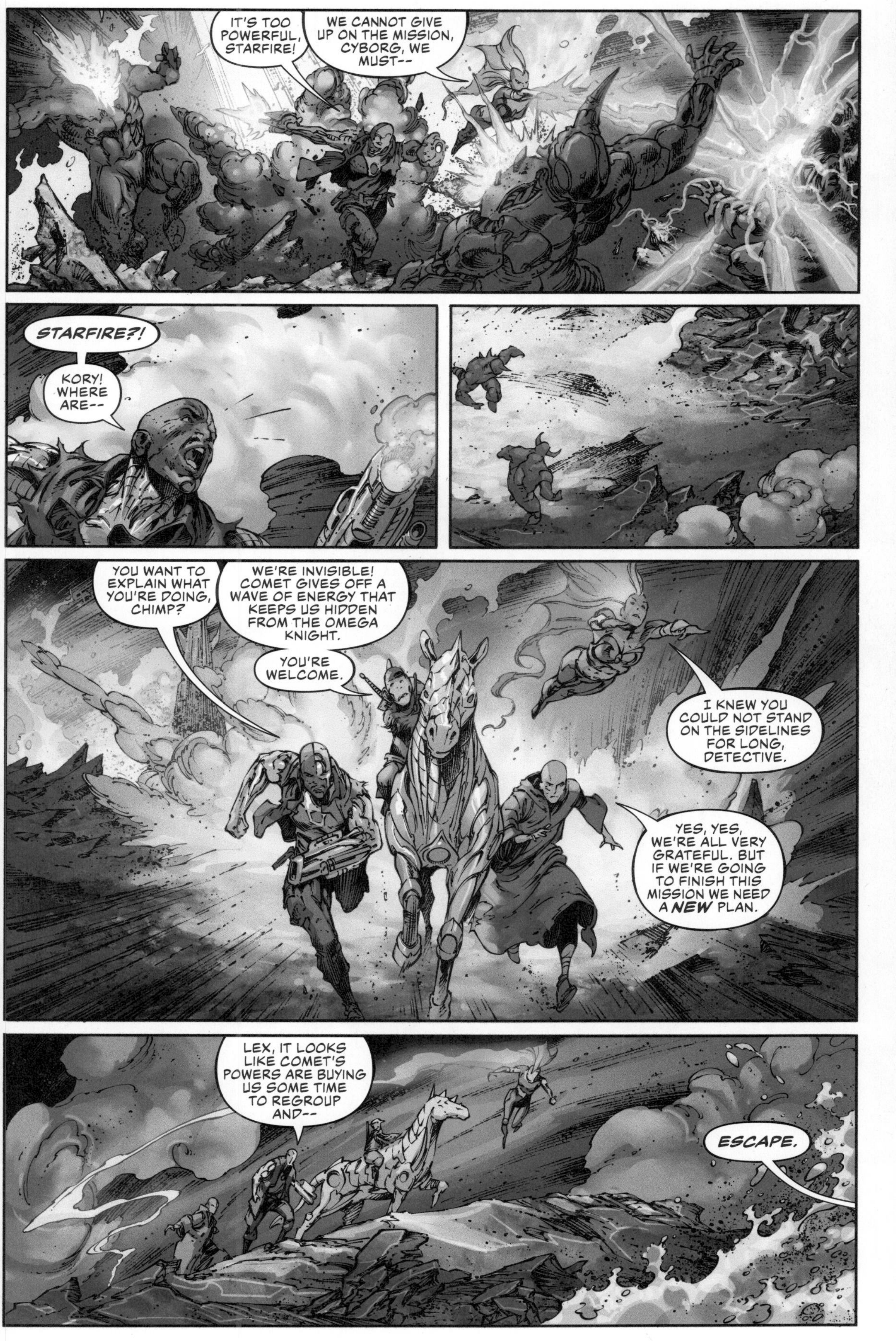
IT'S TOO POWERFUL, STARFIRE!
WE CANNOT GIVE UP ON THE MISSION, CYBORG, WE MUST--
STARFIRE?!
KORY! WHERE ARE--
YOU WANT TO EXPLAIN WHAT YOU'RE DOING, CHIMP?
WE'RE INVISIBLE! COMET GIVES OFF A WAVE OF ENERGY THAT KEEPS US HIDDEN FROM THE OMEGA KNIGHT.
YOU'RE WELCOME.
I KNEW YOU COULD NOT STAND ON THE SIDELINES FOR LONG, DETECTIVE.
YES, YES, WE'RE ALL VERY GRATEFUL. BUT IF WE'RE GOING TO FINISH THIS MISSION WE NEED A NEW PLAN.
LEX, IT LOOKS LIKE COMET'S POWERS ARE BUYING US SOME TIME TO REGROUP AND--
ESCAPE.

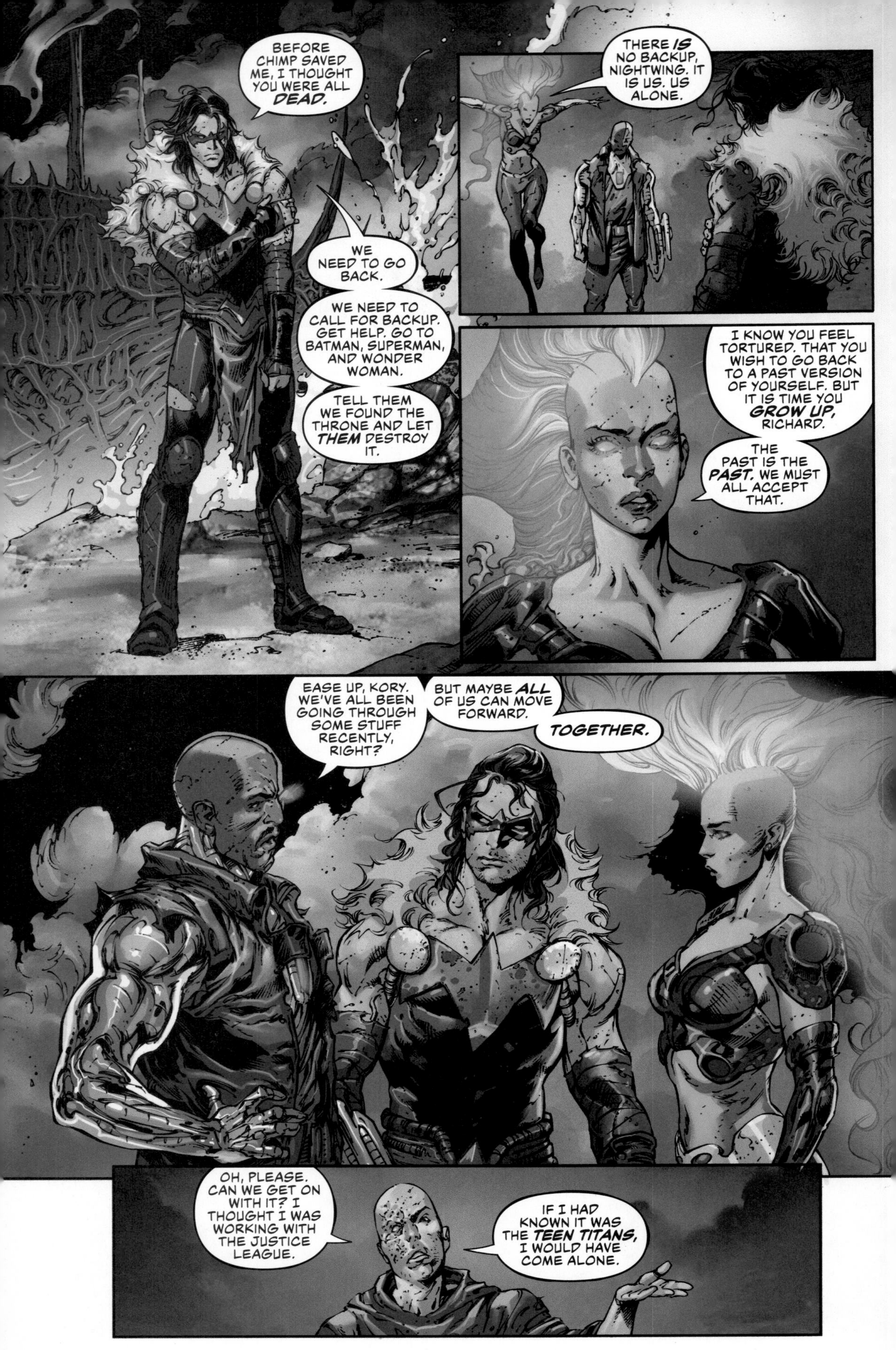
BEFORE CHIMP SAVED ME, I THOUGHT YOU WERE ALL DEAD.
WE NEED TO GO BACK.
WE NEED TO CALL FOR BACKUP. GET HELP. GO TO BATMAN, SUPERMAN, AND WONDER WOMAN.
TELL THEM WE FOUND THE THRONE AND LET THEM DESTROY IT.
THERE IS NO BACKUP, NIGHTWING. IT IS US. US ALONE.
I KNOW YOU FEEL TORTURED. THAT YOU WISH TO GO BACK TO A PAST VERSION OF YOURSELF. BUT IT IS TIME YOU GROW UP, RICHARD.
THE PAST IS THE PAST. WE MUST ALL ACCEPT THAT.
EASE UP, KORY. WE'VE ALL BEEN GOING THROUGH SOME STUFF RECENTLY, RIGHT?
BUT MAYBE ALL OF US CAN MOVE FORWARD.
TOGETHER.
OH, PLEASE. CAN WE GET ON WITH IT? I THOUGHT I WAS WORKING WITH THE JUSTICE LEAGUE.
IF I HAD KNOWN IT WAS THE TEEN TITANS, I WOULD HAVE COME ALONE.

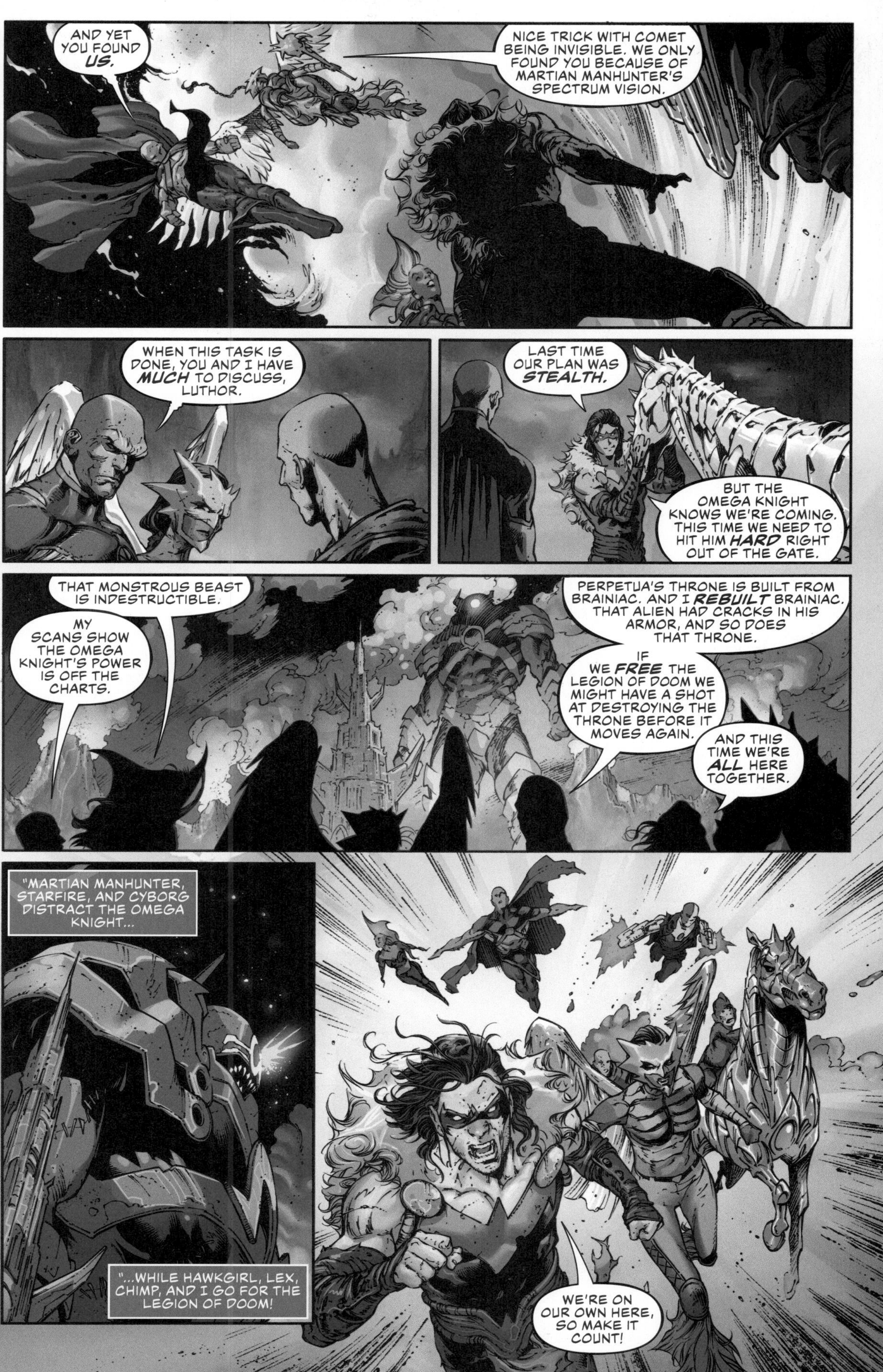
AND YET YOU FOUND US.
NICE TRICK WITH COMET BEING INVISIBLE. WE ONLY FOUND YOU BECAUSE OF MARTIAN MANHUNTER'S SPECTRUM VISION.
WHEN THIS TASK IS DONE, YOU AND I HAVE MUCH TO DISCUSS, LUTHOR.
LAST TIME OUR PLAN WAS STEALTH.
BUT THE OMEGA KNIGHT KNOWS WE'RE COMING. THIS TIME WE NEED TO HIT HIM HARD RIGHT OUT OF THE GATE.
THAT MONSTROUS BEAST IS INDESTRUCTIBLE.
MY SCANS SHOW THE OMEGA KNIGHT'S POWER IS OFF THE CHARTS.
PERPETUA'S THRONE IS BUILT FROM BRAINIAC. AND I REBUILT BRAINIAC. THAT ALIEN HAD CRACKS IN HIS ARMOR, AND SO DOES THAT THRONE.
IF WE FREE THE LEGION OF DOOM WE MIGHT HAVE A SHOT AT DESTROYING THE THRONE BEFORE IT MOVES AGAIN.
AND THIS TIME WE'RE ALL HERE TOGETHER.
"MARTIAN MANHUNTER, STARFIRE, AND CYBORG DISTRACT THE OMEGA KNIGHT...
"...WHILE HAWKGIRL, LEX, CHIMP, AND I GO FOR THE LEGION OF DOOM!
WE'RE ON OUR OWN HERE, SO MAKE IT COUNT!

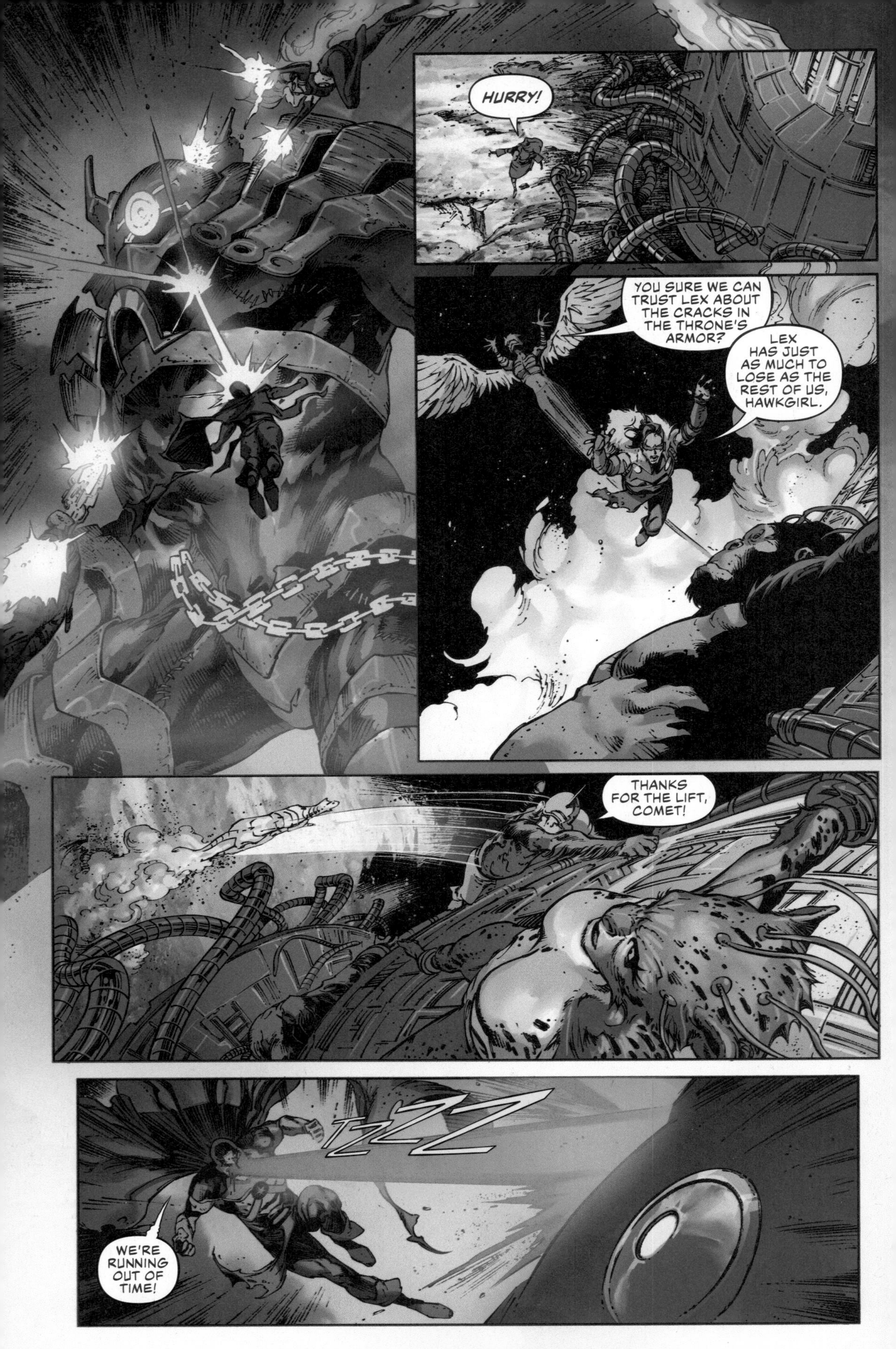
HURRY!
YOU SURE WE CAN TRUST LEX ABOUT THE CRACKS IN THE THRONE'S ARMOR?
LEX HAS JUST AS MUCH TO LOSE AS THE REST OF US, HAWKGIRL.
THANKS FOR THE LIFT, COMET!
TZZZ
WE'RE RUNNING OUT OF TIME!

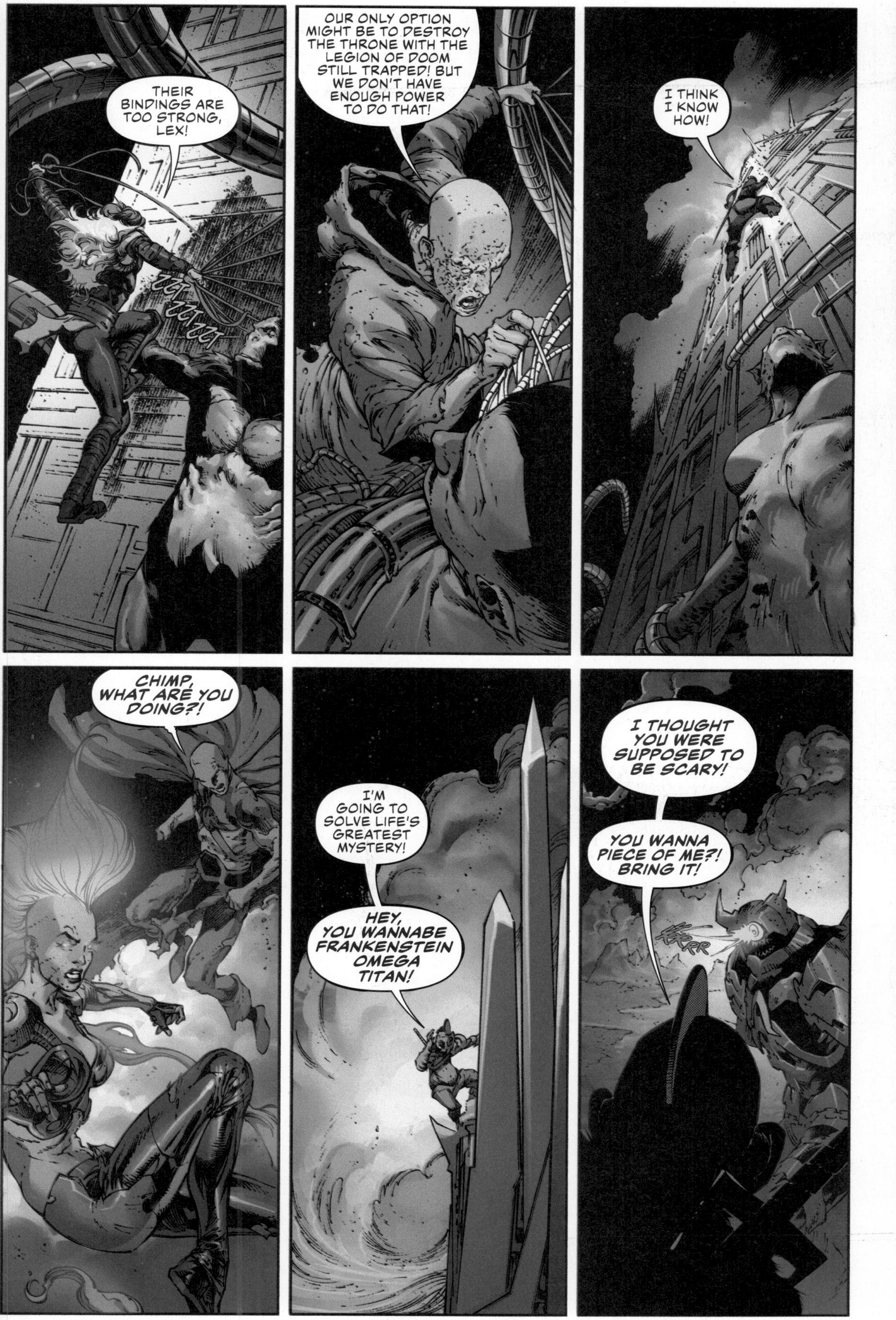
THEIR BINDINGS ARE TOO STRONG, LEX!
ZZZT ZZZT ZZZT
OUR ONLY OPTION MIGHT BE TO DESTROY THE THRONE WITH THE LEGION OF DOOM STILL TRAPPED! BUT WE DON'T HAVE ENOUGH POWER TO DO THAT!
I THINK I KNOW HOW!
CHIMP, WHAT ARE YOU DOING?!
I'M GOING TO SOLVE LIFE'S GREATEST MYSTERY!
HEY, YOU WANNABE FRANKENSTEIN OMEGA TITAN!
I THOUGHT YOU WERE SUPPOSED TO BE SCARY!
YOU WANNA PIECE OF ME?! BRING IT!
KRRRR

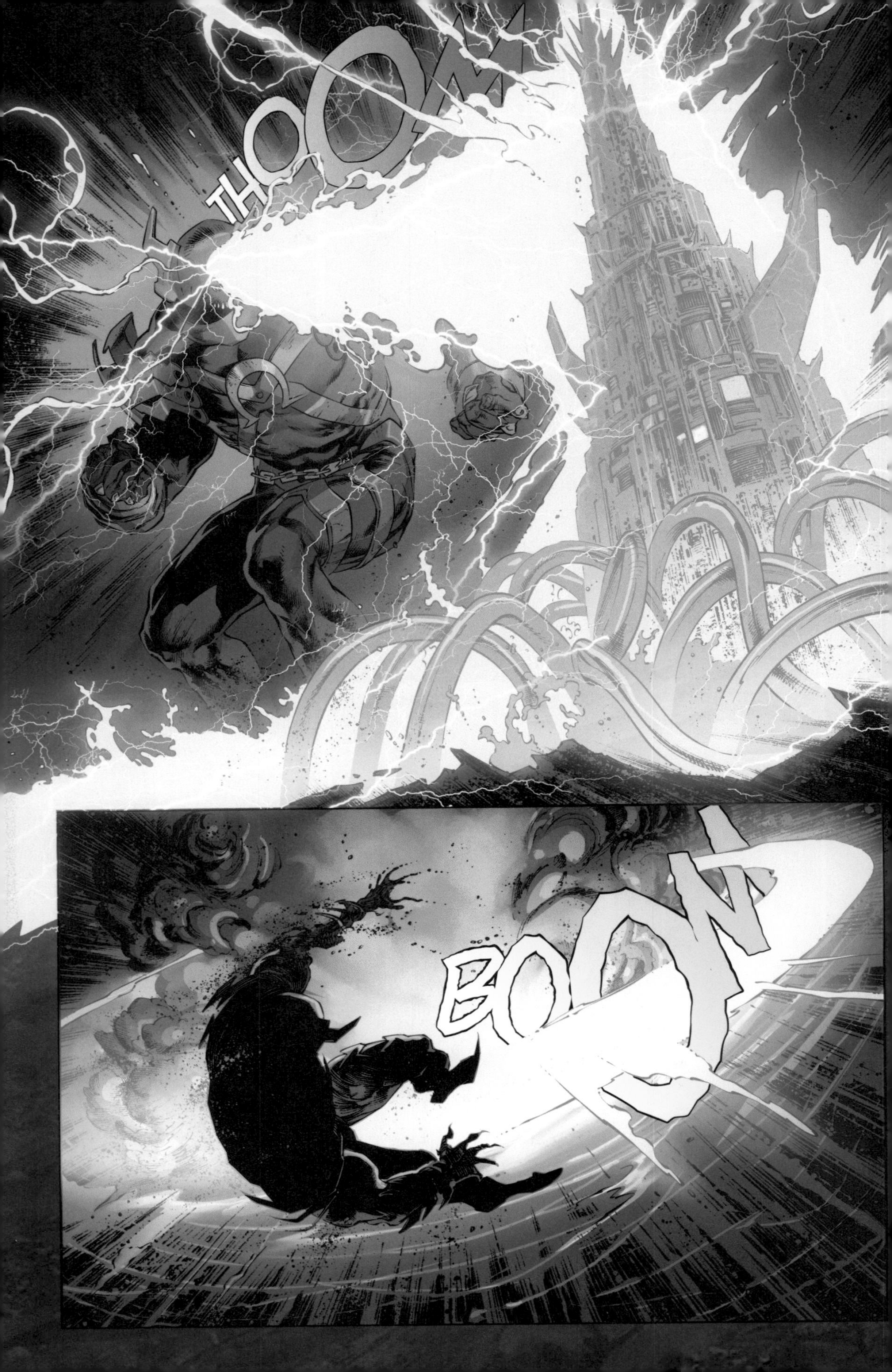
THOOOM
BOOM

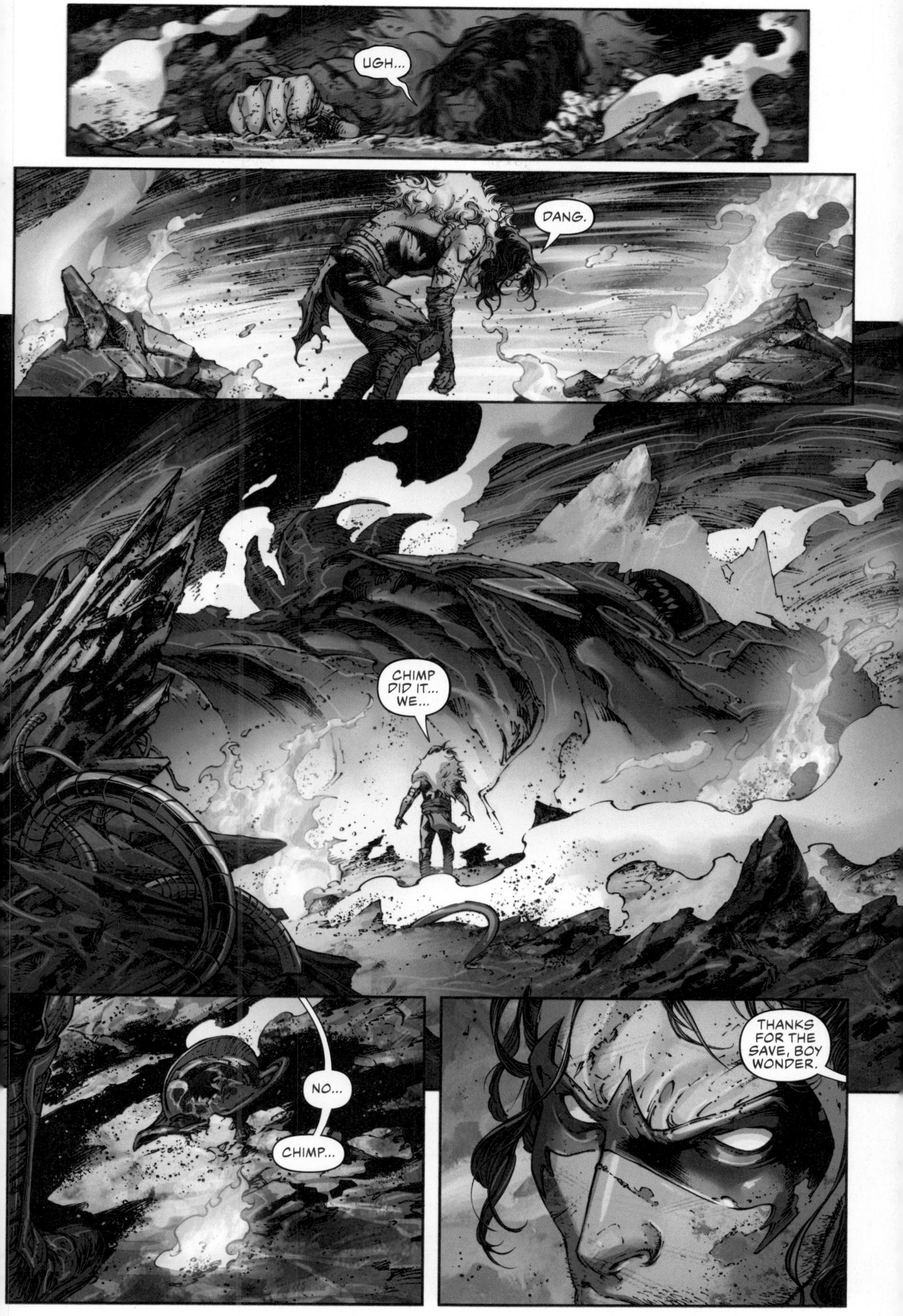
UGH...
DANG.
CHIMP DID IT... WE...
NO...
CHIMP...
THANKS FOR THE SAVE, BOY WONDER.

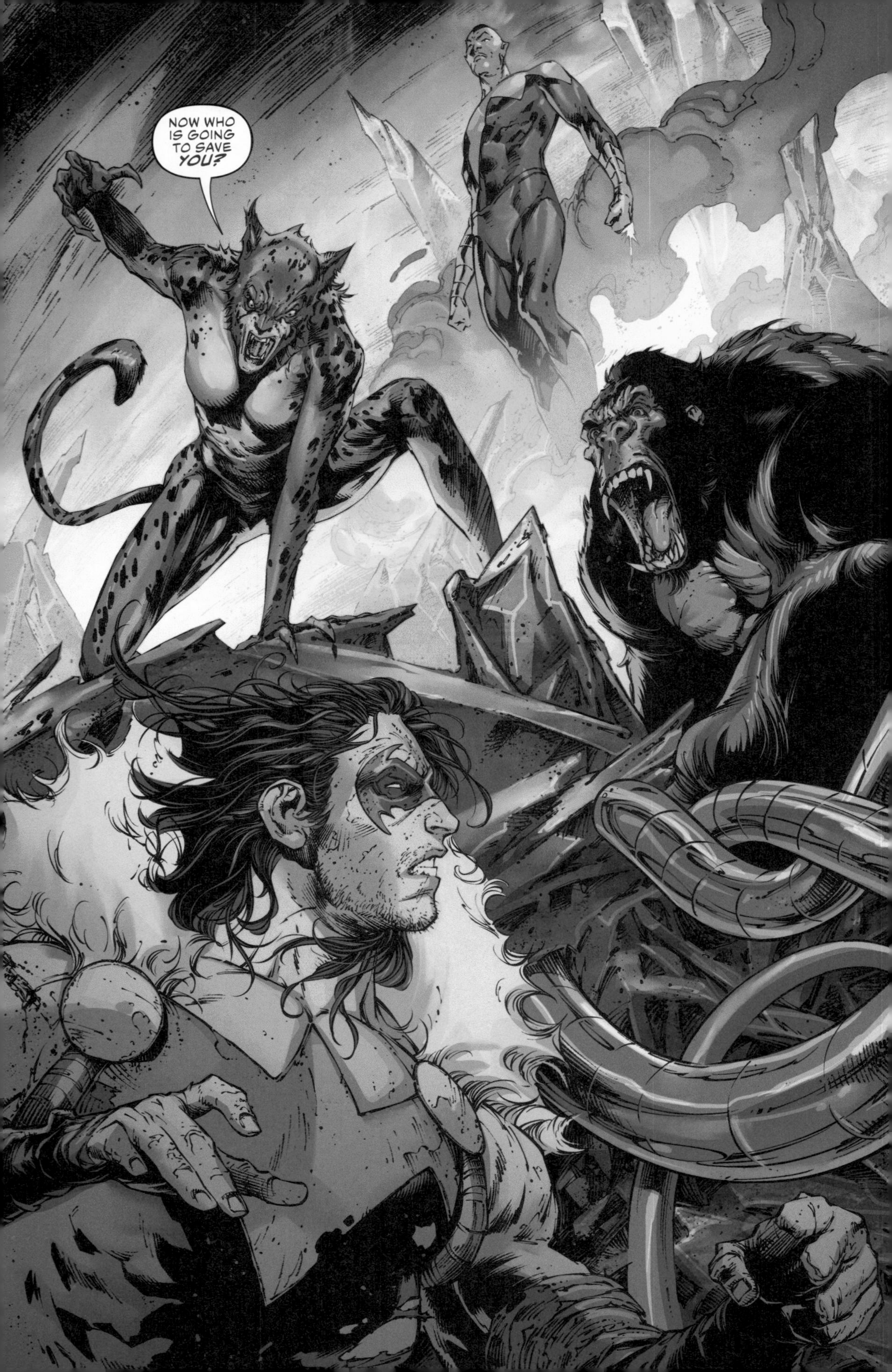
NOW WHO IS GOING TO SAVE YOU?

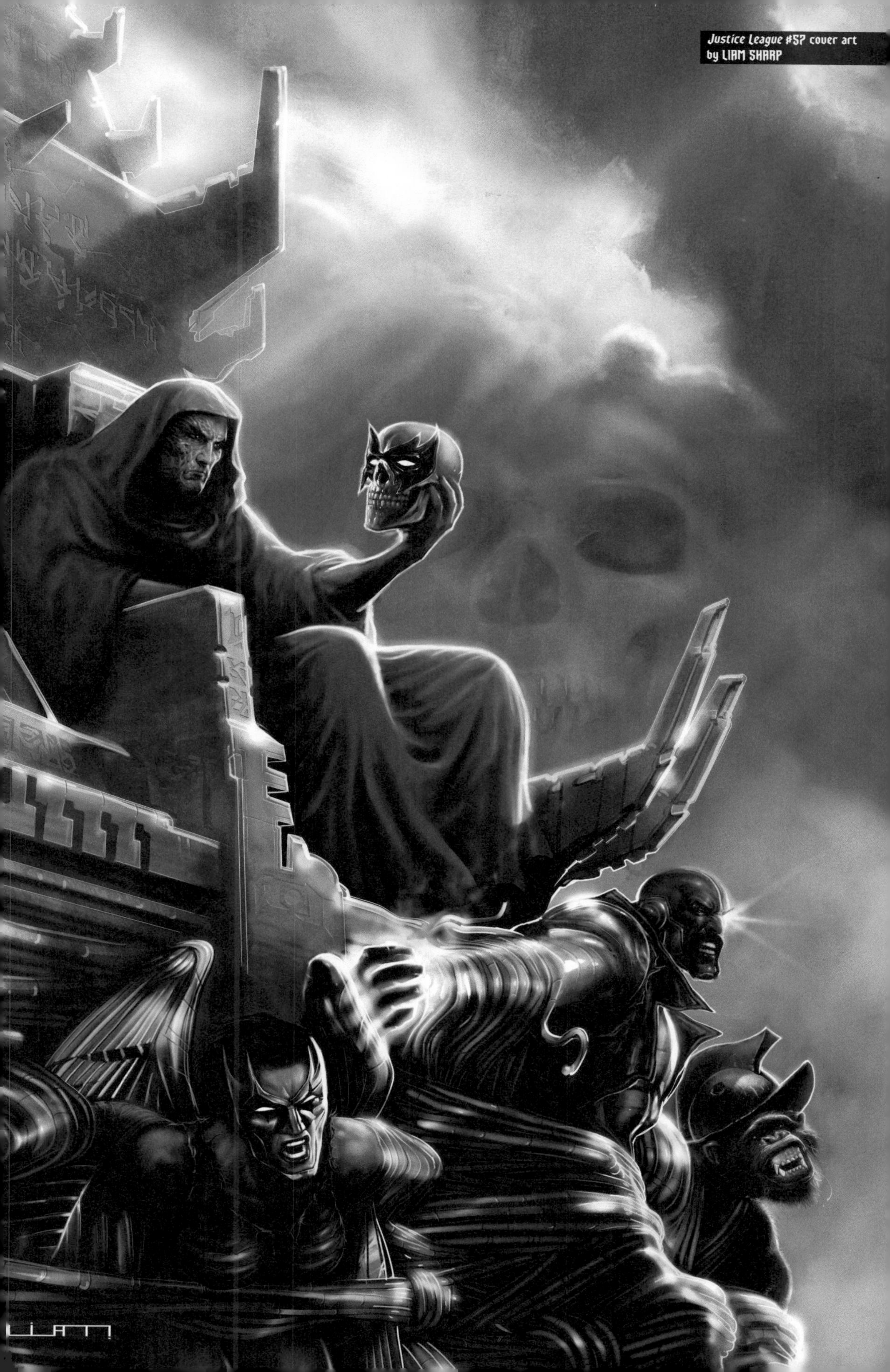
LIAM

Justice League #57 cover art
by LIAM SHARP

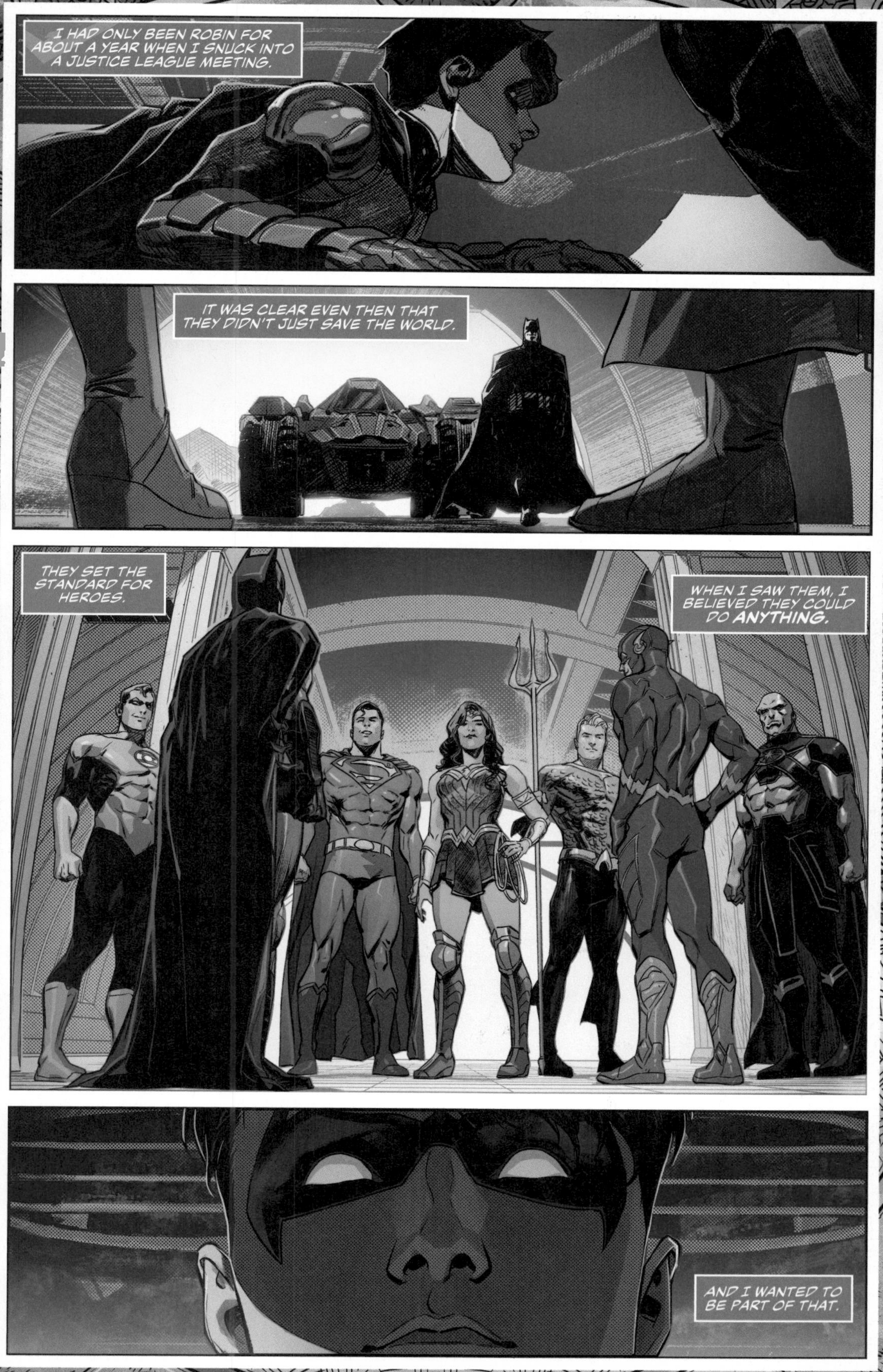
I HAD ONLY BEEN ROBIN FOR ABOUT A YEAR WHEN I SNUCK INTO A JUSTICE LEAGUE MEETING.
IT WAS CLEAR EVEN THEN THAT THEY DIDN'T JUST SAVE THE WORLD.
THEY SET THE STANDARD FOR HEROES.
WHEN I SAW THEM, I BELIEVED THEY COULD DO **ANYTHING.**
AND I WANTED TO BE PART OF THAT.

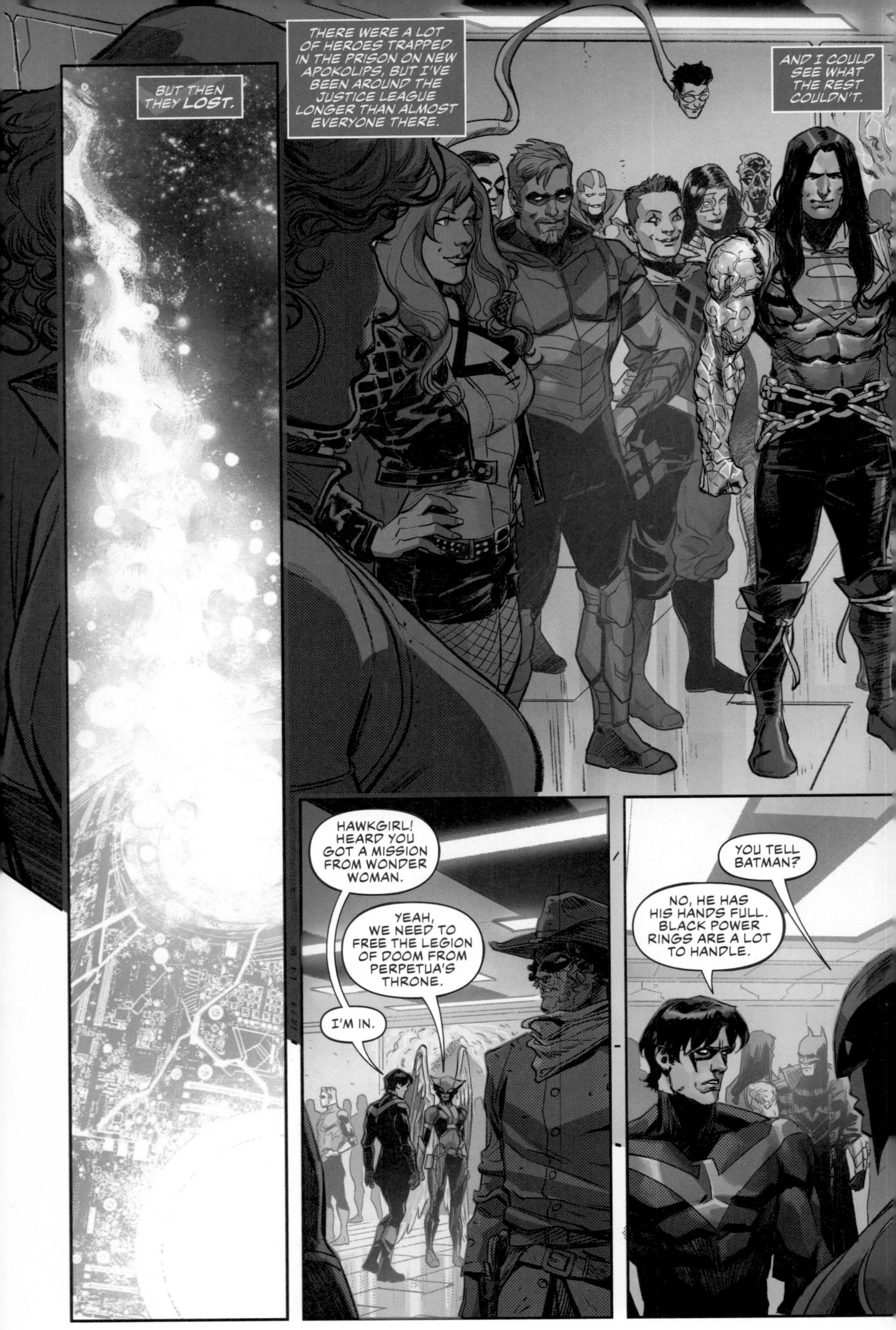
BUT THEN THEY **LOST**.
THERE WERE A LOT OF HEROES TRAPPED IN THE PRISON ON NEW APOKOLIPS, BUT I'VE BEEN AROUND THE JUSTICE LEAGUE LONGER THAN ALMOST EVERYONE THERE.
AND I COULD SEE WHAT THE REST COULDN'T.
HAWKGIRL! HEARD YOU GOT A MISSION FROM WONDER WOMAN.
YEAH, WE NEED TO FREE THE LEGION OF DOOM FROM PERPETUA'S THRONE.
I'M IN.
YOU TELL BATMAN?
NO, HE HAS HIS HANDS FULL. BLACK POWER RINGS ARE A LOT TO HANDLE.

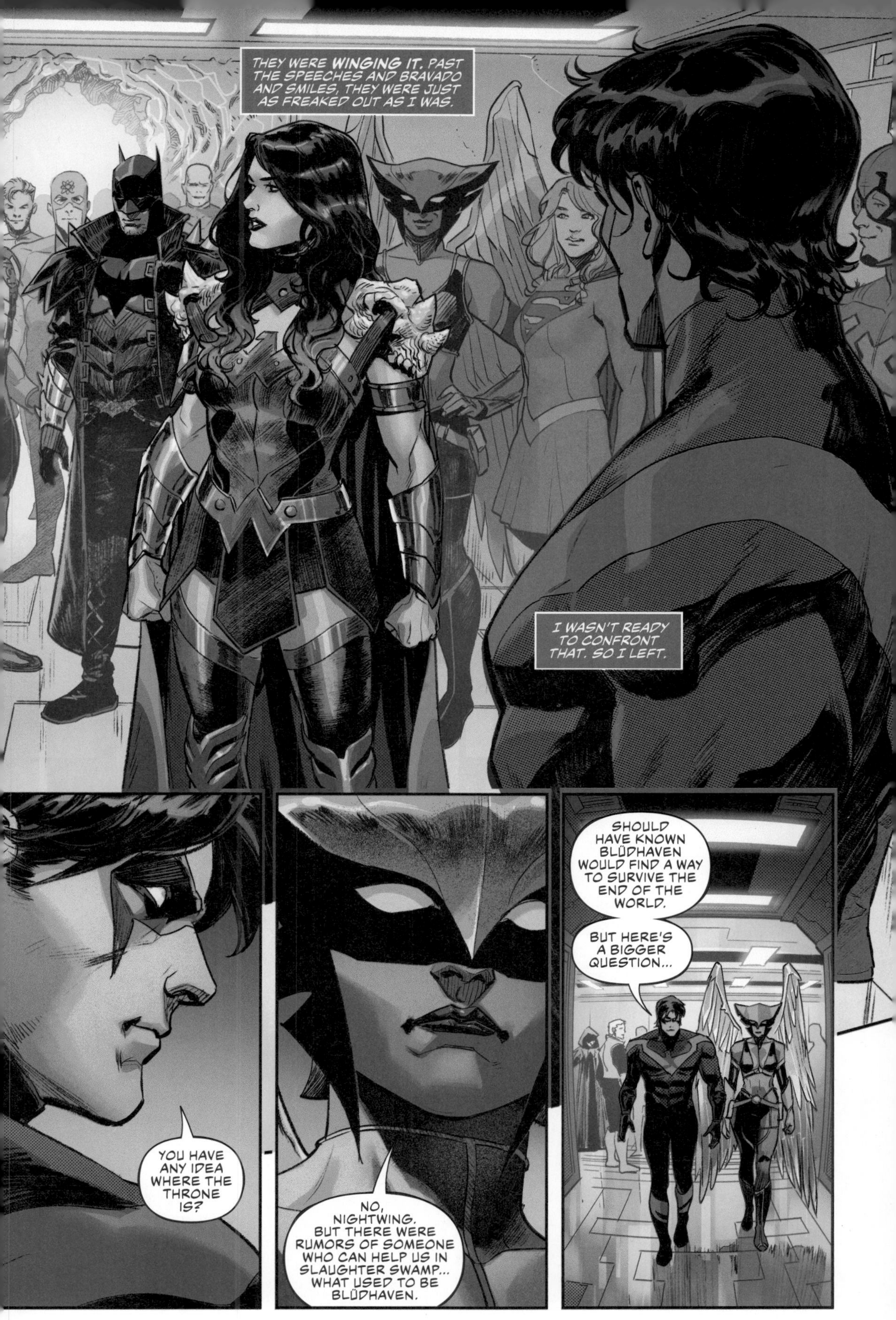
THEY WERE **WINGING IT.** PAST THE SPEECHES AND BRAVADO AND SMILES, THEY WERE JUST AS FREAKED OUT AS I WAS.
I WASN'T READY TO CONFRONT THAT. SO I LEFT.
YOU HAVE ANY IDEA WHERE THE THRONE IS?
NO, NIGHTWING. BUT THERE WERE RUMORS OF SOMEONE WHO CAN HELP US IN SLAUGHTER SWAMP... WHAT USED TO BE BLÜDHAVEN.
SHOULD HAVE KNOWN BLÜDHAVEN WOULD FIND A WAY TO SURVIVE THE END OF THE WORLD.
BUT HERE'S A BIGGER QUESTION...

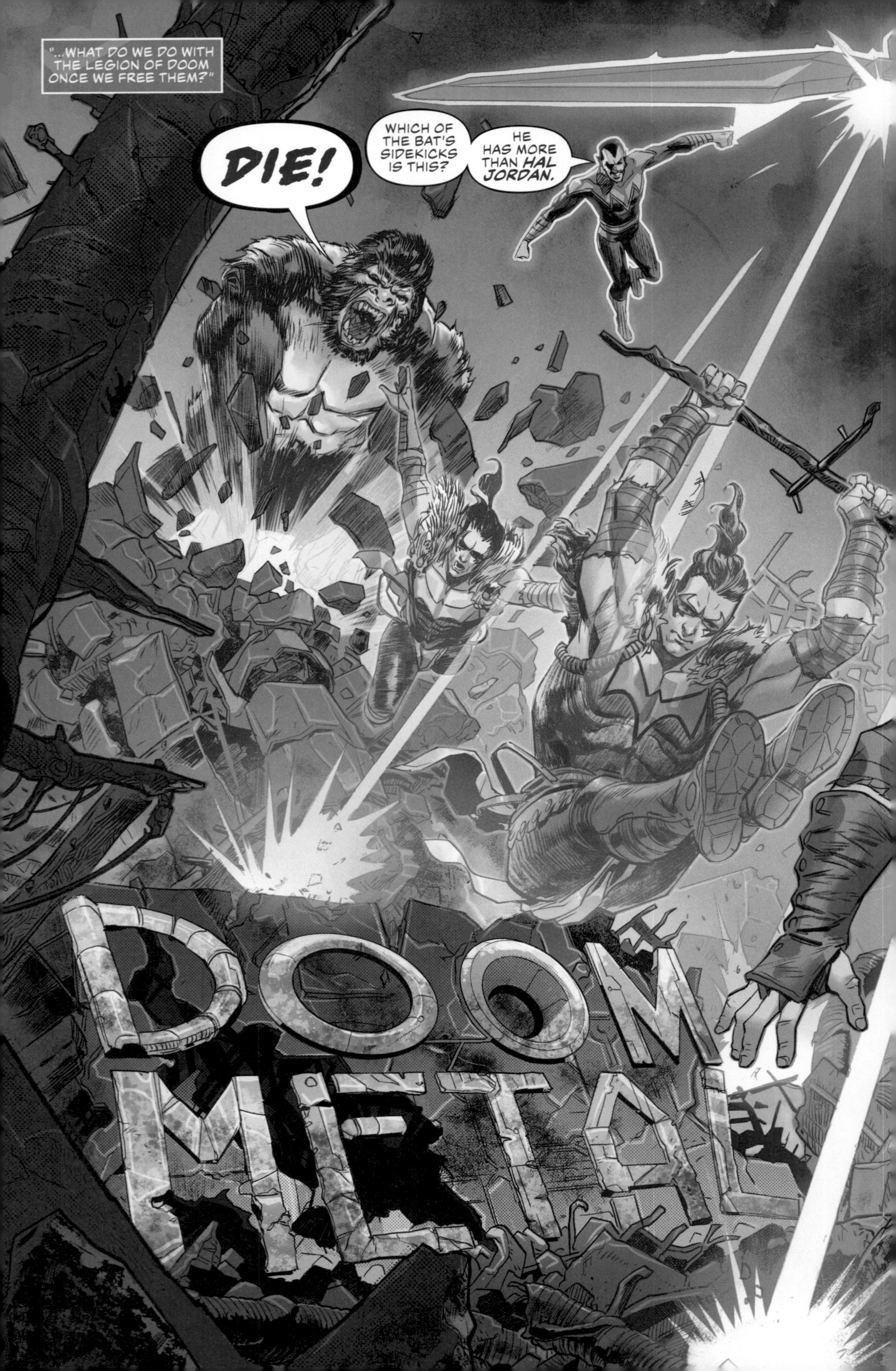
"...WHAT DO WE DO WITH THE LEGION OF DOOM ONCE WE FREE THEM?"
DIE!
WHICH OF THE BAT'S SIDEKICKS IS THIS?
HE HAS MORE THAN HAL JORDAN.
DOOM METAL

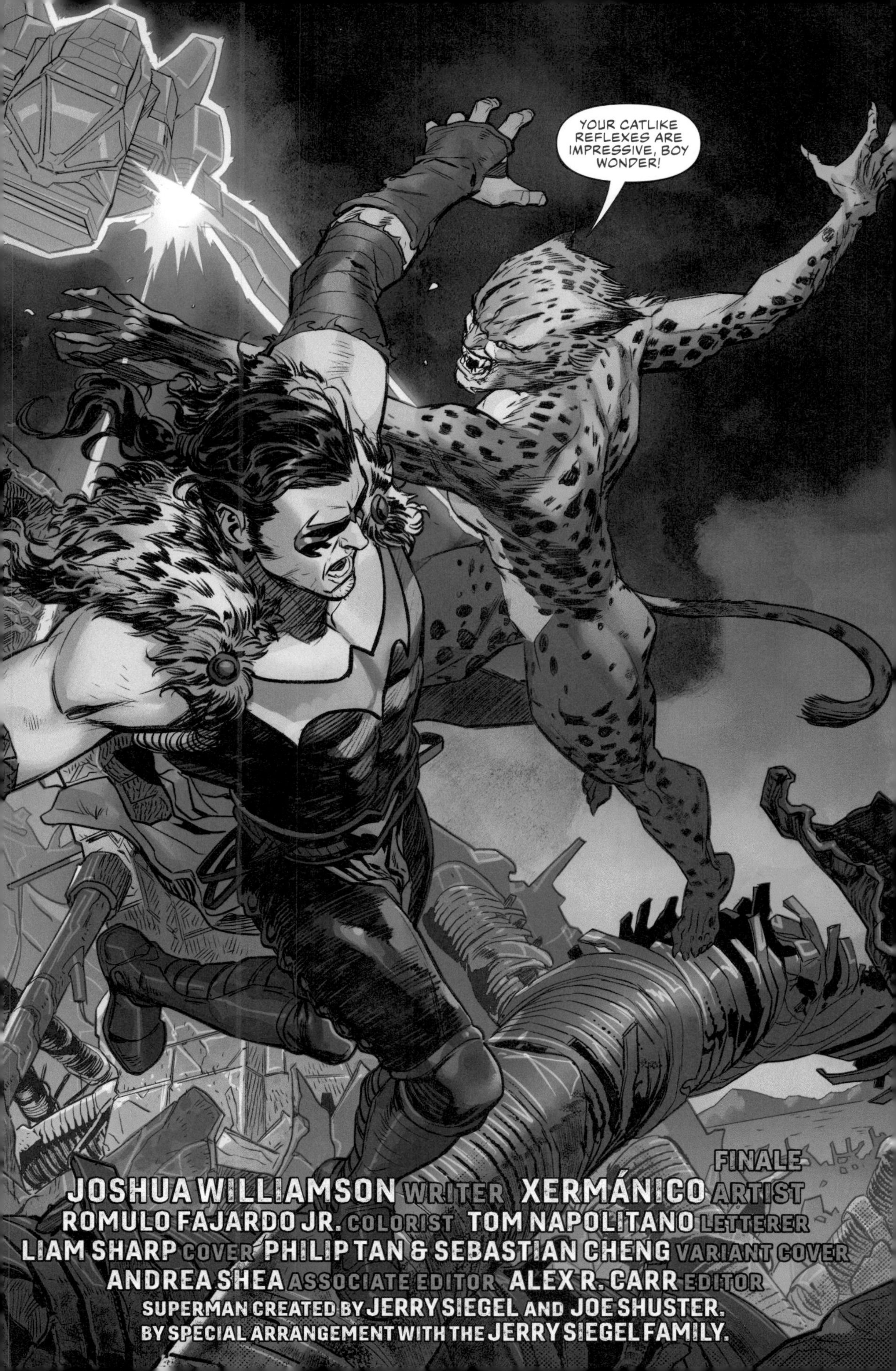
YOUR CATLIKE REFLEXES ARE IMPRESSIVE, BOY WONDER!

FINALE

JOSHUA WILLIAMSON WRITER XERMÁNICO ARTIST
ROMULO FAJARDO JR. COLORIST TOM NAPOLITANO LETTERER
LIAM SHARP COVER PHILIP TAN & SEBASTIAN CHENG VARIANT COVER
ANDREA SHEA ASSOCIATE EDITOR ALEX R. CARR EDITOR
SUPERMAN CREATED BY JERRY SIEGEL AND JOE SHUSTER.
BY SPECIAL ARRANGEMENT WITH THE JERRY SIEGEL FAMILY.

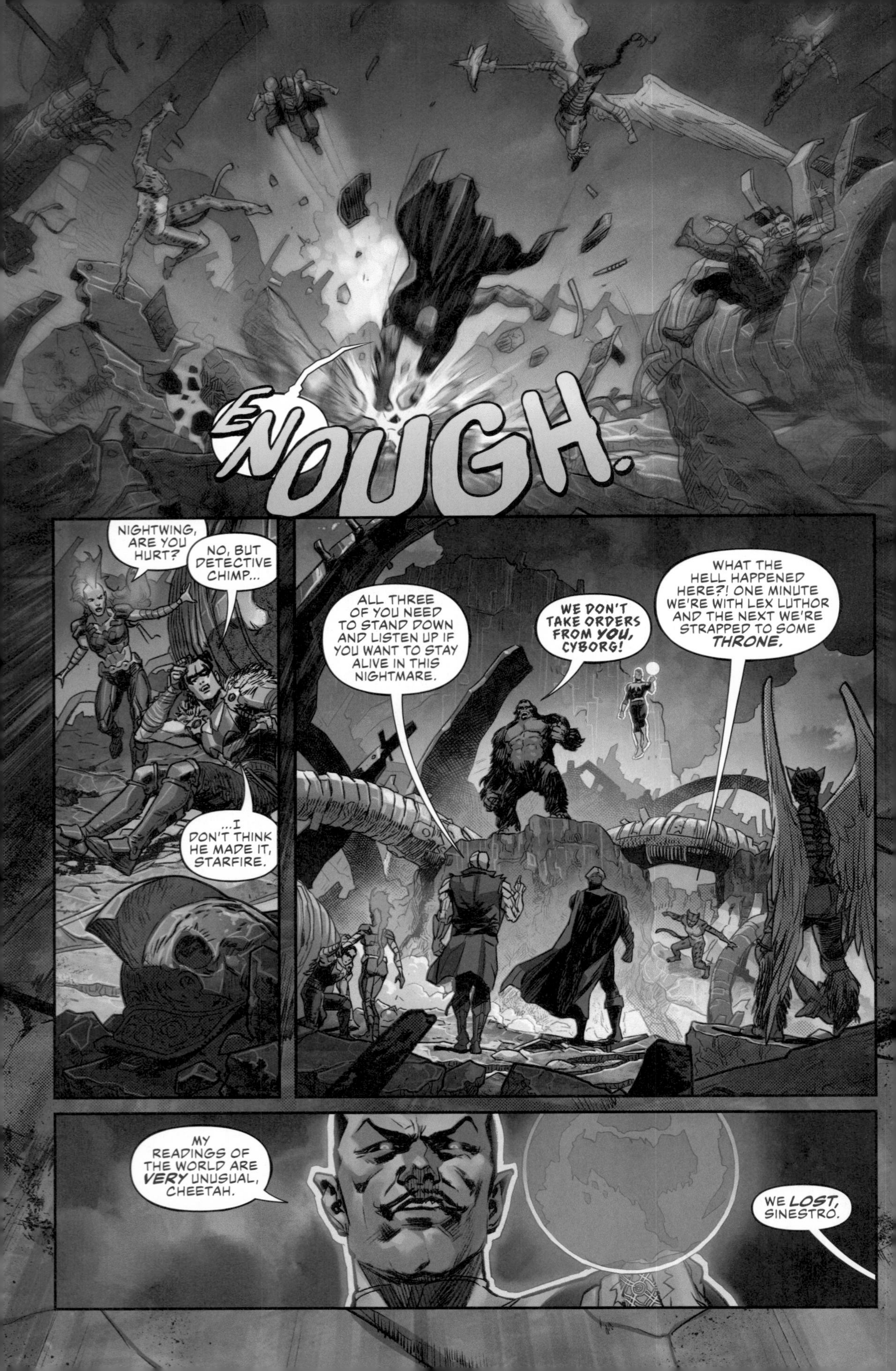
ENOUGH.
NIGHTWING, ARE YOU HURT?
NO, BUT DETECTIVE CHIMP...
...I DON'T THINK HE MADE IT, STARFIRE.
ALL THREE OF YOU NEED TO STAND DOWN AND LISTEN UP IF YOU WANT TO STAY ALIVE IN THIS NIGHTMARE.
WE DON'T TAKE ORDERS FROM YOU, CYBORG!
WHAT THE HELL HAPPENED HERE?! ONE MINUTE WE'RE WITH LEX LUTHOR AND THE NEXT WE'RE STRAPPED TO SOME THRONE.
MY READINGS OF THE WORLD ARE VERY UNUSUAL, CHEETAH.
WE LOST, SINESTRO.

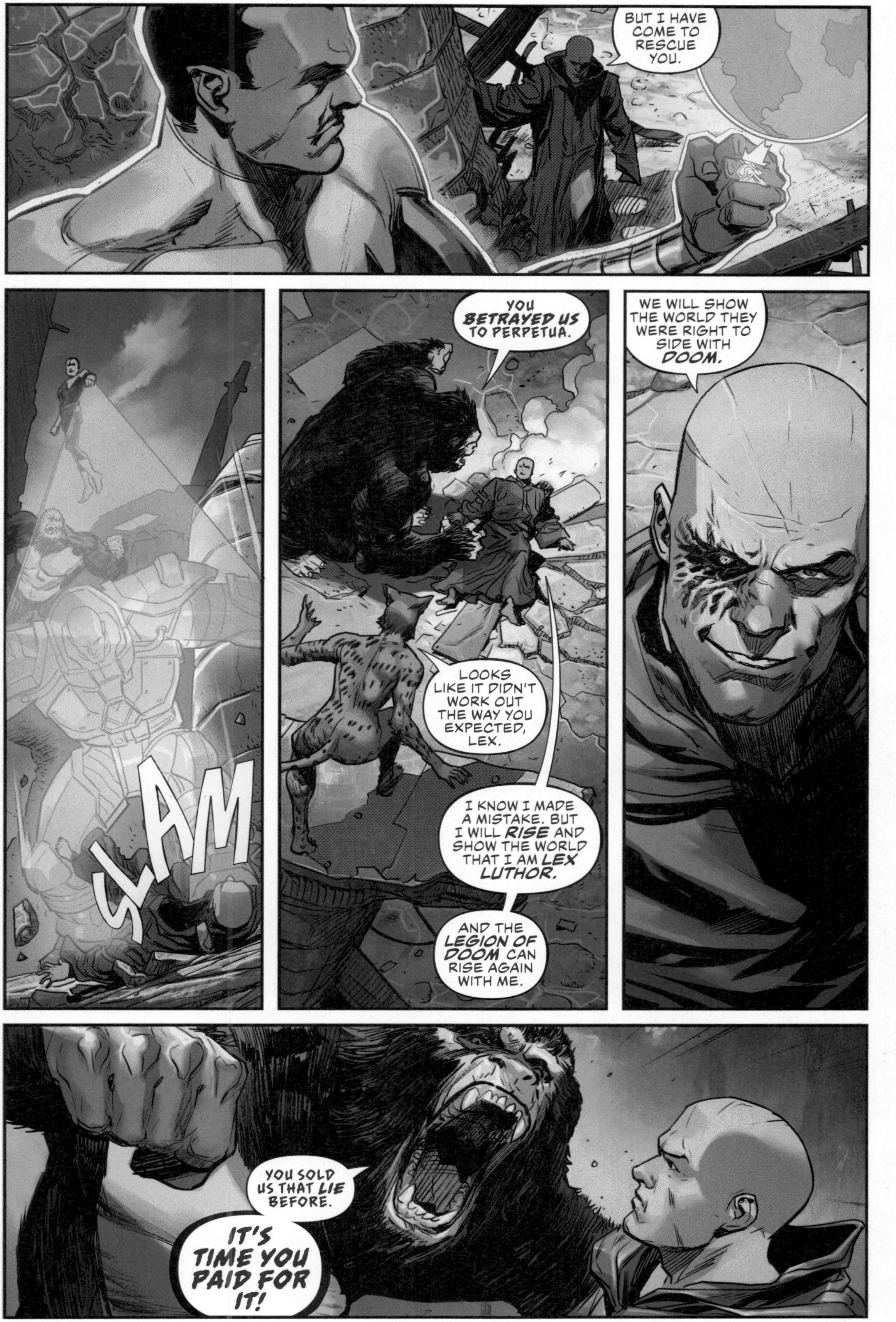

BUT I HAVE COME TO RESCUE YOU.
SLAM
YOU BETRAYED US TO PERPETUA.
LOOKS LIKE IT DIDN'T WORK OUT THE WAY YOU EXPECTED, LEX.
I KNOW I MADE A MISTAKE. BUT I WILL RISE AND SHOW THE WORLD THAT I AM LEX LUTHOR.
AND THE LEGION OF DOOM CAN RISE AGAIN WITH ME.
WE WILL SHOW THE WORLD THEY WERE RIGHT TO SIDE WITH DOOM.
YOU SOLD US THAT LIE BEFORE.
IT'S TIME YOU PAID FOR IT!

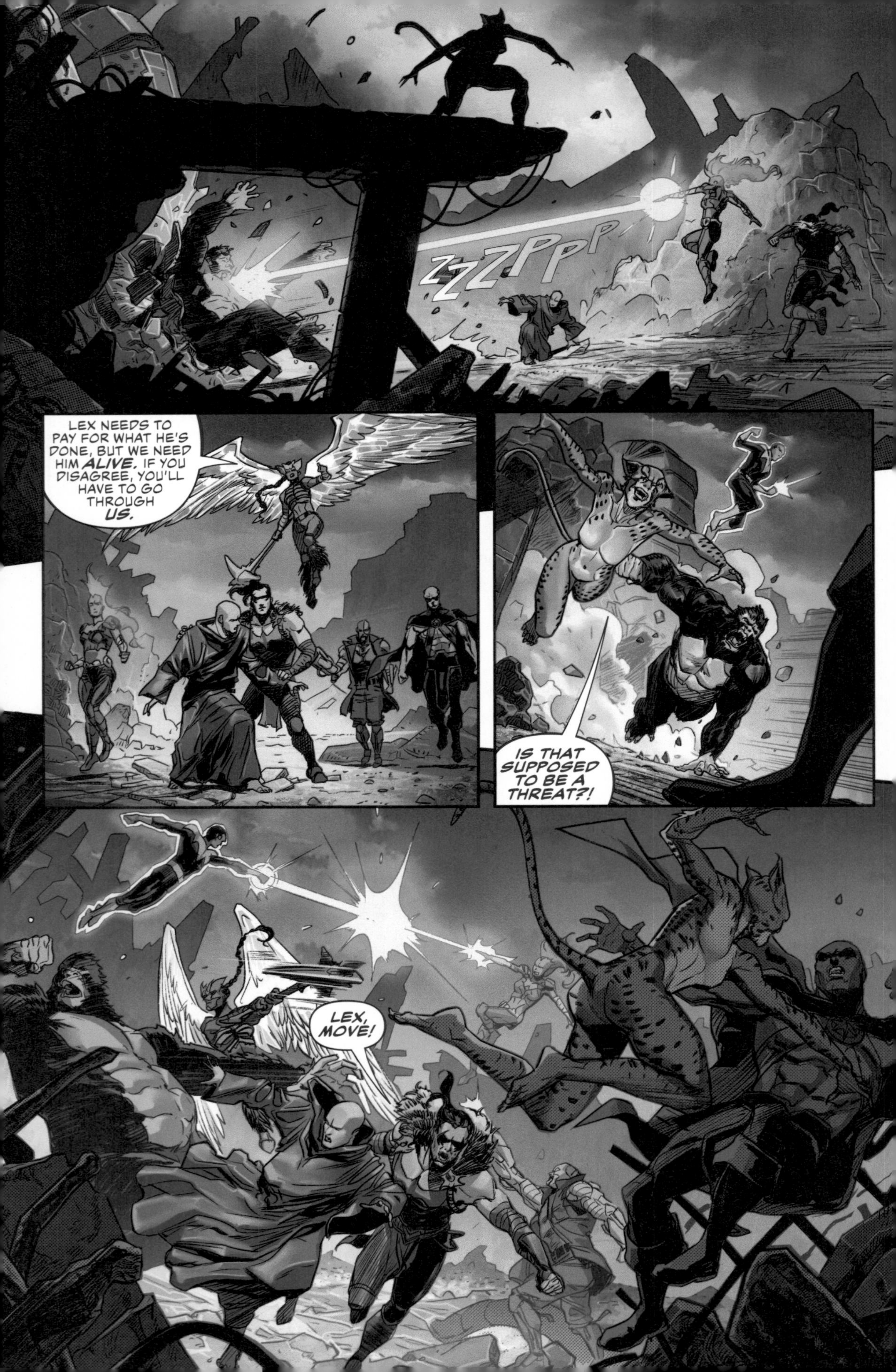
ZZZPPPP
LEX NEEDS TO PAY FOR WHAT HE'S DONE, BUT WE NEED HIM ALIVE. IF YOU DISAGREE, YOU'LL HAVE TO GO THROUGH US.
IS THAT SUPPOSED TO BE A THREAT?!
LEX, MOVE!

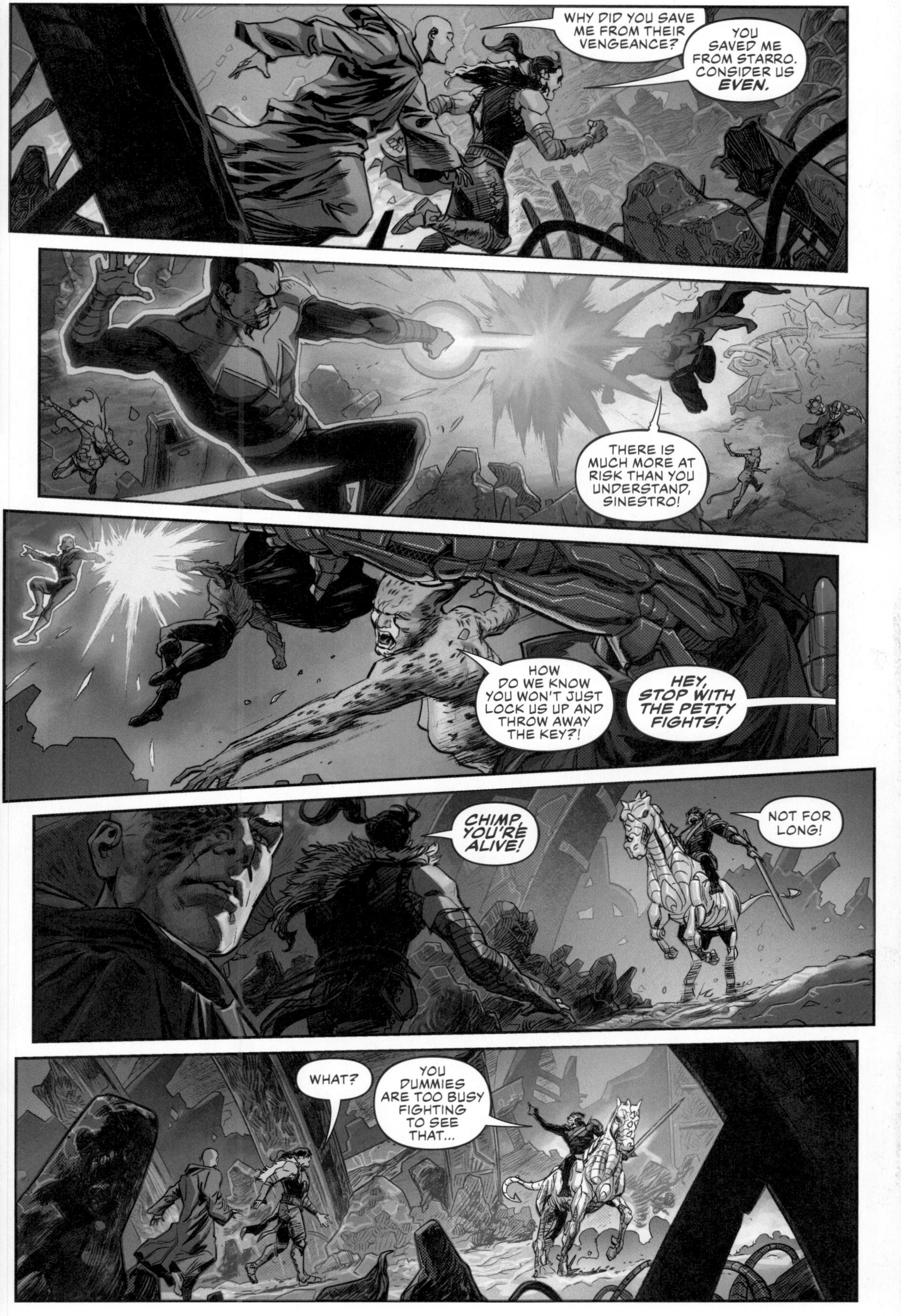
WHY DID YOU SAVE ME FROM THEIR VENGEANCE?
YOU SAVED ME FROM STARRO. CONSIDER US EVEN.
THERE IS MUCH MORE AT RISK THAN YOU UNDERSTAND, SINESTRO!
HOW DO WE KNOW YOU WON'T JUST LOCK US UP AND THROW AWAY THE KEY?!
HEY, STOP WITH THE PETTY FIGHTS!
CHIMP, YOU'RE ALIVE!
NOT FOR LONG!
WHAT?
YOU DUMMIES ARE TOO BUSY FIGHTING TO SEE THAT...

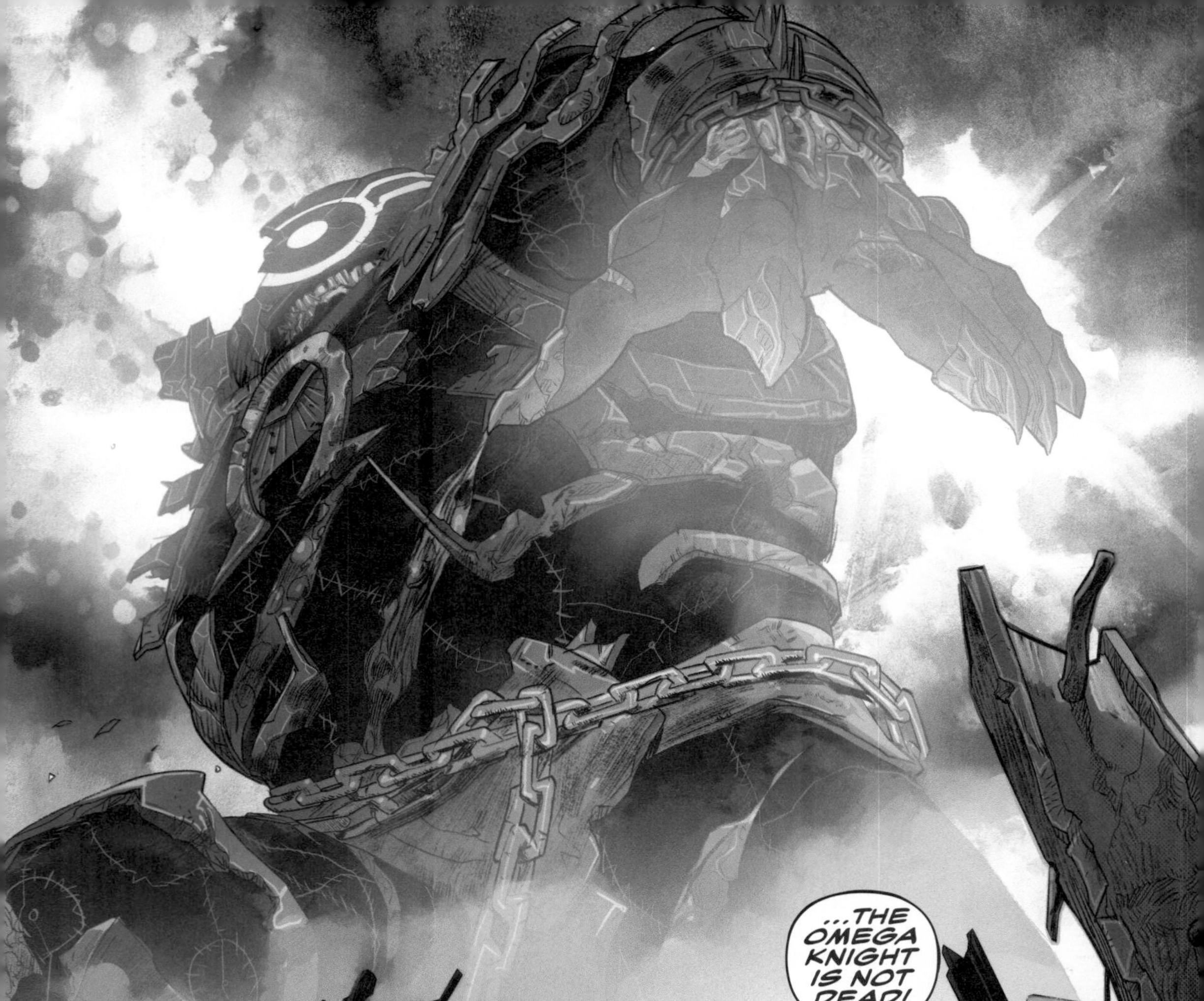
...THE OMEGA KNIGHT IS NOT DEAD!

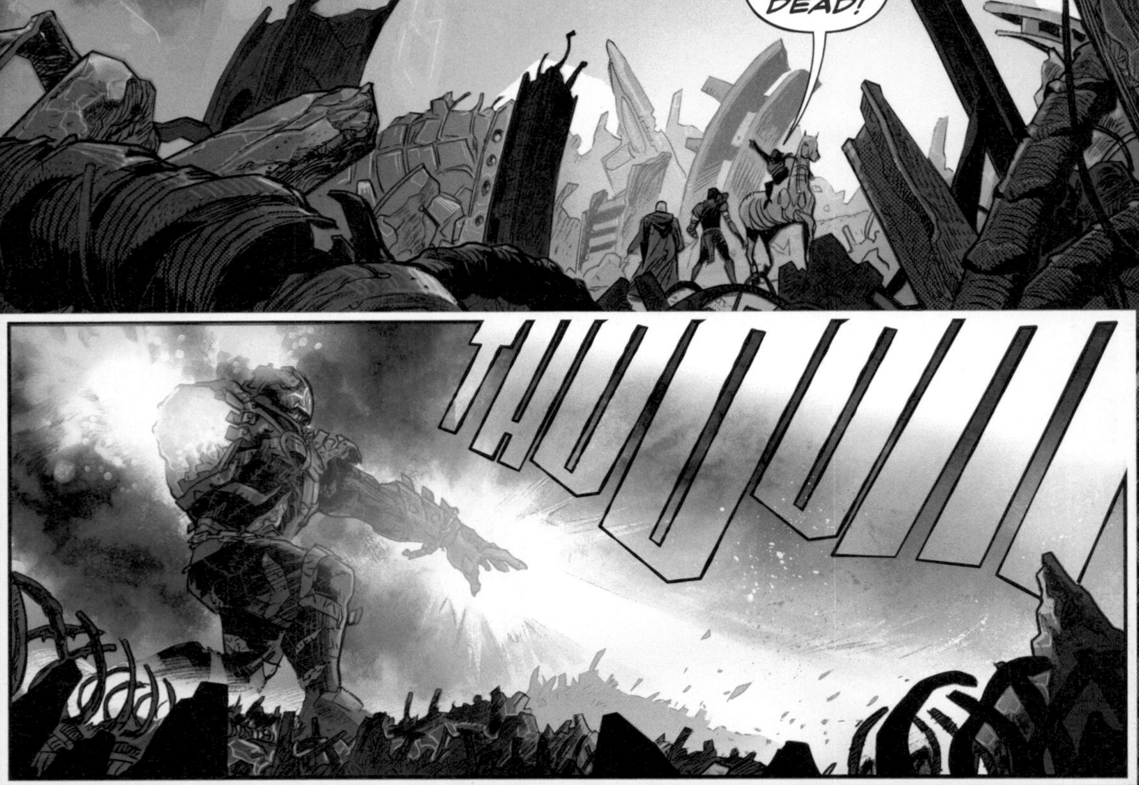
THUDUUU

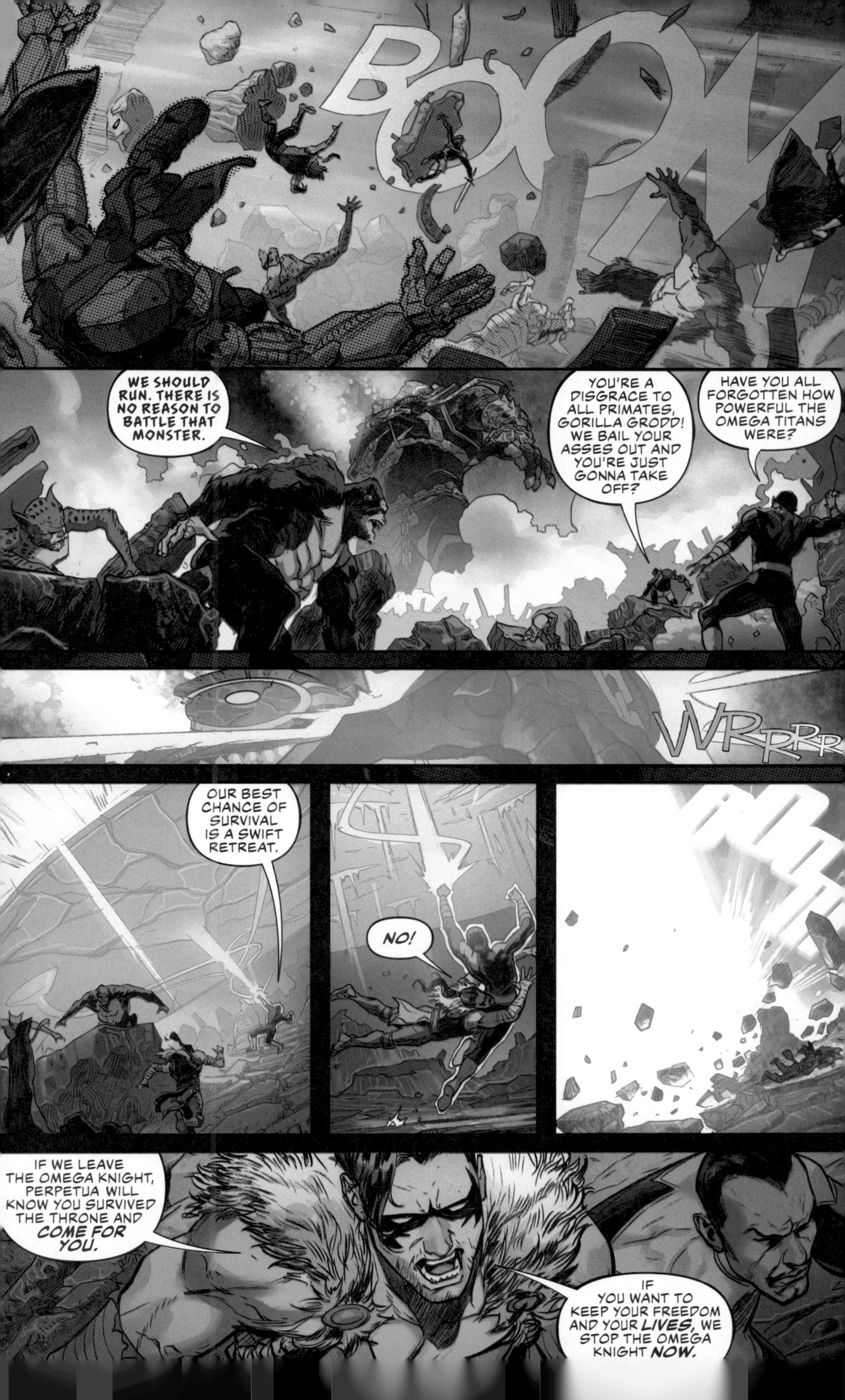
BOOM
WE SHOULD RUN. THERE IS NO REASON TO BATTLE THAT MONSTER.
YOU'RE A DISGRACE TO ALL PRIMATES, GORILLA GRODD! WE BAIL YOUR ASSES OUT AND YOU'RE JUST GONNA TAKE OFF?
HAVE YOU ALL FORGOTTEN HOW POWERFUL THE OMEGA TITANS WERE?
WRRRR
OUR BEST CHANCE OF SURVIVAL IS A SWIFT RETREAT.
NO!
IF WE LEAVE THE OMEGA KNIGHT, PERPETUA WILL KNOW YOU SURVIVED THE THRONE AND COME FOR YOU.
IF YOU WANT TO KEEP YOUR FREEDOM AND YOUR LIVES, WE STOP THE OMEGA KNIGHT NOW.

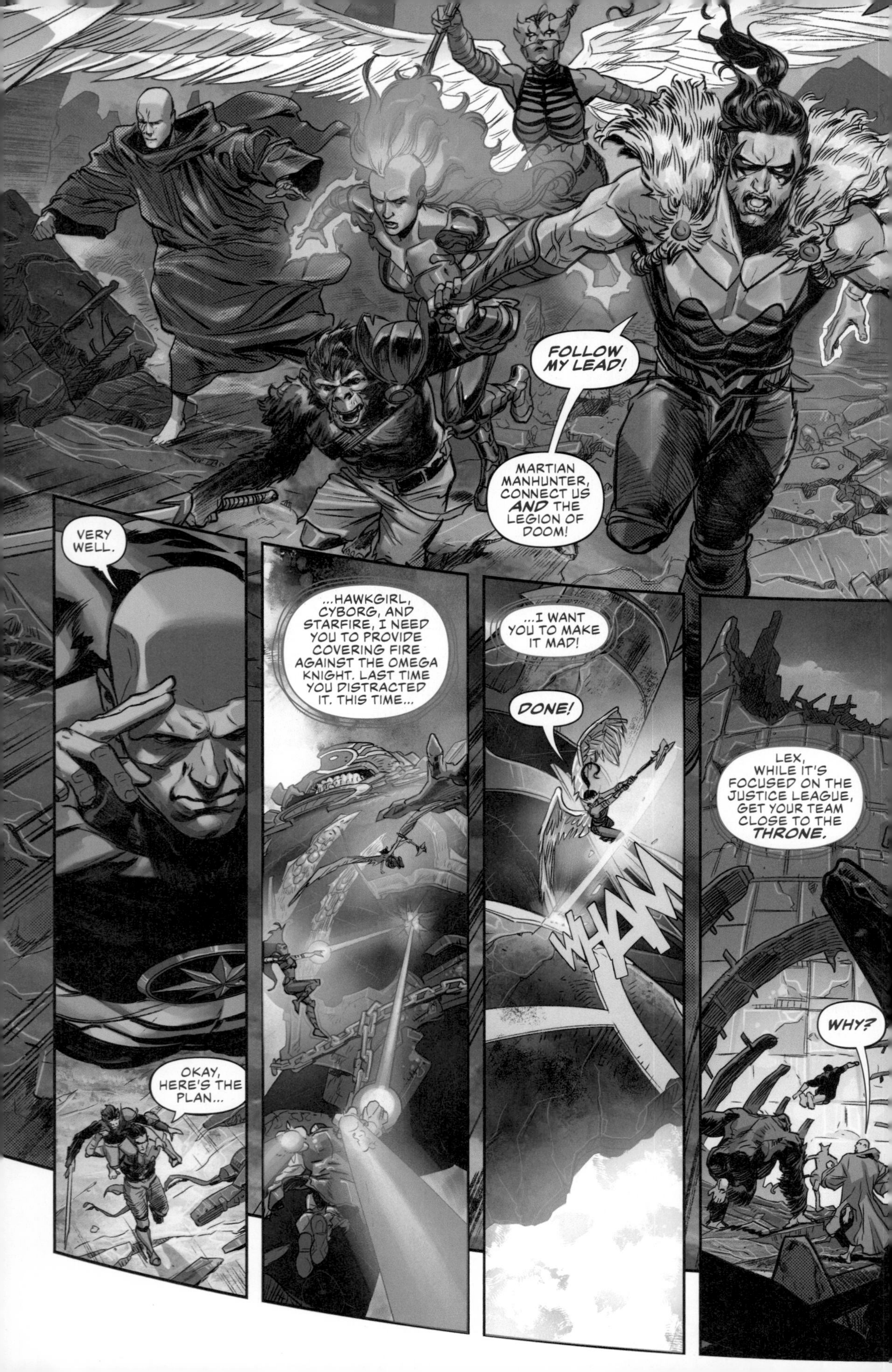
FOLLOW MY LEAD!
MARTIAN MANHUNTER, CONNECT US AND THE LEGION OF DOOM!
VERY WELL.
OKAY, HERE'S THE PLAN...
...HAWKGIRL, CYBORG, AND STARFIRE, I NEED YOU TO PROVIDE COVERING FIRE AGAINST THE OMEGA KNIGHT. LAST TIME YOU DISTRACTED IT. THIS TIME...
...I WANT YOU TO MAKE IT MAD!
DONE!
WHAM
LEX, WHILE IT'S FOCUSED ON THE JUSTICE LEAGUE, GET YOUR TEAM CLOSE TO THE THRONE.
WHY?

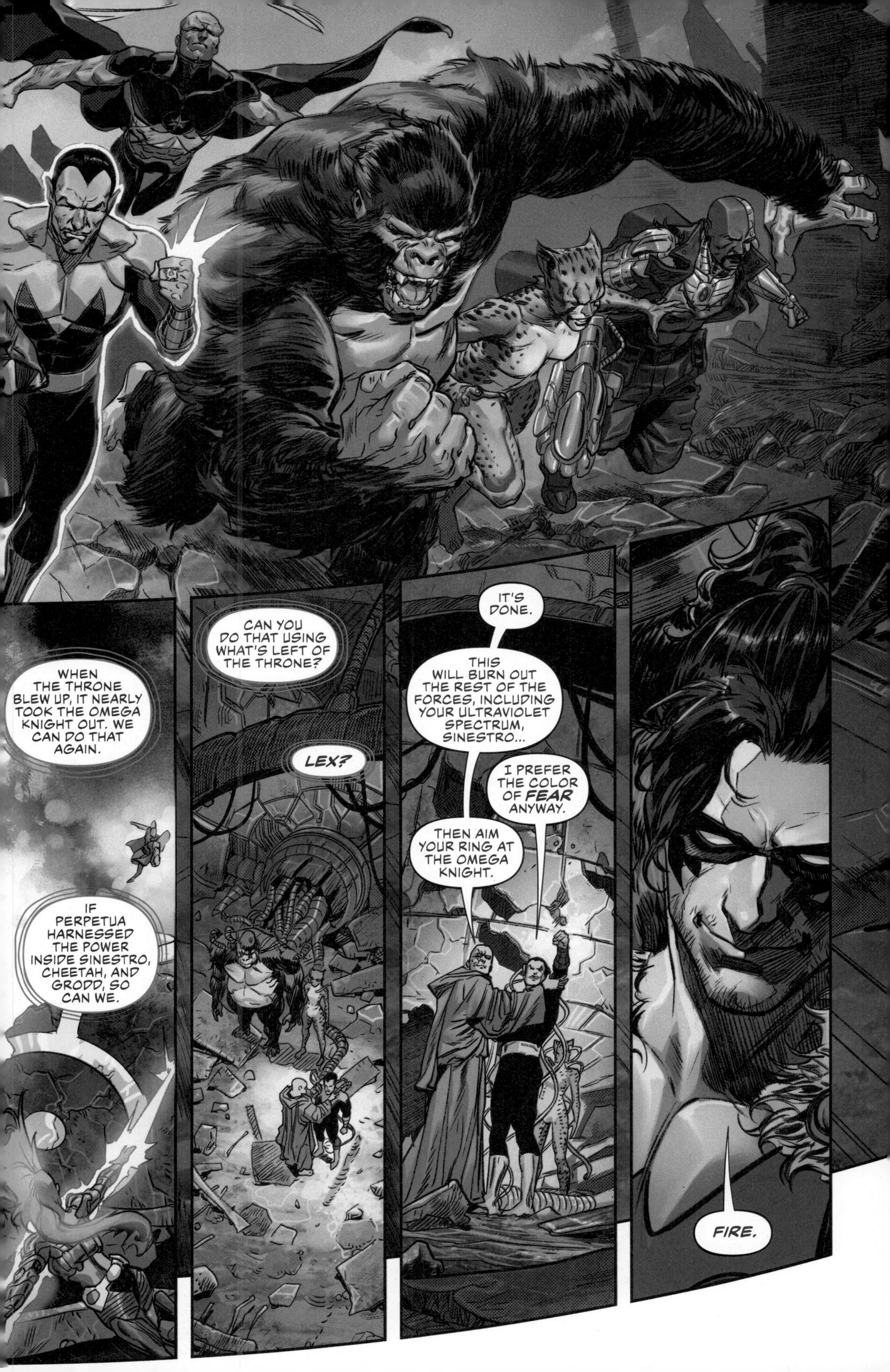

WHEN THE THRONE BLEW UP, IT NEARLY TOOK THE OMEGA KNIGHT OUT. WE CAN DO THAT AGAIN.
IF PERPETUA HARNESSED THE POWER INSIDE SINESTRO, CHEETAH, AND GRODD, SO CAN WE.
CAN YOU DO THAT USING WHAT'S LEFT OF THE THRONE?
LEX?
IT'S DONE.
THIS WILL BURN OUT THE REST OF THE FORCES, INCLUDING YOUR ULTRAVIOLET SPECTRUM, SINESTRO...
I PREFER THE COLOR OF FEAR ANYWAY.
THEN AIM YOUR RING AT THE OMEGA KNIGHT.
FIRE.

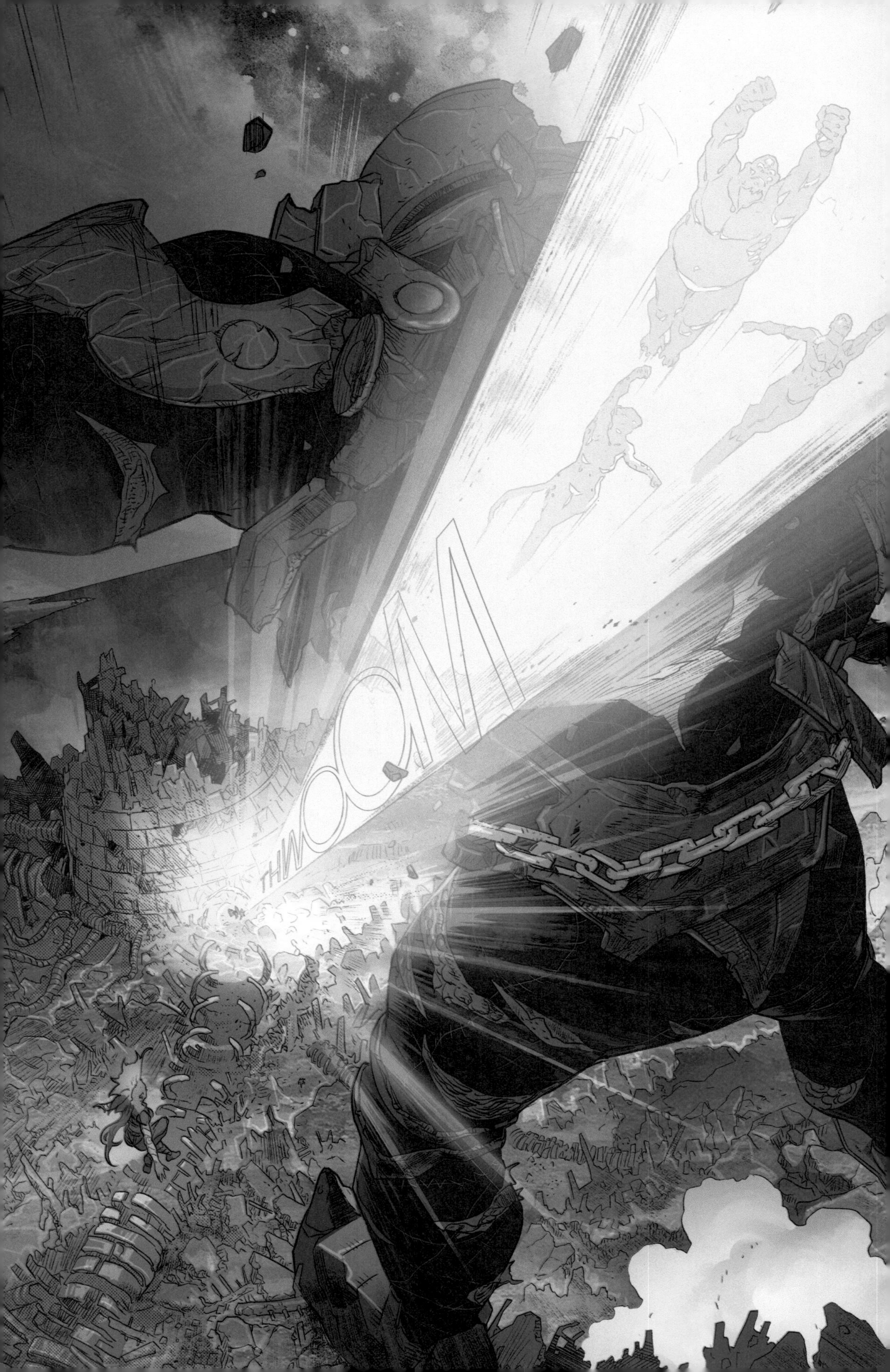
THWOOM

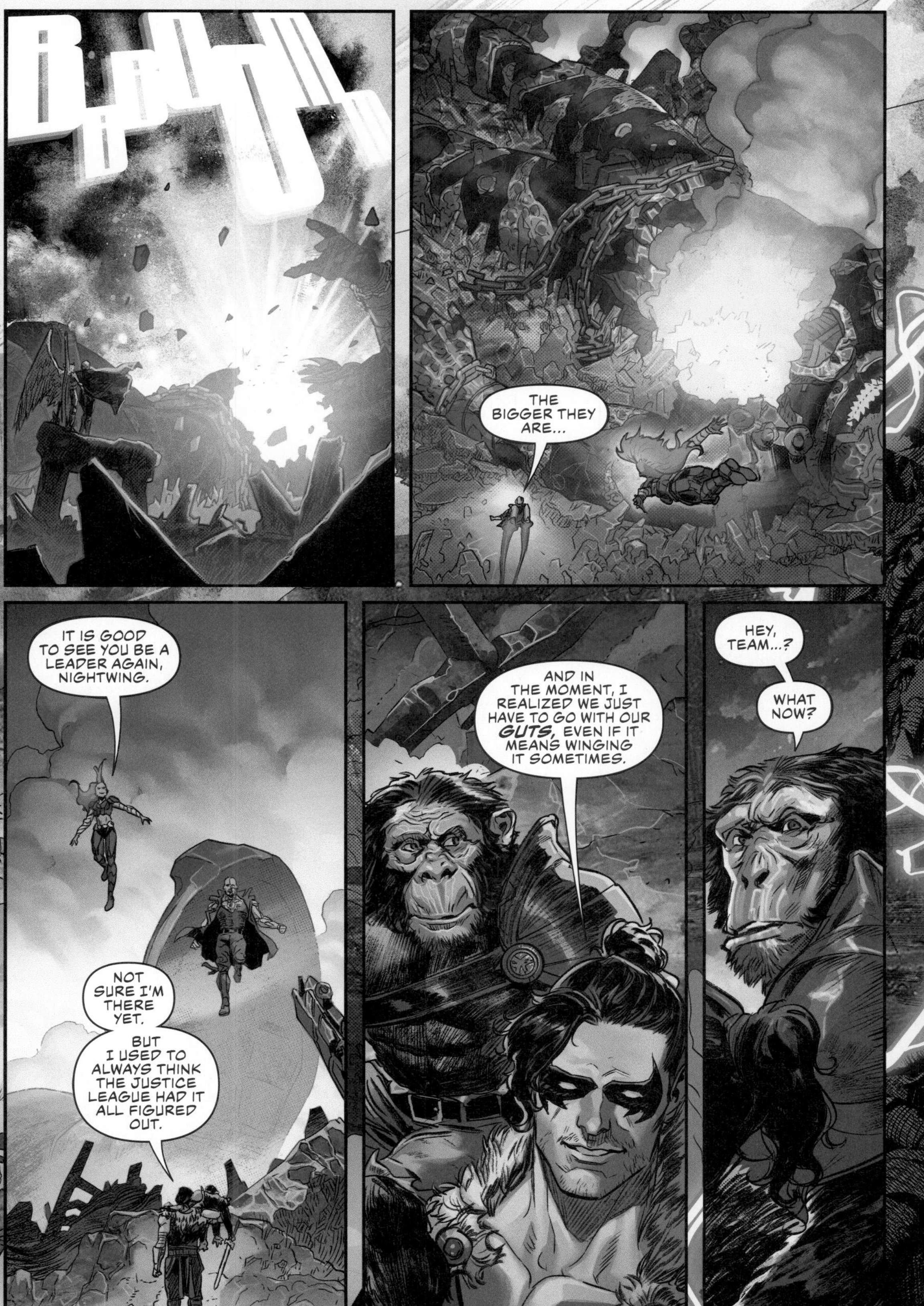
THE BIGGER THEY ARE...
IT IS GOOD TO SEE YOU BE A LEADER AGAIN, NIGHTWING.
NOT SURE I'M THERE YET.
BUT I USED TO ALWAYS THINK THE JUSTICE LEAGUE HAD IT ALL FIGURED OUT.
AND IN THE MOMENT, I REALIZED WE JUST HAVE TO GO WITH OUR GUTS, EVEN IF IT MEANS WINGING IT SOMETIMES.
HEY, TEAM...?
WHAT NOW?

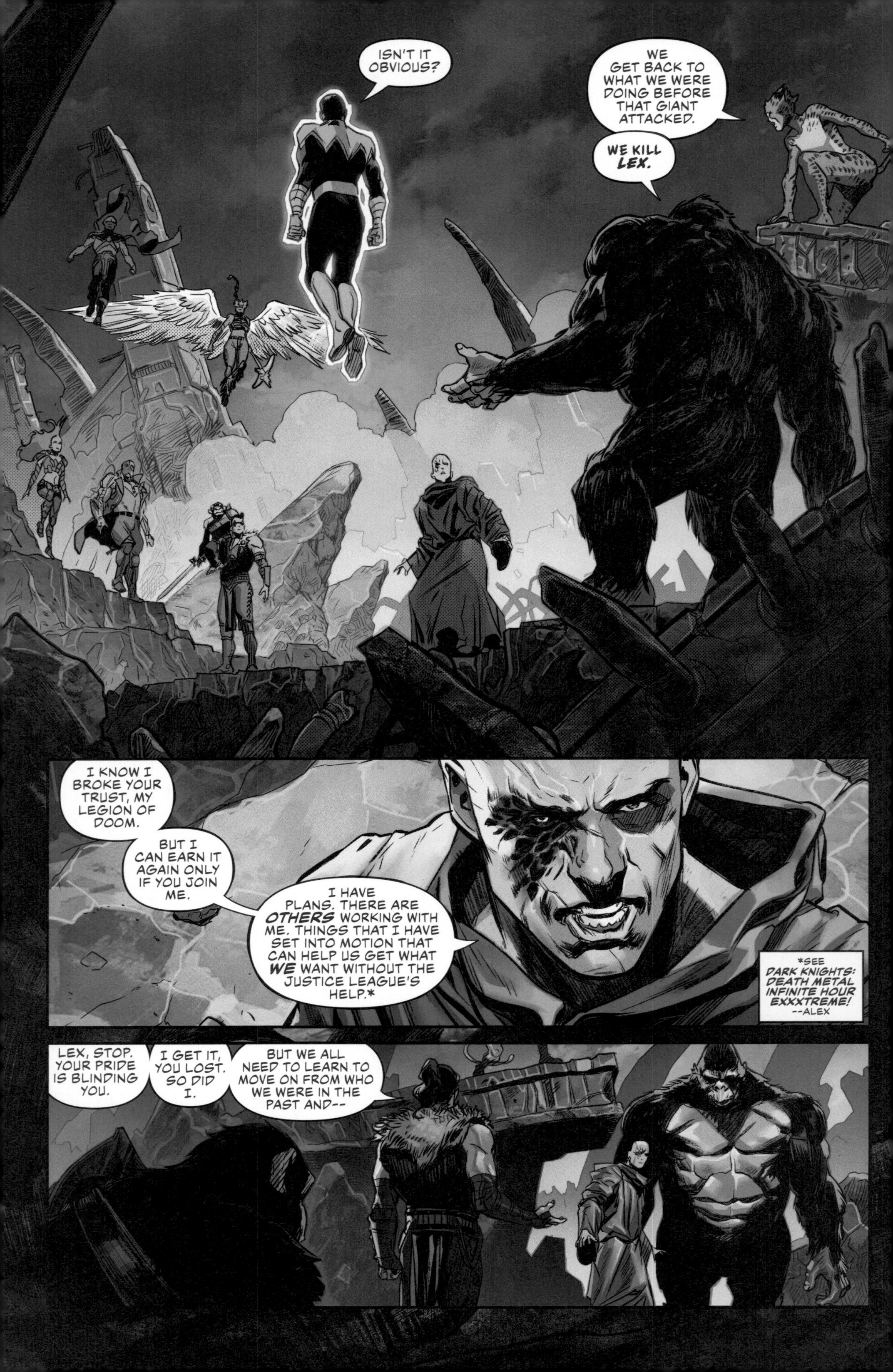

ISN'T IT OBVIOUS?
WE GET BACK TO WHAT WE WERE DOING BEFORE THAT GIANT ATTACKED.
WE KILL LEX.
I KNOW I BROKE YOUR TRUST, MY LEGION OF DOOM.
BUT I CAN EARN IT AGAIN ONLY IF YOU JOIN ME.
I HAVE PLANS. THERE ARE OTHERS WORKING WITH ME. THINGS THAT I HAVE SET INTO MOTION THAT CAN HELP US GET WHAT WE WANT WITHOUT THE JUSTICE LEAGUE'S HELP.*
*SEE DARK KNIGHTS: DEATH METAL INFINITE HOUR EXXXTREME! --ALEX
LEX, STOP. YOUR PRIDE IS BLINDING YOU.
I GET IT, YOU LOST. SO DID I.
BUT WE ALL NEED TO LEARN TO MOVE ON FROM WHO WE WERE IN THE PAST AND--

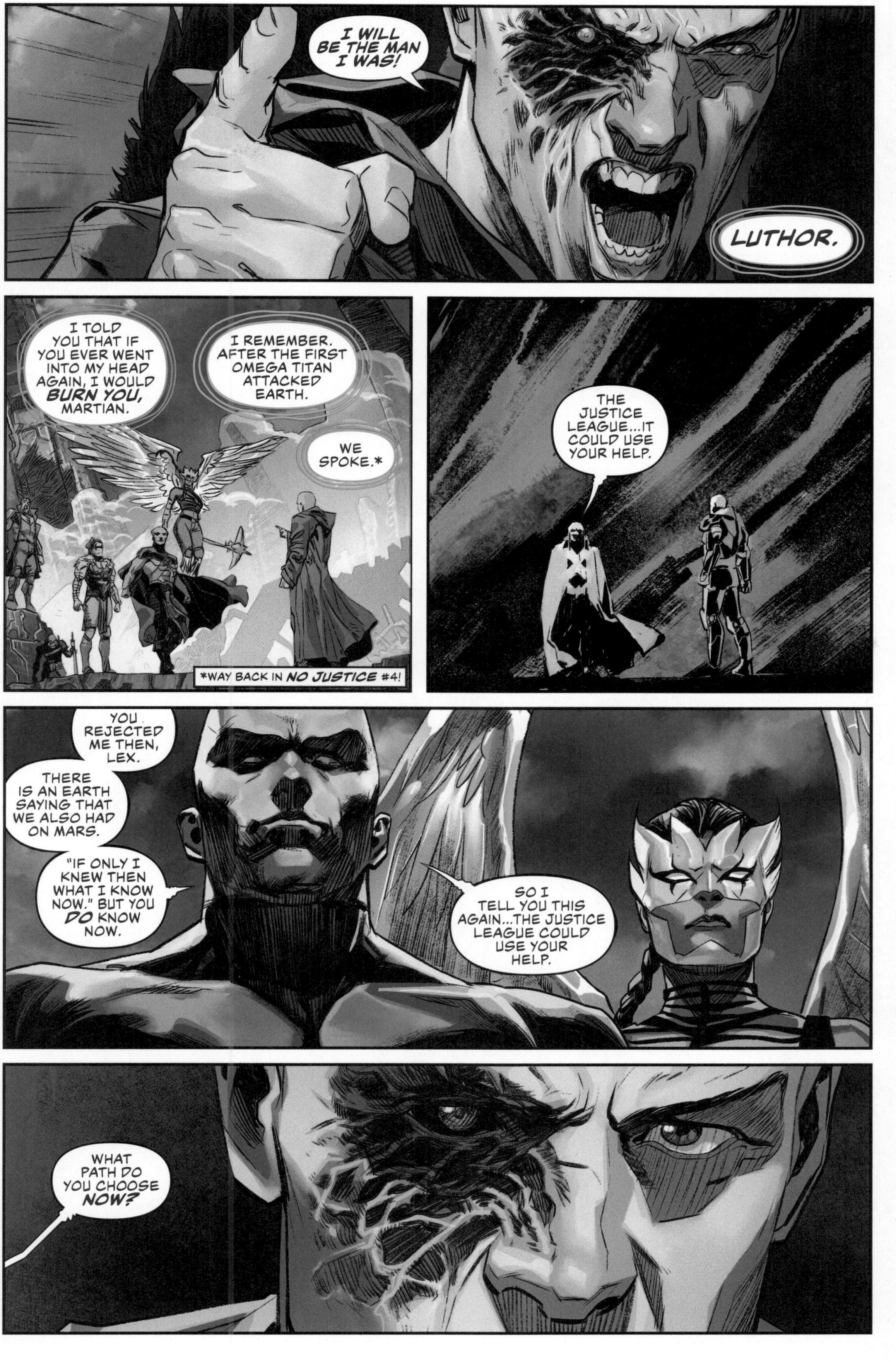
I WILL BE THE MAN I WAS!
LUTHOR.
I TOLD YOU THAT IF YOU EVER WENT INTO MY HEAD AGAIN, I WOULD BURN YOU, MARTIAN.
I REMEMBER. AFTER THE FIRST OMEGA TITAN ATTACKED EARTH.
WE SPOKE.*
*WAY BACK IN NO JUSTICE #4!
THE JUSTICE LEAGUE...IT COULD USE YOUR HELP.
YOU REJECTED ME THEN, LEX.
THERE IS AN EARTH SAYING THAT WE ALSO HAD ON MARS.
"IF ONLY I KNEW THEN WHAT I KNOW NOW." BUT YOU DO KNOW NOW.
SO I TELL YOU THIS AGAIN...THE JUSTICE LEAGUE COULD USE YOUR HELP.
WHAT PATH DO YOU CHOOSE NOW?

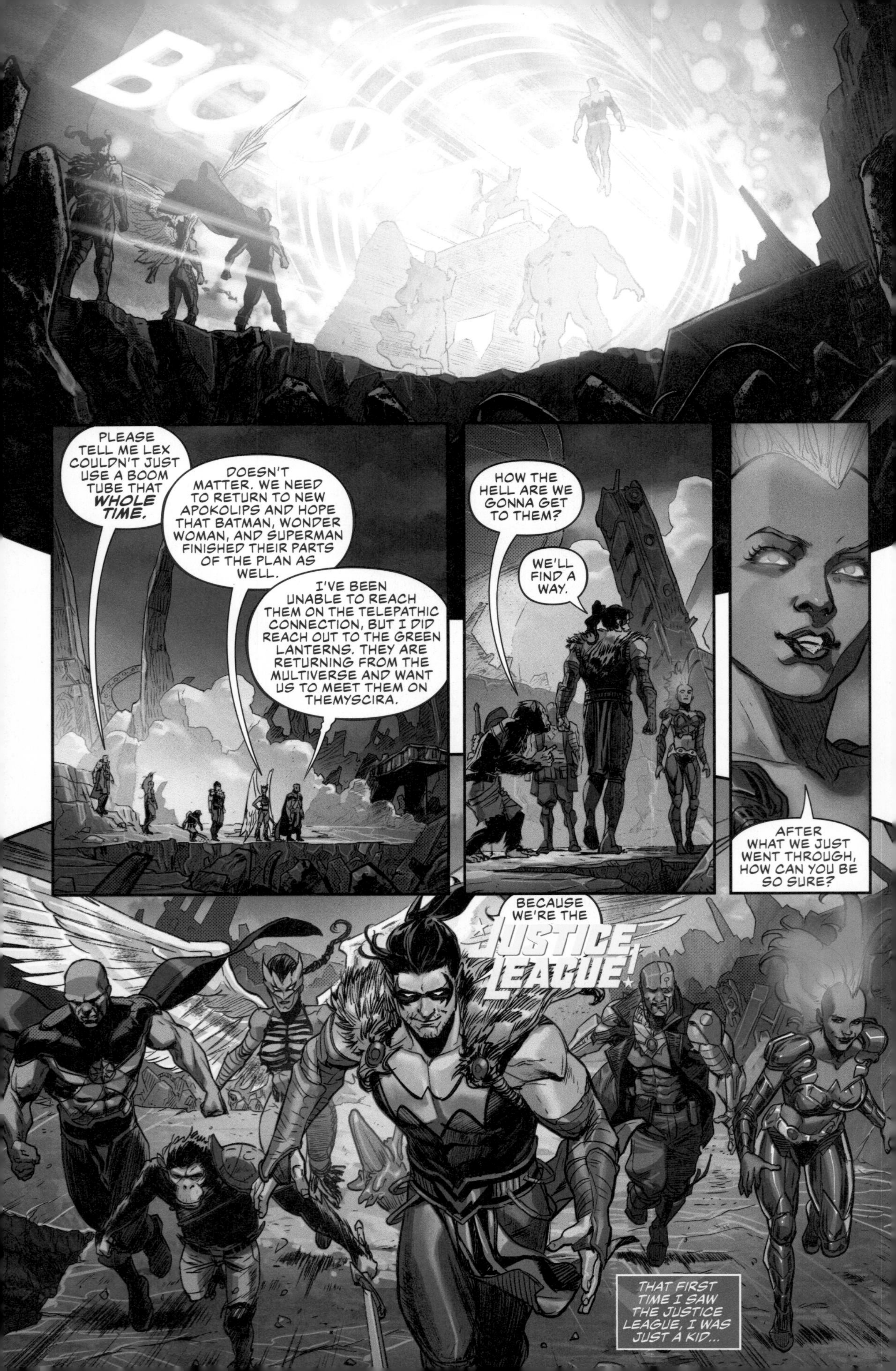
BOO
PLEASE TELL ME LEX COULDN'T JUST USE A BOOM TUBE THAT WHOLE TIME.
DOESN'T MATTER. WE NEED TO RETURN TO NEW APOKOLIPS AND HOPE THAT BATMAN, WONDER WOMAN, AND SUPERMAN FINISHED THEIR PARTS OF THE PLAN AS WELL.
I'VE BEEN UNABLE TO REACH THEM ON THE TELEPATHIC CONNECTION, BUT I DID REACH OUT TO THE GREEN LANTERNS. THEY ARE RETURNING FROM THE MULTIVERSE AND WANT US TO MEET THEM ON THEMYSCIRA.
HOW THE HELL ARE WE GONNA GET TO THEM?
WE'LL FIND A WAY.
AFTER WHAT WE JUST WENT THROUGH, HOW CAN YOU BE SO SURE?
BECAUSE WE'RE THE
JUSTICE LEAGUE!
THAT FIRST TIME I SAW THE JUSTICE LEAGUE, I WAS JUST A KID...

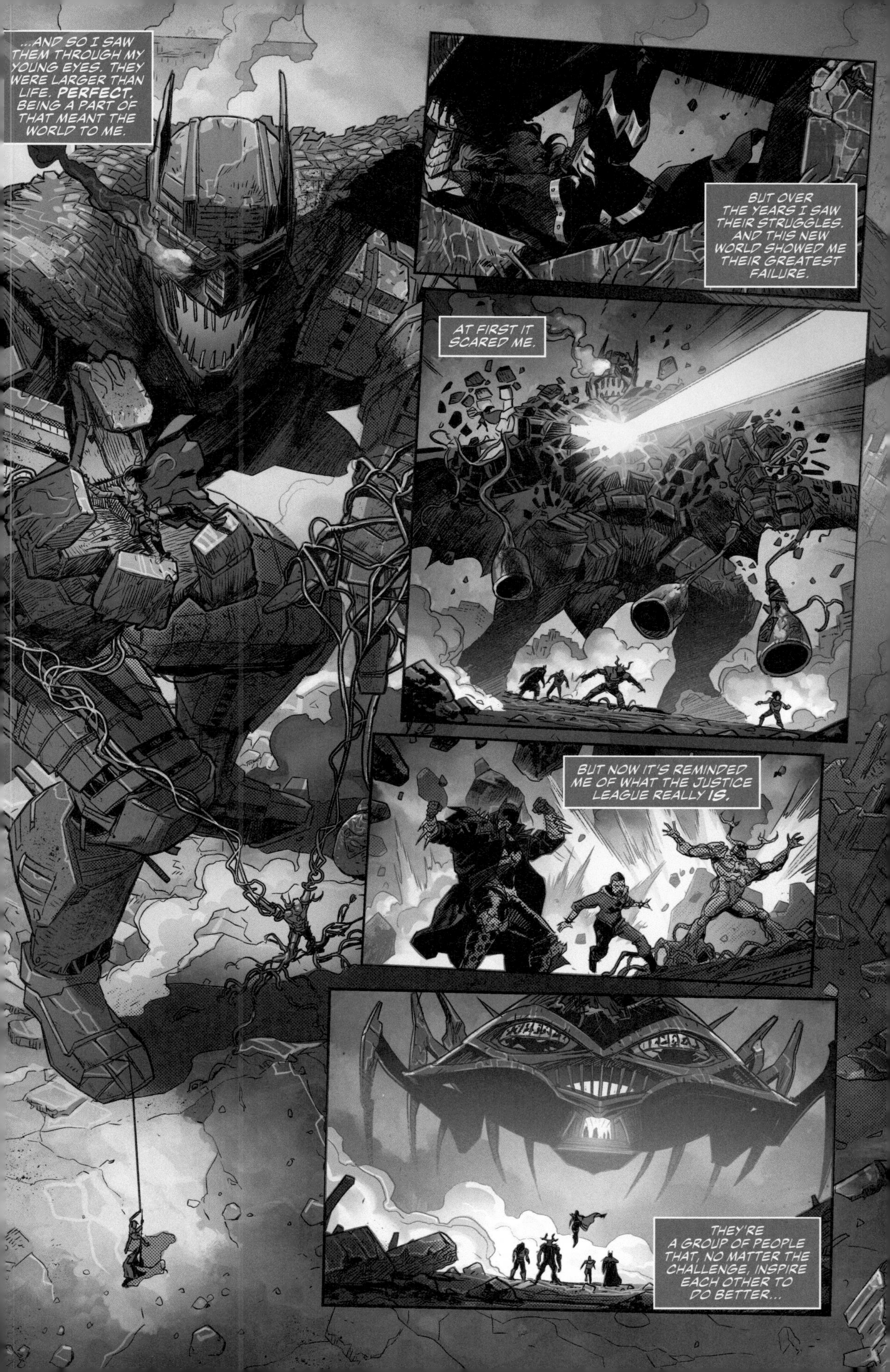
...AND SO I SAW THEM THROUGH MY YOUNG EYES. THEY WERE LARGER THAN LIFE. PERFECT. BEING A PART OF THAT MEANT THE WORLD TO ME.
BUT OVER THE YEARS I SAW THEIR STRUGGLES. AND THIS NEW WORLD SHOWED ME THEIR GREATEST FAILURE.
AT FIRST IT SCARED ME.
BUT NOW IT'S REMINDED ME OF WHAT THE JUSTICE LEAGUE REALLY IS.
THEY'RE A GROUP OF PEOPLE THAT, NO MATTER THE CHALLENGE, INSPIRE EACH OTHER TO DO BETTER...

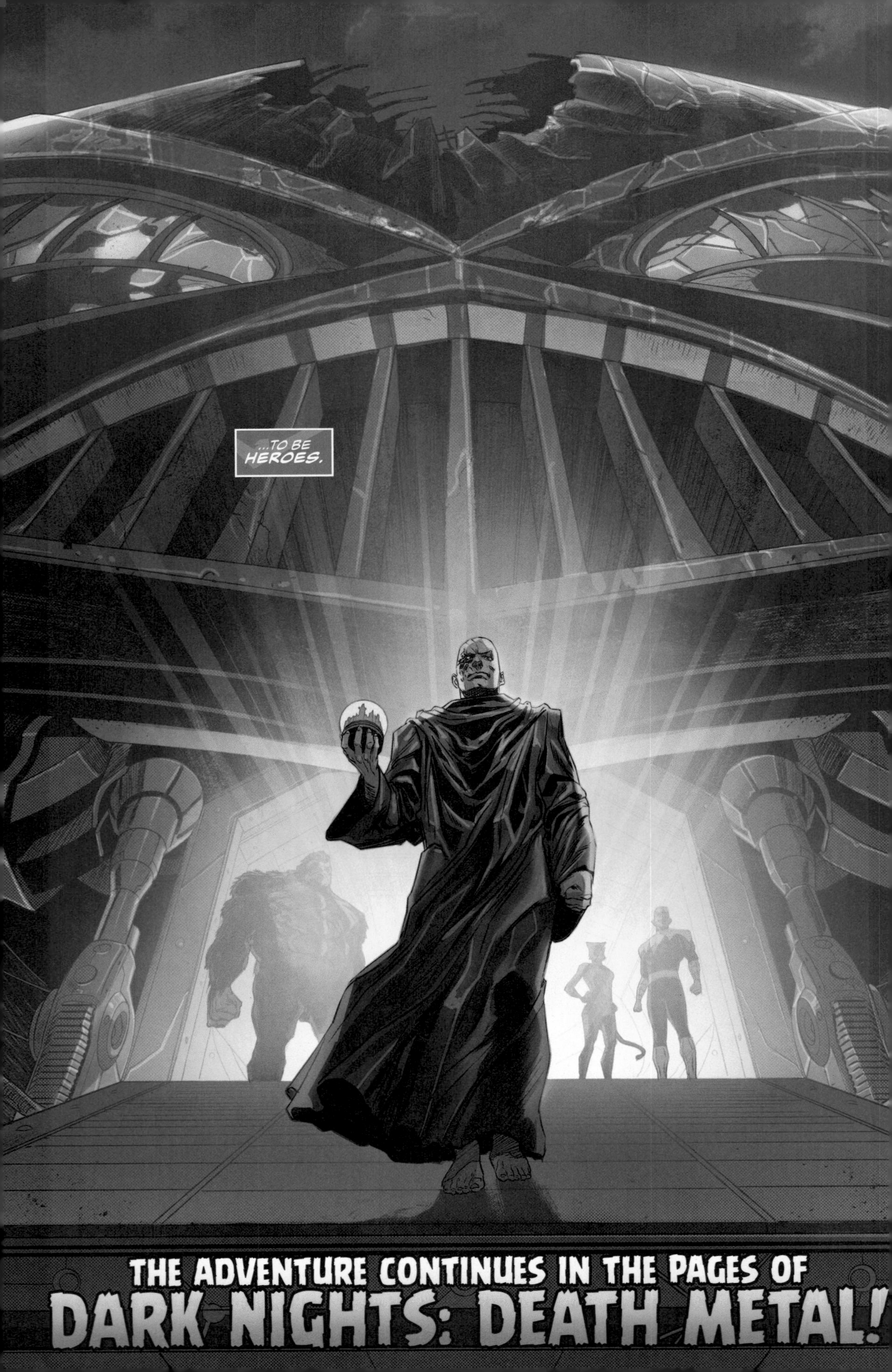
...TO BE HEROES.
THE ADVENTURE CONTINUES IN THE PAGES OF
DARK NIGHTS: DEATH METAL!

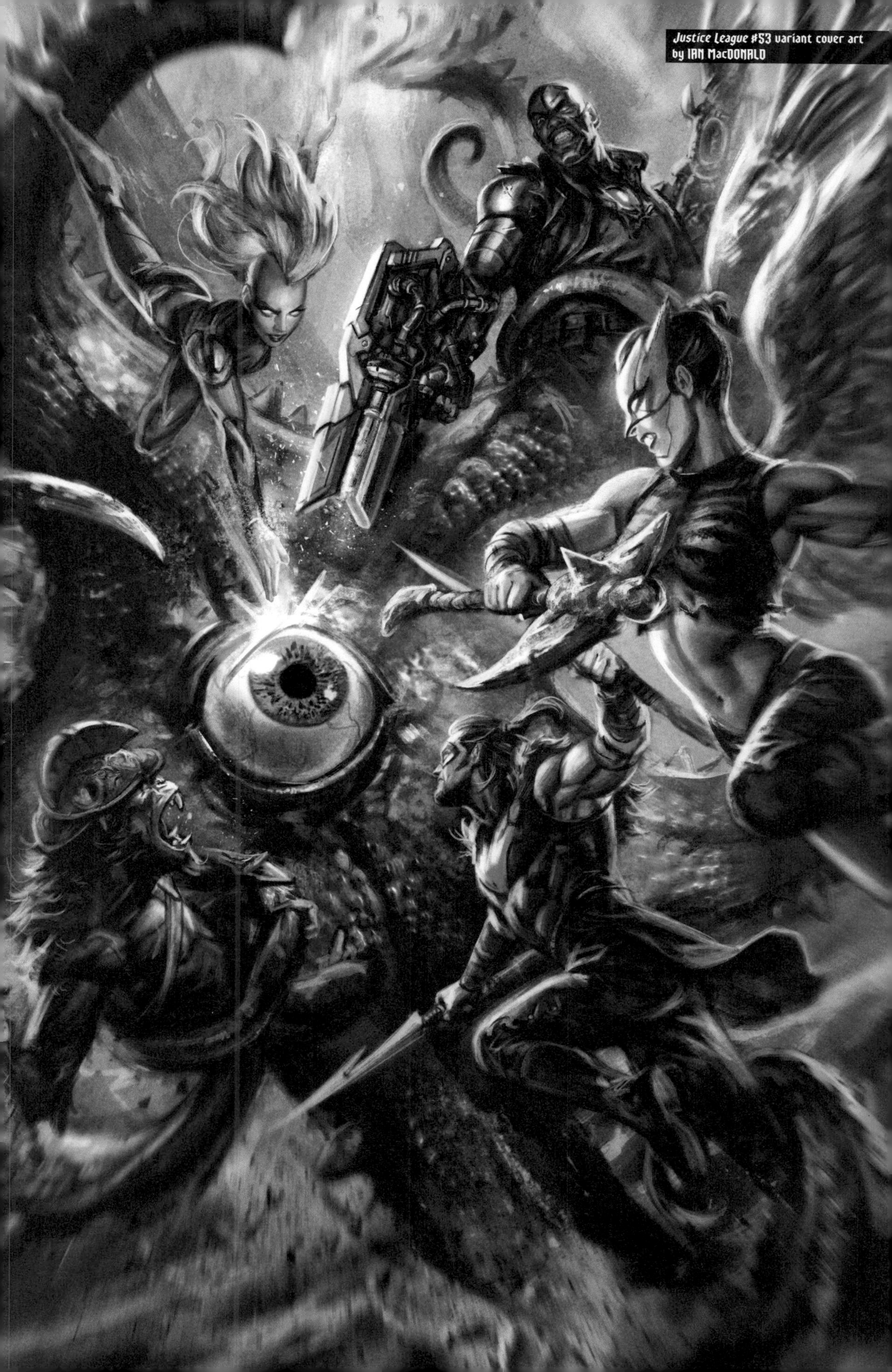

Justice League #53 variant cover art
by IAN MacDONALD

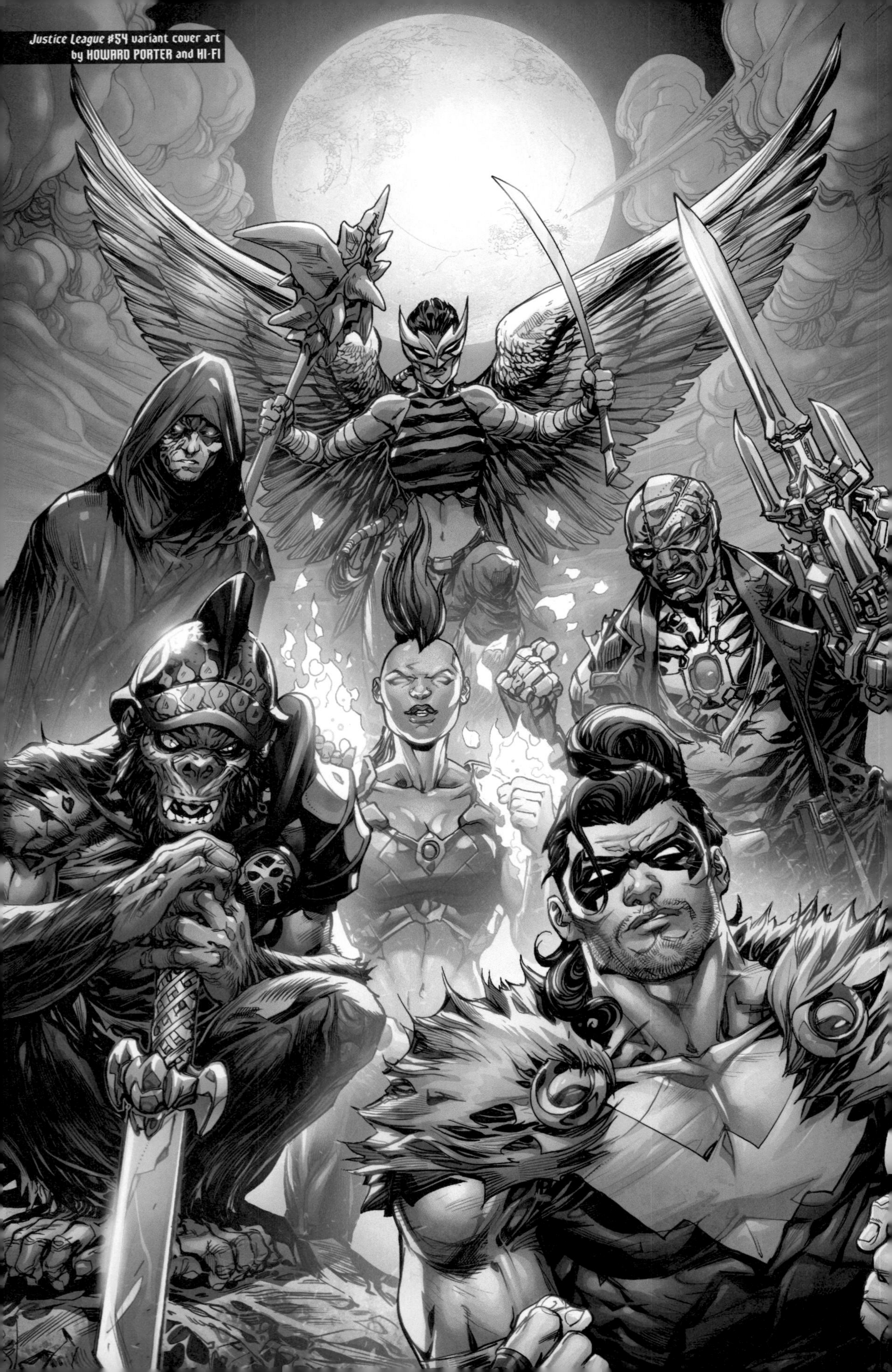

Justice League #54 variant cover art
by HOWARD PORTER and HI-FI

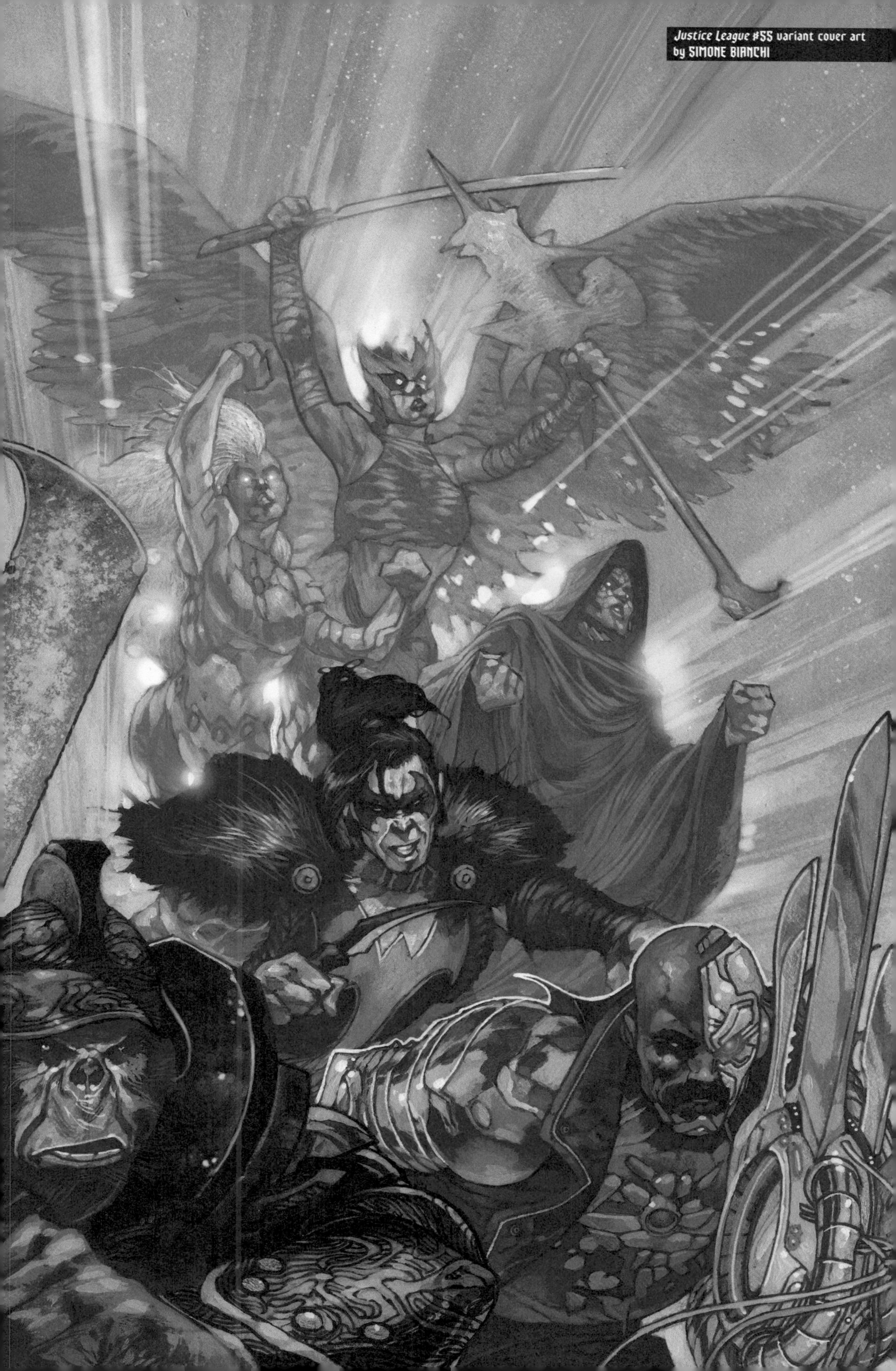

Justice League #55 variant cover art
by SIMONE BIANCHI

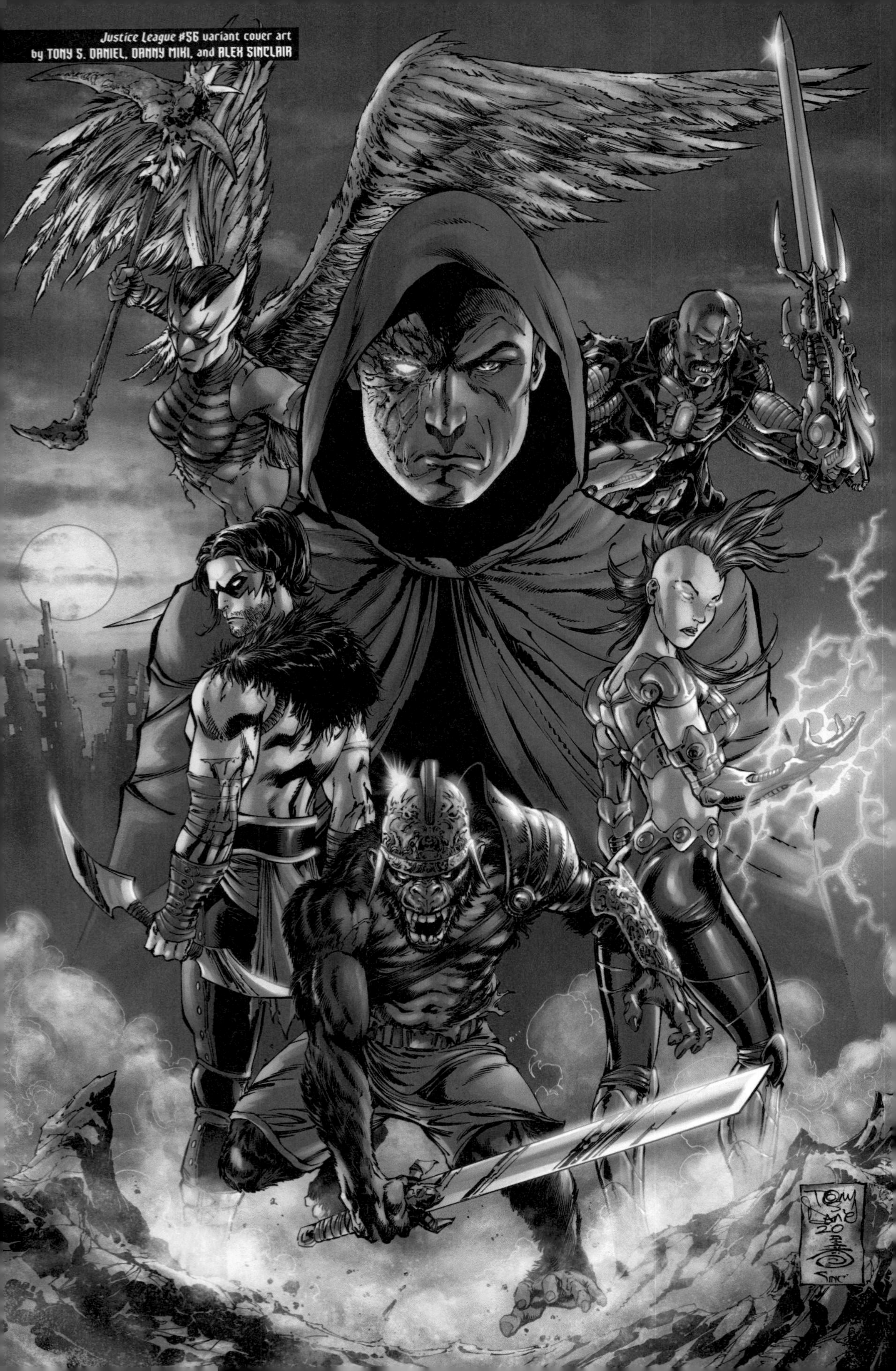

Justice League #56 variant cover art
by TONY S. DANIEL, DANNY MIKI, and ALEX SINCLAIR

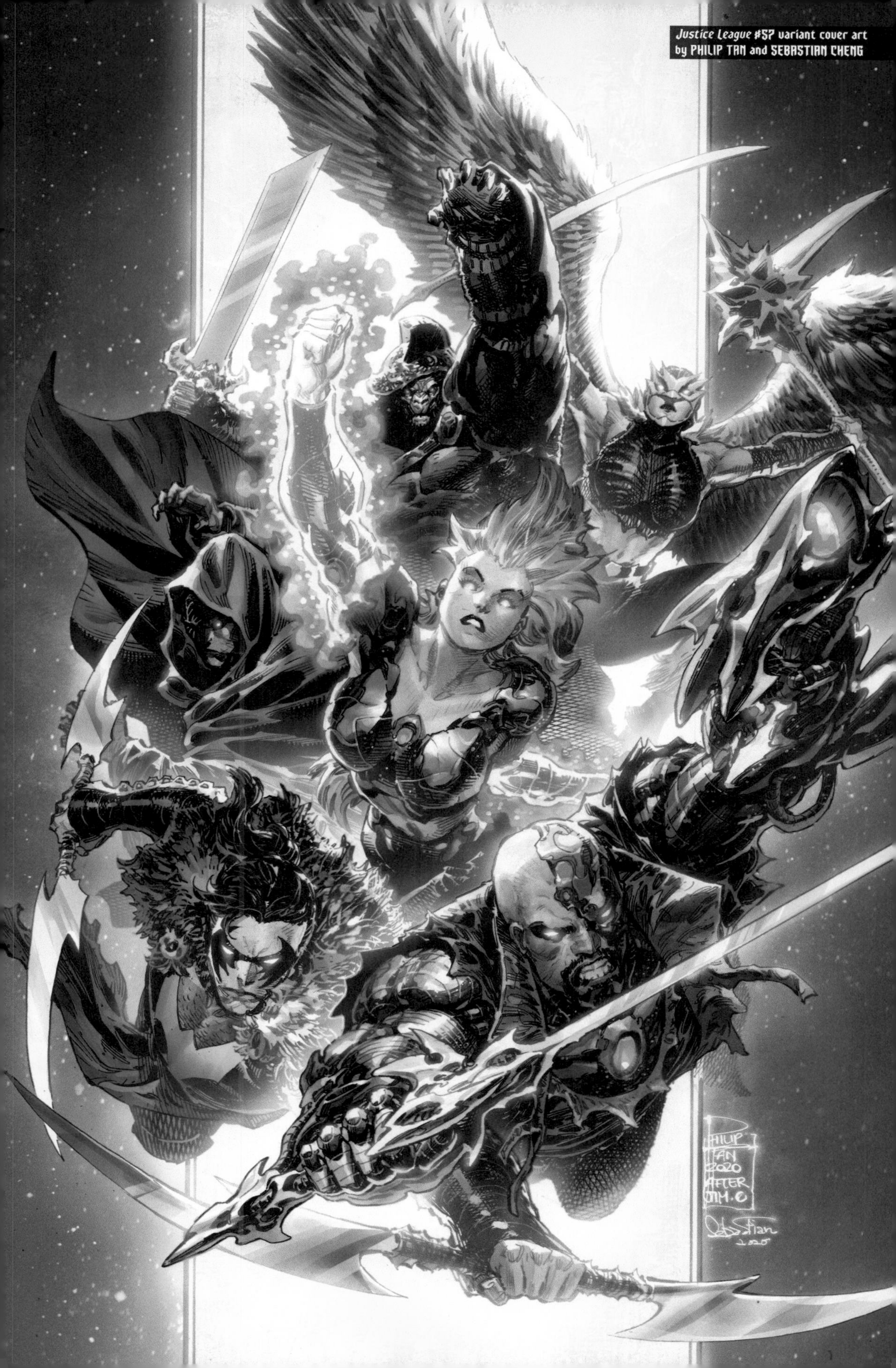
PHILIP TAN 2020 AFTER JIM.C

Justice League #57 variant cover art
by PHILIP TAN and SEBASTIAN CHENG